TWEET
OF THE
DAY

TWEET
OF THE
DAY

A YEAR OF
BRITAIN'S BIRDS
FROM THE ACCLAIMED
RADIO 4 SERIES

BRETT WESTWOOD
& STEPHEN MOSS

SALT·YARD
BOOK C.º

First published in Great Britain in 2014
by Saltyard Books
An imprint of Hodder & Stoughton
An Hachette UK Company

1

Text © Brett Westwood and Stephen Moss 2014
Illustrations © Carry Akroyd 2014

By arrangement with the BBC
The BBC logo is a trade mark of the
British Broadcasting Corporation and is
used under licence.
Radio 4 logo © Radio 4 2008

Quotation from 'Stonechat on Cul Beg' from *The Poems of Norman MacCaig* reproduced by
kind permission of Polygon, Birlinn Ltd.

A CIP catalogue record for this title is available from
the British Library

ISBN 978-1-84854-977-7
Ebook ISBN 978-1-84854-979-1

Book design by Ami Smithson

Printed and bound in the UK by Butler Tanner & Dennis Ltd

Hodder & Stoughton policy is to use papers that are natural, renewable and
recyclable products and made from wood grown in sustainable forests.
The logging and manufacturing processes are expected to conform to the
environmental regulations of the country of origin.

Hodder & Stoughton Ltd
338 Euston Road
London NW1 3BH

www.saltyardbooks.co.uk

TO MY PARENTS,
ANN AND BARRIE WESTWOOD,
FOR BUYING ME MY FIRST PAIR OF
BINOCULARS ... AND A BIKE

*

TO SUZANNE, DAVID, JAMES, CHARLIE,
GEORGE AND DAISY MOSS,
FOR THEIR LOVE AND SUPPORT

CONTENTS

*

TWEET OF THE DAY: THE INSIDE STORY IX

USING THIS BOOK XII

BIRDSONG XIV

BIRDWATCHING: A BRIEF HISTORY XXII

GETTING STARTED XXX

MAY.......... 2

JUNE.......... 22

JULY.......... 44

AUGUST....... 68

SEPTEMBER... 90

OCTOBER......110

NOVEMBER....134

DECEMBER....154

JANUARY......176

FEBRUARY....202

MARCH........224

APRIL........248

EPILOGUE.....270

ACKNOWLEDGEMENTS 273

FURTHER READING AND LISTENING 275

INDEX 277

THIS BOOK IS A CELEBRATION of one of the great wonders of nature: the variety and beauty of British birds and the sounds they make, over the course of the year. It is based on the highly successful Radio 4 series *Tweet of the Day*, which has entertained and informed legions of listeners – on the radio itself and on the web – since it first began broadcasting in May 2013.

Made by the radio arm of the BBC Natural History Unit in Bristol, the aim of the series was to showcase a range of almost 250 British birds. But the species were not chosen simply for their sounds, as Julian Hector, executive producer of Natural History Radio, explains:

> Tweet of the Day *was a daily invitation to listen to the story of a bird, told through its calls and songs. Partly, of course, this focused on the bird's appearance and behaviour. But as the series unfolded, insights also emerged about the crucial part that birds play in our society and culture: through folklore, art, music and literature. Finally, what came through in every brief episode was the huge effect birds have on us and our daily lives: for many people, they are the route that inspires us to get to know and love nature as a whole.*

Two things inspired the series: one traditional, one very contemporary. The first was our nation's long love of, and connection with, birdsong; the second, the rise of the online communication medium known as 'tweeting', which for more and more people is becoming a way of life. We felt that it would be impossible to capture the essence of a bird in just 140 characters, so instead we gave ourselves a time-limit of ninety seconds, just enough to convey succinct and relevant information about each species through words and recordings of their sounds.

Choosing which birds to feature was a challenge. With 265 programmes throughout the year we needed about 240 species, allowing for some birds whose calls and songs were so well known that they would justify a second outing on air: these included the song thrush, cuckoo and nightingale.

The next step was to allocate each species to a month when people were most likely to see and hear them. This wasn't always straightforward, because most British birds sing in spring and reach a peak in April and May, but with roughly forty slots in those two months we would have to allocate the majority of species to other times in the year.

Once we'd debated long and hard, and finally drawn up our provisional calendar, producer Sarah Blunt then spent days combing the NHU sound archives for suitable recordings:

One of my first tasks was to haul bag after bag of recordings from the Natural History Unit sound library up several flights of stairs to my top-floor office, where I listened to over a thousand recordings to see which we might use. Among them were wonderful old recordings dating back to the 1950s, by one of the pioneers of wildlife recording, Ludwig Koch. But there were also gaps – lots of gaps! So we recruited a team of superb wildlife sound recordists – Gary Moore, Geoff Sample and Chris Watson – and set them the daunting task of capturing sounds for the series, either from their own personal archives or out in the field.

Some of our most familiar birds proved unexpectedly challenging. The feral pigeon lives amid such a hubbub of urban sound that Geoff Sample found recording pure calls, without people and traffic in the background, surprisingly difficult. The golden pheasant presented different challenges, as it calls infrequently, usually during late winter and spring nights in the depths of dense conifer woods. Gary Moore spent a freezing April night among prickly pine needles to capture its seldom recorded mating squawk. And Chris Watson, who has travelled the world in search of exotic wildlife, bedded down in the Lincolnshire reedbeds to obtain some exceptional recordings of water rails and bearded tits:

The best moments of my work as a wildlife sound recordist are putting on a pair of headphones and entering into that secret world of animals we can never get that close to. Listening intently, the clattering hiss and rattle of reed stems became much sharper. I heard the distant squeal of a water rail and the sharp warning notes of coot on the water. I could hear all this yet see very little from my position. Eventually, and without much audible warning, they came by. Bearded tits would approach and pass by dancing around the microphone for just a few moments, calling frequently to keep in contact, and then melting away into the forest of reed stems.

Once we had gathered our birdsongs and calls, we started thinking about the different human voices that would present the programmes. Sir David Attenborough would begin the series on 6 May, the day after International Dawn Chorus Day, and would be followed by many well-known names: Miranda Krestovnikoff, Michaela Strachan, Steve Backshall, Brett Westwood, Chris Watson, Martin Hughes-Games, Kate Humble, John Aitchison, Bill Oddie and Chris Packham. The scripts were written by Brett Westwood but many of the presenters contributed their own thoughts and experiences. For Martin Hughes-Games the jackdaw evoked long-forgotten childhood memories:

As a child we had a tame jackdaw, which was brought injured to my father (the local doctor) who managed to patch her up and she became a very colourful, if somewhat demanding member of the family with her very own store of costume jewellery to play with. She lived in the downstairs bathroom.

One year, in my old house, we tried to light the wood burner when winter came but it filled the house with smoke. When the chimney sweep came we removed a vast heap (around five bin bags) of dry twigs from the chimney where the jackdaws had tried to build a nest — unbelievable industry! In my current house I have fitted wire covers on the chimneys to ward off the jackdaws — always in pairs — who come in early spring and try to fill the entire chimney with twigs.'

Once the scripts had been recorded, the programmes were mixed at the BBC Bristol studios. Sarah Blunt produced the first three months and then Sarah Pitt took over the remaining nine months, rising to the challenge of editing a programme of just ninety seconds another 189 times:

There's something very special about our relationship with birds and that's why Tweet of the Day *is a joy to produce. It doesn't matter where you live in the UK, city or country, birdsong and calls are ever present. The magic of* Tweet *is that we capture these voices of the wild and invite listeners to imagine themselves out on an estuary hearing the plaintive call of the curlew or deep in woodland to hear a tawny owl duet. Best of all, for me, is that* Tweet *continues the fine tradition of natural history sound recording and production begun in Bristol by the BBC over sixty years ago. Searching out old recordings or commissioning new ones, the variety of birdsong is staggering, so it's a privilege to be able to share it with so many people.*

Tweet of the Day is, however, about far more than Britain's birds and their sounds, as Julian Hector concludes:

Broadcast first thing in the morning, ahead of the most influential news programme in the country, Today, *the series provided a natural punctuation mark in our busy lives. There is a growing sense that we have to change our relationship with nature, the nature on which we all depend, if we want to avoid losing touch with what matters most in our lives. By allowing us to pause for just ninety seconds, and remind ourselves that our lives are inextricably linked with those of the wild creatures around us,* Tweet of the Day *has created a vital refuge where we could experience joy and delight in a troubled world.*

SO WHY THIS BOOK? The length of the programmes meant that only the briefest flavour of each bird could be given on the radio and there was so much more to say. Indeed, this book could have been four times the length, but we wanted to translate something of the concentrated intensity of the radio programmes on to the page.

In this book, you'll find the birds under each monthly heading as they appeared in the radio series. It is not a field guide, so in these pages you won't find detailed descriptions of bird plumages or distribution, or long lists of statistics. Instead, we have attempted to convey the essence of each bird: its character, the places where it lives, and especially what it is like to see and hear it in the field.

Where appropriate, we have also added stories about how the bird's life intersects with our own: through folklore, history, art, music, literature and culture. We have been immeasurably helped by Carry Akroyd's beautiful and evocative illustrations.

The book is in no way meant to be a comprehensive guide to Britain's birds. There are about 600 birds on the 'British List', defined as having occurred naturally in the wild by the British Ornithologists' Union. This book, like the radio series, includes just under half of these.

Eagle-eyed readers will notice that some fairly familiar birds are missing. These include several ducks, for example tufted duck, pintail and red-breasted merganser, and a few birds of prey such as marsh and Montagu's harriers. The reason for these omissions is that our choice was influenced by sound and though these species are interesting, and indeed very beautiful in many other respects, the sounds they make are not among their strongest features.

While the series was on the air, the question of what makes a bird British became a talking point in the letters column of *Radio Times* and subsequently in some of our national newspapers. A handful of listeners were puzzled about the inclusion of what they regarded as unfamiliar 'foreign' birds: passage migrants and vagrants, that either pass through Britain in small numbers in spring and autumn, or turn up once in a blue moon, having taken the wrong turn on migration. This overlooked the inconvenient fact that the male cuckoo – one of our best-known and most iconic birds – spends barely two months in Britain, arriving in April and heading back south to Africa in midsummer, and that even swallows spend half the year away from our shores.

So, in these pages you'll read about the bobolink as well as the blackbird, the mourning dove as well as the moorhen, among the rich panoply of species that we can see and hear in Britain. But before we get to the birds themselves, there's a short detour to find out why birds sing, a brief history of birdwatching, and a tour around our local patches to explain how and why we became birders and how you can too – that is, if you're not hooked already.

The accompanying Radio 4 website features illustrations of all the birds and the chance to listen again and download each programme. The site has proved very popular – and is the perfect accompaniment to this book.

http://www.bbc.co.uk/radio4/tweetoftheday

BIRDSONG

The language of birds is very ancient, and, like other ancient modes of speech,
very elliptical: little is said, but much is meant and understood.

Gilbert White, 1789

WHY DO BIRDS SING?

Throughout human history we have been fascinated by birdsong. No other
natural phenomenon has quite such power to captivate us; a power displayed
in religion and superstition, poetry and prose, music and folklore, history and
culture – even in the names we give to birds. Of all our innumerable encounters
with the natural world, none is quite so all-pervasive as birdsong, and none
has quite the same power to stir human emotions: of love, longing and loss,
among others.

Yet for the birds themselves, birdsong is simply a means to an end, rather
than an end in itself. Some may sound more musical to our ears than others –
the lush outpourings of the nightingale or the skylark, compared with the
mono-tonous ramblings of the dunnock, for example. But from the birds' point
of view, tunefulness has nothing to do with whether a song is effective. The only
thing that matters is that other members of the same species can hear it, and
respond in the desired way.

What is extraordinary about birdsong is that it performs two different but
equally important functions. On the one hand, birds sing to repel rival males and
stop them invading the incumbent's territory; on the other, they do so to attract
females to form a pair bond and eventually mate with the singer, thus enabling
him to procreate.

For the singing bird, it could hardly be more serious: if he fails to attract a
mate, or allows his rivals to steal a march on him by getting there first, he may die
without ever having reproduced. This is particularly true for songbirds, many of

which have a life expectancy of only a year or two. This could be his one chance to pass his genetic heritage on, so no wonder he sings so loudly and persistently.

You'll notice we say 'he'. That's because with a very few exceptions, all birds that sing are males. But although they are doing the hard work, it is the females that in many ways matter more. For it is they who judge the quality of the song they hear and decide whether to commit themselves to one particular male — or to another. Just as in *The X Factor*, it is the judges who have the real power.

The only exceptions to this rule, in Britain at least, are those birds where the female defends a territory, as with robins in autumn and winter, when females will also deliver their plaintive and unseasonal song. But in the vast majority of cases, the male, and the male alone, is singing.

Birds are able to produce such complex sounds because their vocal mechanism is completely different from ours, which is why we find it so difficult to imitate birdsong with any accuracy. Whereas we use our vocal cords and larynx, a bird's vocal organ is called a syrinx, and is able to produce two sounds simultaneously by separately controlling both sides of the trachea.

The reason why some birds use this sophisticated mechanism to produce a complex series of extraordinary sounds, while others sing something much more simple, is harder to explain. Why a female chiffchaff is happy with the male's rather monotonous song, whereas a female nightingale requires her potential mate to create a tune with dozens of different phrases, is a puzzle.

And if you think the nightingale's song is complex, try listening to a brown thrasher, a thrush-sized member of the mockingbird family from North America. Brown thrashers have been found to sing more than 2,000, and perhaps as many as 3,000, distinct songs — that's ten times as many as the Beatles ever wrote — and although no single male thrasher sings anything like that many, they are still all able to produce a wide range of sounds.

Even more peculiar is why some birds, entirely capable of singing their own compositions, choose to copy other species instead. The starling is the best known British mimic, able to recreate the songs of many common birds, as well as car alarms and telephone ringtones. But the undisputed champion impersonator is the marsh warbler. Each individual male can mimic up to eighty different songs: both British birds and those from its winter quarters in south-east Africa. Overall, marsh warblers have been known to imitate more than 200 different species.

The theory behind such extraordinary complexity — which also applies to birds like the nightingale, which sing many different variations of their own song — is that the ability to perform to such high standards is the accidental result of an evolutionary 'arms-race', in which the females preferred males with a more varied song, and so the ability to perform such complex sounds was passed down from generation to generation.

BIRDSONG

WHICH BIRDS SING?

Not all birds sing. Indeed by a small margin, the majority of the world's ten thousand or so bird species do not sing. Although albatrosses and auks, hawks and herons, and gulls and geese all make distinctive sounds, they do not 'sing' in the sense that we usually use the word.

So what of the rest: the half of all the world's birds that do sing? The vast majority of these are members of the order Passeriformes, sub-order Oscines – the families and species we usually call 'songbirds'. These range across a wide spectrum of shapes, sizes and plumages: from tits to treecreepers, warblers to wrens and finches to flycatchers; all of which produce a series of notes – sometimes simple, sometimes highly complex.

However, if we define 'birdsong' as a learned, vocal tool whose purpose is to defend a territory and attract a mate, then it is true that other species, apart from songbirds, also 'sing'. Waders perform a display flight over their territory, producing a sound at least as complex. The haunting calls of divers, the hooting of owls and the mewing of buzzards, not to mention non-vocal sounds such as the drumming of woodpeckers, all perform the same function as traditional birdsong.

Then there are the various other sounds made by birds, usually referred to as 'calls'. This is a tricky area, for when does a call become a song, and vice versa? Some calls have a very specific function: the ringing alarm made by blackbirds when a predator is nearby; the nocturnal screeches of shearwaters as they try to locate their youngster among the hubbub of the colony; and the contact calls of a winter flock of tits, which enable them to stay in touch and alert the flock to a source of food.

But other calls are performing essentially the same function as a song. Watching a herring gull throw its head back and unleash that famous sound, so redolent of childhood holidays by the seaside, leaves the observer in no doubt that this bird is staking out its nesting territory and warning off its rivals from coming too close.

In *Tweet of the Day* we haven't been too fussy about whether the sound we're hearing is defined as a song or a call; in some ways this is a fairly artificial distinction, especially when it comes to our cultural appreciation of the sounds made by birds. But before we examine this, a little scientific understanding may also be necessary.

WHEN DO BIRDS SING?

Put simply, birds sing in springtime. For most birds, the 'breeding season' is during the spring and summer, so the need to sing – to establish and defend a territory and win and keep a mate – is indeed predominant at this time of year.

But here in the British Isles, where the weather can be so unpredictable, and the seasons so fluid, spring is a rather more elastic concept. Thus the earliest songsters, such as the mistle thrush and song thrush, may begin singing to defend a territory as early as January – even before Christmas in very mild winters. Other resident breeders will start singing in February or March; early migrants such as the chiffchaff and blackcap arrive in March, but others, such as spotted flycatchers and marsh warblers, may not get here until well into May.

The situation is complicated by the fact that many species have two or more broods of young, so continue to defend their territory by singing well into June, July and even August. And as we have already seen, robins hold autumn and winter territories, so sing from September right the way through to the New Year. They're not alone: wrens often burst into song on a mild winter's day, as do reclusive Cetti's warblers, while migrant chiffchaffs call out their name on sunny days in September.

It's a useful lesson, perhaps, that nature doesn't always conform to rigid rules. What we can say, though, is that the peak time for birdsong is the months of April and May, with smaller peaks in March and June. So if you want to hear a truly spectacular dawn chorus, you'll need to get up very early during the first couple of weeks in May, when almost all the migrants have returned and the resident birds are still at their peak.

The effort needed to sing for such a long period – several weeks or even months in some cases – is astonishing. Remember, when a bird is singing he immediately puts himself at a disadvantage: he cannot feed – either himself, his partner as she sits on her clutch of eggs or, later on, his hungry young. He may also be in danger from predators, especially if, like the skylark, he chooses to sing right out in the open.

Then there is the sheer energy singing requires. It has been calculated that if a song thrush sings his brief, repeated phrases for a few hours every day, by the time the breeding season is over that one bird will have sung more than 1 million separate phrases. That's a lot of effort. But we are lucky that birds are so single-minded, because their resulting songs have huge resonance for us.

WHAT DOES BIRDSONG MEAN TO US?

As the Chinese proverb goes: 'A bird does not sing because it has an answer. It sings because it has a song.' However much we study the science behind birdsong, one inescapable truth remains: that despite all the evidence to the contrary, we still subconsciously believe that in some way the birds are singing to please us.

On spring mornings up and down the country, legions of enthusiasts get up well before sunrise and head out into the woods to listen to what has been described as the best free entertainment in the world, the dawn chorus. There is even an International Dawn Chorus Day, held on the first Sunday in May, to commemorate this very British obsession. The dawn chorus is often portrayed as the 'tuning up of the orchestra', but this ignores the inconvenient fact that each bird only listens to the songs made by its own species, and ignores all the rest.

One of the very first written references to birds comes in the Old Testament's Song of Solomon, and refers to the soporific cooing of the turtle dove. The Greeks and Romans were likewise fascinated by birdsong. Aristotle, in the fourth century BC, proposed that young birds learned how to sing from their parents, inaccurately claiming that 'a mother nightingale has been observed to give lessons in singing to a young bird'. Pliny the Elder, writing in the first century AD, noted the rivalry between singers, though like Aristotle (and many others since) he subscribed to the misguided notion that it was the female, not the male, that sings.

But down through the ages, nowhere is the connection between birdsong and art more deeply embedded than in poetry. This goes back even earlier than Aristotle, to the ancient Greek poet Homer, whose Iliad and Odyssey (probably written in the ninth century BC) feature a number of references to singing birds, including the nightingale, which 'sings sweetly in the early spring'. The Roman poet Catullus wrote a moving elegy for Lesbia's pet sparrow that chirped for her alone.

In English poetry, the first references to bird sounds come in the Anglo-Saxon poem known as 'The Seafarer', whose anonymous author (translated by the ornithologist, author and broadcaster James Fisher) summons up a springtime visit to a noisy seabird colony:

There heard I naught but seething sea,
Ice-cold wave, awhile a song of swan.
There came to charm me gannets' pother
And whimbrels' trills for the laughter of men,
Kittiwakes singing instead of mead.
Storms there the stacks thrashed, there answered them the tern
With icy feathers; full oft the erne wailed round
Spray-feathered . . .

It is perhaps not surprising that the oral tradition of Anglo-Saxon poetry ('The Seafarer' was not written down until the year 1000, some three centuries after it was first created) includes so many references to the sound, rather than simply the appearance, of birds.

In these days when optical equipment is so advanced, it is hard for us to remember that until very recently our encounters with birds would have been primarily through hearing, rather than seeing them. Gilbert White, in the mid-eighteenth century, took great delight in identifying the three similar-looking 'leaf warblers' through their distinctive songs, rather than by the more subtle differences in their plumage. Shakespeare liked his birdsong, too, though he mistakenly thought that the tawny owl's 'tu-whit, to-whoo' was made by a single bird, whereas in fact it is a duet between the female and male.

But it wasn't until the late eighteenth and early nineteenth centuries that birdsong really became a focus for poets. The writings of the Romantic poets are full of birdsong: Wordsworth's 'To the Cuckoo' ('While I am lying on the grass I hear thy restless shout'); Shelley's 'To a Skylark' ('Hail to thee, blithe spirit, bird thou never wert') and Keats's 'Ode to a Nightingale':

> *Adieu! Adieu! Thy plaintive anthem fades*
> *Past the near meadows, over the still stream,*
> *Up the hill-side; and now 'tis buried deep*
> *In the next valley-glades . . .*

The Romantics may have written evocatively about nature, but the birds they describe are often more symbolic than real. Keats is not even particularly interested in the nightingale; his poem is actually a complex meditation on death. Given that he composed it in Hampstead, north London, more than one birder has pointed out that the subject of his poem might not have been a nightingale at all, but a blackbird or song thrush.

The poet who best understood birds, and wrote about them more consistently and evocatively than any other, was John Clare. Born in 1793, Clare was a contemporary of Keats, but was somewhat contemptuous of his peer who, he said, 'often described nature as she appeared to his fancies and not as he would have described her had he witnessed the things he describes'.

For Clare, genuine field observation of the bird itself was the key, as opposed to the Romantics' fevered imagination, and nowhere is this truer than in his descriptions of birdsong, as in the poem 'Birds in Alarm':

> *The firetail tells the boys when nests are nigh*
> *And tweets and flies from every passer-by*
> *The yellowhammer never makes a noise*
> *But flies in silence from the noisy boys . . .*

> *The nightingale keeps tweeting-churring round*
> *But leaves in silence when the nest is found*
> *The peewit hollos 'chewrit' as she flies*
> *And flops about the shepherd where he lies;*
> *But when her nest is found she stops her song*
> *And cocks [her] coppled crown and runs along.*

Wrens cock their tails and chitter loud and play,
And robins hollo 'tut' and fly away.

At times the very rhythm of his poetry appears to mimic the sound of the bird he writes about, as in 'The Skylark':

Up from their hurry, see, the skylark flies,
And o'er her half-formed nest, with happy wings
Winnows the air, till in the cloud she sings,
Then hangs a dust-spot in the sunny skies,
And drops, and drops, till in her nest she lies . . .

The song of the skylark has inspired musicians as well as poets: Ralph Vaughan Williams's *The Lark Ascending* (itself inspired by George Meredith's poem of the same title) was written in the 1920s, and remains very popular today.

Vaughan Williams wasn't the only composer to have turned to birdsong for inspiration. In his book *Was Beethoven a Birdwatcher?* David Turner muses on whether the opening notes of the last movement of Beethoven's Symphony No. 2 were inspired by the explosive song of Cetti's warbler. This isn't as far-fetched as it sounds, as they share the same rhythm, and we know that parts of the same composer's Symphony No. 6, the 'Pastoral', imitate various birdsongs, including the cuckoo, quail and (inevitably) the nightingale. The twentieth-century French composer Olivier Messiaen went one step further, frequently incorporating almost note-by-note transcriptions of birdsong into his musical compositions.

Nor has birdsong only inspired classical composers. From Leon René's 'Rockin' Robin' (later sung by Michael Jackson), to Paul McCartney, whose 1968 song 'Blackbird' includes a snatch of the bird's actual song, it is a running strand in our musical consciousness. And when the digital radio station Oneword closed down in 2008, the frequency was kept open by playing recordings of birdsong, which ironically attracted far more listeners than the programmes it replaced.

HOW CAN WE LEARN BIRDSONG?

Many people who consider themselves birdwatchers, or simply enjoy feeding birds in their garden or seeing them when on a country walk, baulk at the idea that they could ever learn to identify birds by their sound alone. Yet it really is not all that difficult to learn the calls and songs of birds.

Rather like mastering a foreign language, it does take some time and effort – but just as beginners soon find they can scrape some basic French phrases

together, so you will rapidly be able to identify more birds than you ever thought possible.

You may be surprised at how many you know already. Most people can distinguish the chirp of the house sparrow from the plaintive song of the robin, or the deep, measured tones of the blackbird from the more assertive, repetitious song thrush.

Then there are the songs and calls you know without even having to think about them: the unmistakable two-note call of the cuckoo, the jaunty song of the chiffchaff, or the echoing cries of the kittiwake – just three birds that call out their own name.

Many others do so too, even if it's not quite so obvious. Choughs call 'chow' – the sound 'chough' would make if we rhymed it with 'plough', as it may originally have been. Jackdaws say 'jack', while rooks, crows and ravens all shout out an approximation of their name – and indeed all three names originally derive from their call. You can use this to help you remember bird sounds: when you learn that the word 'finch' comes from the chaffinch's 'pink' call, you can associate this sound with the bird.

Other mnemonics are based not on the bird's name, but simply on its sound. Thus the great tit is, for generations of schoolchildren, the 'teacher bird', because it sings a syncopated 'tea-cher, tea-cher', with the stress on the second syllable. Pied wagtails are known in London as the 'Chiswick flyover', because they call 'chis-ick' as they pass overhead.

Once you start using mnemonics to help you learn and remember bird sounds, the sky's the limit. You don't need to follow convention: not everyone thinks that yellowhammers call out 'a-little-bit-of-bread-and-no-cheeese' but if it helps you remember what they sound like, that's fine. And when you discover that reed buntings remind you of bored sound engineers, chaffinches have the rhythm of a cricketer running up to bowl, and wrens perform like opera singers, a whole new world of birding will open up for you.

There's no right or wrong way to remember a bird's call or song, just the way that works for you. Next time you hear the bird, you'll be amazed at how you can identify it without hesitation. So if you hear what you think might be a lesser whitethroat, try singing the last line of the first verse of the Spice Girls' hit 'Wannabe' – it works for Stephen every time, even if he does get some funny looks from his fellow birders.

BIRDWATCHING: A BRIEF HISTORY

All sorts of different people seem to watch birds. Among those I know of are a Prime Minister, a President, three Secretaries of State, a charwoman, two policemen, two Kings, two Royal Dukes, one Prince, one Princess, a Communist, seven Labour, one Liberal, and six Conservative Members of Parliament, several farm-labourers earning ninety shillings a week, a rich man who earns two or three times that amount in every hour of the day, at least forty-six schoolmasters, an engine-driver, a postman, and an upholsterer.

James Fisher, *Watching Birds* (1940)

A Royal Duke, three pop stars, a postwoman, a landscape gardener, several university lecturers, at least three former Conservative cabinet ministers, a trades union leader, four comedians (three living, one dead), a quiz show host, ITV and BBC weather forecasters, a fashion photographer, a nurse, a grandmother, two ten-year-old boys, the news editor of the *Daily Star*, an Australian musician, and a retired worker from Ford's of Dagenham.

List updated by Stephen Moss, *A Bird in the Bush* (2004)

TODAY, when millions of people in Britain and around the world enjoy watching birds, it's hard to believe that it is only in the past few decades that people have had the spare time, the money and the inclination to take part in this hobby, pastime or – for some – obsession.

For most of human existence, people did of course watch birds, but when our distant ancestors did so, it was for a number of (mostly) practical reasons. Were they good to eat and, if so, would they be easy to catch? Could their behaviour help predict the weather, at least in the short term? Did some of them arrive back on a regular date in the calendar, and if they did, could that help decide when to plant or harvest crops? Could they be worshipped, or used in other religious or superstitious rituals?

Later, as civilizations rose and fell across the ancient world, so our ancestors' interest in birds became more complex. Thus the philosophers of ancient Greece and Rome studied the behaviour of birds, and tried to incorporate this into their view of the world. But Aristotle and Pliny, though they observed birds carefully and often perceptively, were still not 'birdwatching', if we define this as looking at birds primarily for pleasure.

Deciding who was 'the first modern birdwatcher' will always be contentious, but our vote goes to the Reverend Gilbert White, vicar of the parish of Selborne in rural Hampshire. White's life spanned much of the eighteenth century, during which our society and culture were undergoing huge and unprecedented changes, first through the Enlightenment, and then the Industrial Revolution.

The former encouraged new ideas, which laid the ground for the kind of observation of birds and other wildlife that White pioneered, and has lasted to this day. The latter paved the way for a wholesale change in British society, including the huge shift in population from the countryside to the city, and the rise of a new 'middle class', with the time, money and inclination to pursue a range of leisure activities, including birdwatching.

What made White different from all his predecessors was that although scientific enquiry was always an important motivator, his main purpose when wandering the byways of his country parish was to find, watch and above all enjoy birds. The passion he feels when observing an individual bird is really modern, as shown in this extract from his bestselling book *The Natural History of Selborne*:

> *The most unusual birds I ever observed in these parts were a pair of hoopoes (upupa) which came several years ago in the summer, and frequented an ornamental piece of ground, which adjoins my garden, for several weeks. They used to march about in a stately manner, feeding in the walks . . .*

After White's death in 1793, other people began to watch birds in the same way. They included Thomas Bewick, whose two-volume *History of British Birds*

(1797 and 1804), with its neat engravings and clear, concise text, could claim to be the very first 'field guide'; and John Clare, whose acute observations of the birds around his Northamptonshire home stand comparison with any modern birder.

Over the course of the late eighteenth and early nineteenth centuries these and other pioneers managed to establish which birds were found in Britain, where they lived, and what their official names should be, setting the groundwork for the huge rise in interest in birds and birdwatching during the late nineteenth and early twentieth centuries.

In the meantime, though, the invention of the breech-loading shotgun in the mid-nineteenth century had a profound influence on the accumulation of our knowledge of birds. 'Collecting' became the watchword, as hordes of Victorian gentlemen set forth at dawn to blast every bird they could find out of the sky. Their unfortunate victims were then stuffed, mounted and put on display.

Collecting was especially influential in our understanding of rare birds: vagrants to our shores from far-flung corners of the globe. Unless a bird was shot, its identity would not be accepted, a custom that gave rise to the saying: 'What's hit is History, what's missed is Mystery.' From a modern perspective it is easy to condemn the practice of killing rare and unusual birds, but in the days before optical aids such as binoculars and telescopes it was often the only way to be absolutely sure of a bird's identity.

Shooting birds wasn't universally popular, however, especially when it was done for profit and fashion: to obtain skins and feathers to adorn the hats and clothes of high society ladies. The Victorian era saw a huge shift in attitudes towards nature, and by the end of the nineteenth century the fightback against this wanton slaughter had begun.

The Society for the Protection of Birds (later the RSPB) was founded in 1889, and in the following decades the practice of 'collecting' birds gradually gave way to simply watching them. Even so, it was not until the first year of the twentieth century that the phrase 'bird watching' first appeared, as the title of a book by a young naturalist named Edmund Selous. Thus the term we use for our pastime is barely a century old.

The new 'birdwatchers' were aided by the invention of the piece of equipment we all take for granted, prismatic binoculars. Invented by the Italian

Ignacio Porro in the 1850s, the first mass-production binoculars were marketed by Carl Zeiss in 1894 – featuring the same 'Porro prism' design many people still use today. Binocular technology was hugely advanced by the need for soldiers to see the enemy during both the First and Second World Wars, and indeed many older birdwatchers active today learned their craft using ex-military binoculars.

During the course of the twentieth century, birdwatching went from being the preserve of a small minority of mainly educated, affluent, upper-class British men, to a pastime anyone can enjoy, regardless of their sex, class or background. The changes that led to this extraordinary boom began in the early decades of that century, when some key institutions were established that brought these pioneering birdwatchers together and enabled them to develop their hobby. These included the monthly magazine *British Birds* (founded in 1907 and still going strong); the start of bird ringing in Britain in 1909; and the scientific study of bird behaviour in the field, pioneered by Julian Huxley (see Great Crested Grebe for more on this) in 1912.

During the twentieth century people's horizons broadened, as first the private car and later the development of air travel and package holidays enabled them to explore new locations at home and abroad. There was also a huge increase in the amount of free time available to most Britons. As early as 1939 George Orwell wrote about this new boom in leisure activities:

> *Another English characteristic which is so much a part of us that we barely notice it, and that is the addiction to hobbies and spare time occupations . . . We are a nation of flower-lovers, but also a nation of stamp-collectors, pigeon-fanciers, amateur carpenters, coupon-snippers, darts-players, crossword-puzzle fans . . .*

In the decades following the end of the Second World War birdwatching began to move towards the head of this list. Six long years of wartime had sharpened Britons' passion for making the most of the peace, and many of those who had survived the conflict had been given unprecedented opportunities to travel abroad while serving in the armed forces, opening their eyes to a global array of birdlife. When they returned they continued to watch birds in their more

pedestrian, domestic surroundings. These new birdwatchers were encouraged by advances in optical equipment and the first proper field guides, both of which enabled them to identify birds without having to kill them first.

Wartime had another unexpected legacy: the invention of radar enabled ornithologists to track the mass movements of migrating birds; and in the 1950s and 1960s the passion for observing migration became a major aspect of birdwatching, manifested in a growing network of bird observatories all around our coasts. Hordes of people flocked to these migration hotspots, from Fair Isle in the north to the Isles of Scilly in the south, to observe both rare and common birds.

This in turn led to the pastime of 'twitching'. Wilfully misunderstood by the media, who often use the word as synonymous with birdwatching, twitching is in fact the single-minded pursuit of rare birds, in order to add them to your own personal 'British List'.

The heyday of twitching was the 1980s and 1990s, when new technological breakthroughs such as information phonelines and portable pagers enabled twitchers to get up-to-the-minute knowledge of the presence – or absence – of a rare bird. The importance of this cannot be overestimated; thirty years earlier, news of a rare bird hardly ever leaked out at all, and if it did, was often communicated by postcard.

But with the arrival of these new means of rapid communication, thousands of people could gather at very short notice to watch a single vagrant, such as the golden-winged warbler from North America – still the only one of its kind ever seen in Britain – that turned up in the unlikely surroundings of a Tesco's car park in Kent in February 1989. Thousands more made the annual pilgrimage to the Isles of Scilly, where rare birds from North America, Europe and Siberia converge each autumn.

Twitching may not be quite as popular as it used to be – perhaps because for the price of a charter flight to Shetland you can spend a fortnight in North America, seeing the birds where they actually belong – but it still has many thousands of dedicated adherents. In some ways, they are like a benevolent version of the Victorian collectors, using digital cameras and telescopes to add a new species to their 'collection' instead of shotguns.

Other developments in birdwatching during the second half of the twentieth century included bird racing, a competitive version of birding in which teams try to see or hear as many species as possible during a twenty-four-hour period; local patch watching, a more environmentally friendly obsession than twitching, in which a birdwatcher observes the birds on a defined area of land near where they live; and the polar opposite, world listing, in which a tiny cohort of very rich people try to see as many different species as they can out of the ten thousand or so in the world.

For some, this can turn into a kind of mania, in which the chances of adding a new species to their world list diminish with every trip they make, and for whom the momentary buzz of pleasure and relief is almost immediately replaced by the anxiety regarding where the next 'tick' will come from.

Fortunately, birdwatching – now largely known by the American term of 'birding' – is a broad church, with a global network of like-minded people united by their passion for birds. This is manifested both in the virtual and real worlds, with Internet forums catering for every aspect of birding, and local societies and bird clubs bringing people together face to face.

Today, two out of three Britons feed birds in their garden – and though not everyone calls themselves birders, they are nevertheless part of the wider community. There are more than 1 million members of the RSPB, and over half a million people take part in the RSPB's annual Big Garden Birdwatch, making it the biggest Citizen Science project anywhere in the world. One survey suggested that there are almost 3 million active birders in Britain. This has important economic consequences: 'wildlife tourism', both at home and abroad, now makes a significant contribution to local, regional and even national economies.

As a result of this rise in popularity, the kind of people who watch birds has changed too. No longer is birding the preserve of white, educated, middle-class men; vast numbers of women and children regularly go birding. Other distinctive social groups include the Gay Birders Club, set up in the mid-1990s, and Birding for All (originally the Disabled Birders' Association), founded in 2000.

Things are changing very fast in other ways, as well. Already the technology that drove the twentieth-century birding boom looks very old-fashioned: why would you take a heavy, cumbersome book out into the field when you can use smartphone apps to browse online? Indeed why would you bother to identify a bird in the field at all, when you can simply snap a picture of it with your digital camera and work out its identity later on, at your leisure? Birders – especially younger ones – are also using social media sites such as Twitter and Facebook to link up with one another and share details of their sightings.

Old hands sometimes complain that young birders 'don't take field notes any more', but the ability to access information instantly while watching the bird, in real time, has in some ways made this practice redundant. The Internet also provides accurate, up-to-date information on birding sites, rendering 'site guides' (which themselves are less than half a century old – John Gooders's celebrated *Where to Watch Birds* first appeared in 1967) more or less obsolete.

Technology is having other, even more profound, effects on the way we watch birds. Advances in DNA technology are revealing that there may be far more species of bird out there than we ever imagined: so-called 'cryptic species', which look virtually identical but are in fact very subtly different. How this might affect the way we watch birds hasn't perhaps been appreciated. But if we can no longer identify birds in the field will we then need to 'collect' them, just like the Victorians? Or might our obsession with a bird's identity begin to decline, allowing us to take a greater interest in its behaviour and ecology, as the early birdwatchers used to do.

The bad news is that with the constant pressure on their homes, food and habitats, there may not be all that many birds left to see. Global climate change, invasive alien species, habitat loss, persecution and pollution are all major threats to the health of bird populations in Britain and around the globe. With the world's population continuing its seemingly unstoppable growth, with the resulting pressure on natural resources, the picture does look rather gloomy.

BirdLife International estimate that about 2,000 species – about one in five of all those on earth – are now under threat, and that 200 of these could go extinct by the end of this century, more than have disappeared in the 400 years since modern records began in the year 1600. Other studies have suggested that the figure could be much higher; in the worst-case scenario, as many as 2,500, or one in four of all the bird species in the world, could have vanished by the year 2100.

To finish, though, on a more positive note, there can be no doubt that the rise of birding has brought a great degree of pleasure and fulfilment to millions of people. An engagement with the natural world has been shown to benefit our physical, mental, emotional and spiritual health: put simply, birders live longer, feel better and enjoy life more. This is something those of us for whom birds and birding are a lifelong passion have always known; as the pioneering field guide author and artist Roger Tory Peterson wisely observed:

> *The truth of the matter is, the birds could very well live without us, but many – perhaps all – of us would find life incomplete, indeed almost intolerable, without the birds.*

GETTING STARTED

You can know the name of a bird in all the languages of the world: but when you're finished, you'll know absolutely nothing about the bird . . . So let's look at the bird and see what it's doing – that's what counts. I learned very early the difference between knowing the name of something and knowing something.

Richard Feynman

ANYONE can call themselves a birder or birdwatcher, because anyone can enjoy watching birds. However, if you want to make the most of being a birder, there are some things it's worth knowing. So we have tried to distil our own knowledge and experience – we've got almost a century of birding between us – to help you enjoy the pastime to the full.

We both began birding very young. Both born in 1960, we belong to a generation who were allowed to be free-range children, going outdoors at an early age, climbing trees, building dens, and encountering wildlife.

Looking back, it sounds like something out of Enid Blyton, but neither of us lived in some rural idyll. In fact we both grew up in the suburbs – Brett on the edge of the West Midlands, Stephen on the fringes of west London – so we cut our birding teeth in that 'messy limbo which is neither town or country', as Kenneth Allsop so memorably described it. We watched birds in our gardens and in the area immediately around our homes: Brett on north Worcestershire farmland and Stephen on gravel pits and reservoirs in Middlesex. Family holidays around various parts of Britain enabled us to broaden our horizons, and discover a wider range of British habitats and their birdlife.

As Brett remembers:

For me, the first realization that the birds so beautifully portrayed in the field guides really were out there beyond the garden gate came at the age of fifteen, when I was given a pair of battered binoculars as a birthday present. On the first spring bike ride on 5 April 1975, around the lanes near my home in Hagley, I was amazed to see flocks of fieldfares and redwings – obligingly facing left to right just as they did on the plates of my identification guide – roaming the fields just before they set off for Scandinavia. They weren't the free-and-easy garden familiars like blue tits or robins, content to peck at whatever we put out for them. These alert and angular thrushes were the real thing — wild and wary worm-stabbers from foreign lands whose imminent departure and strange markings gave them an irresistible allure.

The next day they were gone, but in the same field were two red-legged partridges, birds so fabulous and exotically marked that they could have stepped off a Chinese tapestry. I couldn't believe that these tiger-striped birds were living and breeding almost on my doorstep and from that day, I was hooked.

For Stephen, some particular highlights stick in the memory too:

Like Brett, redwings feature large in my childhood memories, the first one I ever saw, at the age of eight or nine, on the grassy verge by my home as I biked off to play with friends; my first great crested grebe, sailing serenely past as I tagged along in a crocodile of junior school pupils on a nature walk around the local gravel pits; and the most special of all, my first ever red kite — then a truly rare bird — soaring high overhead after we had searched the valleys of mid-Wales for three long and frustrating days.

Both of us came from families with no obvious interest in birds or wildlife. Brett's long-suffering mother and father tolerated a range of household reptiles and amphibians including a python and, at one point, a captive adder which temporarily hospitalized him; while Stephen's mother, a single parent doting on her only child, ferried him around Britain to the best places to see new birds, thus encouraging his interest without ever really sharing it.

Birding in those days wasn't anything like as popular or mainstream as it is now. At school, we both benefited from meeting like-minded peers, who helped foster and share our interest and stop it petering out, as happens with so many young birders. At Brett's school the ornithological society, which had been founded by Bill Oddie, helped him to focus his interest on different aspects of birding, especially identification and travel to new and exciting places. On Stephen's very first day at grammar school he sat next to Daniel, who turned out to be the only other birder there:

Daniel's family more or less adopted me and took us all around the country during school holidays, including some memorable visits to north Norfolk where we saw clouds of snow buntings and, on one early morning walk, stumbled across a rare great grey shrike on top of a thorn bush. By our teenage years we were going away on our own: cycling around southern England on trips to the New Forest and Dungeness, where we saw even more exotic and wonderful birds, including Ross's gull, rough-legged buzzard and firecrest, to name just a few. Daniel and I remain close to this day.

We have many deep and special memories; not just of the birds, but also of the places we visited and the people we met. For birding is about far more than just the birds themselves: it is a way of life, and a way of connecting with the human as well as the natural world. We have also both been lucky enough to have been able to turn our hobby into work: Brett as a radio producer/presenter and writer, and Stephen as a writer and TV producer.

If you are new to birds and birding, this may seem rather daunting. After all, we were able to try things out, learn from our mistakes and gain experience and expertise over many years, whereas you may feel you need to learn everything at once.

It may sound like a cliché, but the more you learn about birds and wildlife as a whole, the more you realize you don't know. That's one of the great joys of natural history: none of us will ever run out of things to do and to experience. It really comes down to two things: seeing and hearing birds for yourself, in the field; and having an enquiring mind, always questioning both what you see for yourself and what others tell you.

By far the best – and satisfying and enjoyable – way of learning more about birds is to find a local patch. In an ideal world, this will be within a few minutes' walk, cycle or drive of your home; have a range of mini-habitats, preferably including some water; and be small and self-contained enough to visit and cover thoroughly in an hour or less. That way you will visit little and often, and can get to know the birds that live there, and especially the changes they undergo from week to week, season to season and year to year.

Stephen was in his mid-thirties, and had been birding for more than three decades, when he found two local patches that transformed the way he watched birds:

Lonsdale Road Reservoir was a modest little nature reserve along the banks of the Thames in south-west London, while Kempton Park nature reserve was a few miles to the west. Over the course of a few years I visited these places a couple of times a week. Gradually I found myself getting more in tune with the subtle rhythms of nature: the changes of the seasons, the comings and goings of migrant birds such as sand martins and swallows, and the more familiar, resident species, including breeding lapwings and little ringed plovers. It was during that period that I first began to appreciate that common species can be just as exciting as rare ones; as a local patch-watcher I was always far more excited by the first willow warbler of the spring than the prospect of travelling hundreds of miles to see some obscure rarity with a crowd of twitchers.

A few years ago, Stephen and his family moved down to the Somerset Levels, a fabulous place for birds and other wildlife. He lives not all that far from the Avalon Marshes, a vast area of reclaimed wetland with an extraordinary range of species, including such exciting new arrivals as the great white egret and bittern. But to his surprise, he discovered a very different kind of local patch, much closer to home:

In 2010 I decided to spend a year just watching, enjoying and noting down the birds and other wildlife in my own country parish. I deliberately chose it because I knew I could experience nature there every single day – either in my own garden or by walking and cycling around the lanes and droves that crisscross the village and its surroundings. Another reason was that I knew that nothing rare or unusual lives here, which forced me to look harder at common and familiar species, and what they do in their day-to-day lives.

I wrote up my experiences in my book Wild Hares and Hummingbirds, *which deliberately mirrored the most famous literary work on nature in the English language, Gilbert White's* Natural History of Selborne. *Focusing on the creatures on my doorstep helped me to learn a great deal more about the way nature works* than if I had cast my net more widely. It also confirmed my long-standing belief that to understand the global you need to focus on the local; for however small or modest your local patch may be, it is a crucial part of the greater whole.

Stephen has spent the last eight years getting to know the wildlife of his parish and the surrounding area, but he is a mere beginner compared with Brett, who has spent more than half a lifetime getting to know his local patch:

For nearly forty years, I've been watching a rectangle of countryside about three kilometres by two kilometres at the extreme south-western tip of the West Midlands conurbation. It's mostly anonymous farmland with a few copses, a section of the Staffordshire and Worcestershire Canal that shadows the silt-laden River Stour, and two small pools. In that time I've seen 144 species of birds in an area that isn't exactly a rarity magnet. Here a reed warbler is more notable than a goshawk.

I was originally lured there by sewage. Up to the 1980s, the local sewage farm broadcast the slurry widely over large fields. Not only did this attract invertebrates, but in cold weather the warmth kept the ground free of ice. That combination made it attractive to wintering waders, and as a teenage birder I was soon spell-bound by flocks of up to 250 snipe and nearly as many curlews probing for worms and grubs.

In the very harsh winter of 1979 one slurry patch lured in twenty-one wigeon, a pintail and a pink-footed goose, all exceptional birds for the area. One February day in 1976, when I was very much a beginner, two pale and elegant waders loitering near a cattle trough caught my eye and sent me scurrying for the field guides. Against all the rules, they appeared to be spotted redshanks, rare at the best of times, but especially in winter in the West Midlands. Those in the know were understandably sceptical, but spotted redshanks they turned out to be and finding them here cemented my links with this extraordinary place. Those redshanks were my first self-found rarities and working out their identity and having my observation published was an experience that nowadays would be trendily described as 'empowering'.

Spurred on by my find, I deluged the West Midlands Bird Club with wads of records. The club's annual reports gave me an idea of what to expect and what was locally noteworthy. Gradually the patch total began to mount.

There have been some exciting and unexpected moments. One April morning an Alpine swift scythed downriver. Marsh harrier and honey-buzzard have put in appearances and once three little buntings from Scandinavia turned up in a patch of crops planted as pheasant food, pulling in twitchers from as far afield as London.

But it's not really about rarity. The excitement of 'patchworking' is that over the years, by keeping notes, you chart changes not just in your chosen area, but also across the UK. So through my notebooks I can now re-live the moment when I saw my first ravens and buzzards, part of their re-colonization of lowland Britain after centuries of persecution. Here too, though I didn't know it when I wrote them, are my final entries for turtle dove, a bird that has now disappeared from much of the UK.

You also learn over the years to deal with loss. When I began birdwatching, one particular route took me along a green lane where grey partridges creaked and lapwings tumbled in spring. In summer the hedgerow trees jangled with corn buntings and chirping tree sparrows. All were so familiar I took them for granted, but now they are very rare or lost as breeding birds. Tree pipits, whinchats and wood warblers were all regular in the 1980s, but had gone by the turn of the century. On the credit side, however, hobbies, sparrowhawks and cormorants have increased and, unimaginable forty years ago, red kites float over at least annually. Along with the birds, new insects have moved in and polecats – unknown back in the 1970s – are now common.

The real benefits of patch visiting come as you get to know a place really well. That spot where the first celandine leaves come trowelling up through the soil each spring, the horse-paddock where migrant wheatears sprint after insects and the bend in the path where you know you'll be snared by the musky reek of a fox-trail. It's about letting go of our self-imposed rhythms and tapping into other non-human patterns out there. When this happens, it's a revelation. Your perception of the seasons becomes defined by natural events such as the arrival of summer and winter migrants, birdsong and the buzz of insects, and as you observe more, your visits provoke new questions. Why do those blackbirds with dark bills become so obvious in late autumn? Where have the cuckoos gone? Why are barn owls more obvious in some years than in others?

There will be quiet days of course, but the more you see – or don't see – the more questions arise and the more your curiosity will grow.

Getting to know birds and other wildlife on such an intimate basis as this – whether on your local patch or simply in your back garden – really does make you look at them in a different way. It's not merely about identification or ticking off birds on lists. The real thrill is in discovering, as Thomas Hardy put it, 'the ancient pulse of germ and birth', the stuff of life that makes your local patch tick. It's also about the sheer pleasure of seeing birds in their element, a woodcock flushed from beneath a coverlet of bracken or a singing willow warbler after April rain: some things simply are priceless.

To say that birds are special would be a gross understatement; they are – for us, and for millions of others – what makes the world go round. To quote some familiar lines from the poet Ted Hughes, about the swifts that return each spring to the skies above our homes:

> *They've made it again,*
> *Which means the globe's still working . . .*

May birds always refresh us, inspire us, and fill us with joy.

Brett Westwood and Stephen Moss
March 2014

TWEET
OF THE
DAY

Cuckoo
Swift
Wood Warbler
Pied Flycatcher
Nightingale
Garden Warbler
Blackcap
Grey Heron
Dartford Warbler
Shag

 MAY

Reed Bunting
Whimbrel
Greenfinch
Garganey
Redshank
Spotted Crake
Guillemot
Storm Petrel
Sedge Warbler

INTRODUCTION

ASK ANY NATURALIST about the month of May and they will invariably tell you they wish it could be twice as long. Here in the temperate British Isles, where the seasons jostle impatiently with each other, so much is crammed into May's thirty-one precious days of breeding, brooding, feeding and singing that it's hard to know where to look or listen first.

New arrivals, such as warblers and flycatchers, are clamouring for attention among the swelling chorus of the resident tits, blackbirds and thrushes. May is the month when all our summer migrants either arrive or settle down to breed. It's the time to reacquaint ourselves with highly visible old friends, such as the swifts that, exactly on schedule, tear across city skies, screaming as they go. It's a chance to brush up on birdsong: is that really a garden warbler fresh in from West Africa, or just a particularly virtuoso blackcap? It's also time to celebrate the sheer frenzy of the breeding cycle in city gardens and country hedgerows as, right across the UK, countless billions of insects are being stuffed into millions of eagerly begging throats.

May can deliver marvellous cameos and memorable set-pieces, along with one-off, never-to-be-repeated special offers. The trickle of bluebells through our woodlands, which began in April, becomes a flood. Above their spreading pools, moss-green wood warblers effervesce with song, while in the limelight beneath the unfurling leaves, pied flycatchers flit from branch to branch, and redstarts flash their fiery tails.

Taking centre stage in the coppiced woods and thickets of blackthorn, south and east of a line between the Severn and the Humber, is one of the finest – if not *the* finest songster of all – the nightingale. To hear one in full flow on a calm May evening, while hawthorn blossom scents the air and bats flicker in the dying light, is a sublime and unforgettable experience. It's not just the crystalline quality of the song that is so impressive, but as the author and nightingale connoisseur H.E. Bates noted, it's also the pauses the bird leaves between phrases, silences with 'a kind of passion in them, a sense of breathlessness and restraint'.

May is the month to experience the sheer richness and variety of our birdsong. Chris Watson, the doyen of wildlife sound recordists, who has contributed many of the sounds featured on *Tweet of the Day*, believes that our woodland dawn chorus is the finest in the world. It's no surprise that International Dawn Chorus Day is on the first Sunday in May, when all over the UK people gather in little covens before daybreak to witness this extraordinary natural event.

May isn't all about woods and forests, though. In farmland throughout Britain hedgerows are rimmed with a tidemark of creamy cow parsley and, where they haven't been cut back too ferociously, you'll find whitethroats launching themselves into the air to deliver their scratchy song.

In the more luxuriant, thorn-strewn hedgerows, lesser whitethroats rattle. Cuckoos are also at their most insistent now. If you're lucky you'll see one perched on a treetop, its long tail swinging from side to side as it scans for females or rivals. Cuckoos are also regular visitors to marshes and reedbeds, which have filled up with migrants including reed warblers, into whose nests the parasitic cuckoos lay their eggs. If you're really lucky, on a night-time visit to that same marsh, you might hear a whiplash in the dark from an invisible spotted crake.

All these birds are migrants, but many of our commonest residents have eggs or young in the nest by May. That doesn't preclude singing, however, and you'll still hear plenty of song thrushes, mistle thrushes and blackbirds advertising their territories. Some birds have already reared their first brood and by the month's end young long-tailed tits have left their ball-shaped nests of feathers and lichen and are streaming like flying tadpoles through our gardens, chattering softly to each other as they go. Tawny owls are also early breeders. Bearing remnants of fluffy juvenile down, the owlets have left their nests and are 'branching': sitting out at night and wheezing loudly, constantly demanding to be fed. On the coast, sea cliffs bustle with shags, kittiwakes and auks, either incubating eggs or welcoming their first nestlings into their vertiginous world.

Although May is crammed with breeding activity, many birds are still on the move. On coastal and inland marshes, there's a steady trickle of north-bound waders, fuelling up before heading out to sea on the journey to Iceland or Scandinavia. They include wood sandpipers, red-necked phalaropes and spotted redshanks, all Arctic breeders that often linger here for a day or two to delay their arrival in the north until insect populations have emerged. Here in the UK, though, it could hardly be busier, as wildlife shucks off winter with a vengeance and May, with all its delights and distractions, gets into full swing.

CUCKOO

*

The sound is quite unmistakable. A percussive, double-noted call immediately tells you that the best known of our summer visitors is back: the cuckoo. Finding the bird itself is another matter; for such a large bird cuckoos can be surprisingly shy, and that call can carry further than you think. Eventually you catch a glimpse of a steel-grey bird, with long wings and tail and a distinctive horizontal posture, bouncing back and forth as it bestows that famous sound on the springtime air.

The cuckoo is a paradox. Few other birds are so familiar, and yet so rarely seen. It's as much a part of the British countryside as dog roses and cow parsley, and is ingrained in our culture as a harbinger of the coming season.

The anonymous thirteenth-century poem that begins 'Sumer is ycomen in, loude sing, cuckoo!' is a testament to this, and to this mysterious bird's unique sound. No wonder William Wordsworth wrote: 'Shall I call thee bird, or but a wandering voice?'

Cuckoos are indeed great wanderers. Far from being British, they're really African birds, spending well over half the year there, and only gracing us with a brief visit each year. In fact until recently their winter quarters, and the long journey they make to get there, remained a mystery.

Now technology, in the form of tiny tracking devices attached to the cuckoos, has allowed scientists to follow their flightpath as they head south through Europe, across the Mediterranean Sea and the vast Sahara Desert to the dense, equatorial forests where they spend the winter.

To our ancestors, who believed that the cuckoo turned into a sparrowhawk each autumn, this would have come as a surprise. That ancient belief is not so silly as it sounds, given that the cuckoo and the sparrowhawk are roughly the same size, share a greyish plumage, barred underparts and long tails, and have a similar low, direct flight.

After wintering in these African forests, the cuckoo's migratory urge propels it northwards, to arrive back in Britain in the middle of April – a welcome sign that spring is well and truly here. Our ancestors held 'cuckoo fairs' to celebrate its return, something we'd find hard to do now as the species is declining fast, especially in the south. The long-running custom of people writing letters to *The Times* when they hear the first cuckoo of the year is now in danger of coming to an end, as many people never hear a cuckoo nowadays.

Despite its decline, most people are still familiar with the call of the male cuckoo, but how many of us have heard that of the female: a bubbling sound some-times likened to 'bathwater gurgling down the plughole'?

Female cuckoos famously lay their eggs in the nests of smaller songbirds; here in Britain, the reed warbler, meadow pipit and dunnock are the three main hosts. Almost a century ago pioneering film-makers Oliver Pike and Edgar Chance managed to capture unique footage of a cuckoo placing her eggs in the nests of meadow pipits – and revealed that a single female can lay as many as twenty-five eggs in a single season, one in each nest.

Bald and blind, the young cuckoo may look helpless, but it is hard-wired to eject any remaining eggs or chicks from the nest. Begging frantically for food from its unwitting foster parents, it imitates the sound made by their own young – only much more loudly. By the time it is ready to fledge, it is so huge it appears to be wearing the nest, rather than sitting in it.

Most extraordinary of all, the newly fledged young cuckoo then migrates all the way to the heart of Africa – a distance of 4,000 miles – without ever meeting its own parents.

SWIFT
*

Each year, some time around the last week of April or first week of May, city-dwellers are jolted into the realization that spring is well in place, and summer is just around the corner. Swifts, our most visible urban migrants, are back in town.

You may hear them first: a diabolic frenzy of high-pitched screaming above the rooftops. Then you see them, black anchors in the spring skies: a gang of tearaways, scudding through the air like miniature space-rockets, as if they intended to pierce through the firmament to reach the heavens beyond.

Swifts are the ultimate aeronauts: their scythe-like wings and cigar-shaped bodies are the pinnacle of aerial prowess, giving these birds the unique ability to live most of their lives up in the atmosphere, well above our own earthbound existence, where they feed, mate and even sleep.

Swifts only have to come to land to breed. They do so by finding a crevice beneath the eaves of a building, and constructing a shallow cup of grass, leaves and feathers, all these fragments caught on the wing as they float in the air and cemented together with the bird's own saliva, into which the female lays two or three eggs.

To sustain their growing chicks, the parent swifts will fly up to 800 kilometres in a single day, trawling through the air for flying insects and tiny spiderlings, which they store as a food-ball, or bolus, in their throat-pouches.

When rain threatens, and insect food is hard to find, swifts will fly around the edge of the oncoming weather front, often staying away from their nest for several days before the conditions clear and they are able to return. In the meantime their young have the extraordinary ability to lower their metabolic rate and enter a state of torpor until their parents finally return with food.

After between five and eight weeks, when the young are fledged and ready to leave the nest, they launch themselves into the unknown and may not land for more than eighteen months, during which time they will fly to Africa and back. In a swift's lifetime – typically about nine years – they can fly as much as 1.5 million miles.

Swifts are the laggards of spring: late to arrive yet early to depart. The adults head south by early August, with the young following soon afterwards. Throughout the long European autumn and winter they hurtle through African skies until spring finally comes once again, and they're back – bringing a taste of the tropics to town.

WOOD WARBLER
*

'A spinning coin on a marble slab', 'a sweet-sounding, shivering trill', 'waves of pearls dropped … on a shore of pearls': these are all descriptions of one of the most memorable and delightful of all our bird sounds, the song of the wood warbler.

It is a sound that tugs us westwards, to the oak and birch woods of Wales, Scotland and the west of England, where this lemon and lime sprite is one of our most welcome returning migrants in spring.

The wood warbler is the largest of the three 'leaf warblers' to breed in Britain, the other two being the far more familiar willow warbler and chiffchaff. Superficially the three can be hard to tell apart; indeed when Gilbert White wrote in the late eighteenth century of the wood warbler's 'sibilous, shivering noise' he had not yet managed to identify the mysterious bird singing in the beech woods above his Hampshire village.

The wood warbler's blend of moss-green, snow-white and citrus-yellow plumage is perfect camouflage as it darts among the unfurling foliage of the spring woods. Even in song, it's not always easy to pick out in the aqueous shade of the young leaves. But look closely and you'll see that as the male wood warbler sings, he trembles – fizzes, almost – with the effort of producing that shivering sound. If that weren't enough, there then follows a delicate, almost tearful-sounding 'piu, piu, piu', as though the bird were grieving for some unknown loss.

Wood warblers may sing from high in the trees, but they build their nests from grass and dead leaves on the woodland floor, making them very vulnerable to predators. Studies have shown that when the males arrive at potential nesting sites, they spend their time not just singing, but also watching from their high viewpoint for signs of any mammal activity on the ground. If there are too many predators about, they soon move on to find a less risky place to breed.

PIED FLYCATCHER

*

The pied flycatcher is one of the western oak woods trio (along with the wood warbler and the redstart), welcome summer visitors to the venerable ancient woodlands that cloak the hills and crowd the dingles of the rainier, western half of Britain. The bird's song – a tripping series of sharp, melodic notes – is as much a part of the scenery as lichen-covered branches, gnarled trunks, mossy boulders and clear, tumbling streams.

The male pied flycatcher returns here in mid to late April, after the long journey from his wintering grounds in the forests of western Africa. On arrival, he takes up position in his woodland territory, singing lilting arpeggios from the tree canopy, the dappled sunlight illuminating his pied plumage as he flicks his wings and tail.

In between bouts of singing he will launch himself into the air to snatch a passing insect – shutting his bill with an audible snap – to give him the energy to continue serenading potential mates and fending off rival males.

Like other woodland species such as blue and great tits, pied flycatchers nest in holes in trees. Having found a suitable cavity, the male flits repeatedly in and out, flashing white wing-patches to advertise his choice of home to the brown and white females.

Pied flycatchers happily take to ready-made homes, and nestbox schemes have helped boost their population in some places. Overall though, numbers have fallen by between a quarter and a half in recent years, partly because of habitat loss in their winter quarters, but also because a run of wet summers has meant that the adults have struggled to find insects to feed their hungry young. Even so, a walk in May through the sunlit glades of a western oak wood should be enlivened by the sight and sound of one of our most charismatic songbirds.

NIGHTINGALE

*

Imagine a jazz musician, improvising on a theme. Then imagine that he is able to play half a dozen instruments – not one after another, but almost simultaneously, switching effortlessly between both instruments and musical styles with hardly a pause for breath. If you can countenance that, you are halfway towards appreciating the performance that is the extraordinary song of the nightingale.

The beauty, purity and sheer gusto of the nightingale's song has earned it the premier place in our avian orchestra. No other bird – not the song thrush, the blackbird or even the skylark – sings so loudly, so persistently, and with such a varied, and frankly sometimes bizarre, repertoire of sounds. Like many virtuoso singers, the nightingale isn't all that much to look at: a rather drab, russet-brown bird with a rufous tail, often held cocked upwards at an angle to its body.

It's not hard to see – or hear – why the nightingale has inspired so much literature and music and carries such a cargo of symbolism. This is Keats's 'immortal bird', and Joseph Warton's 'chantress of night'. Nightingales were once thought to sing as they impaled themselves on thorns: true beauty, according to the Romantics, comes only with suffering. They are birds of love and longing – one reputedly sang in London's Berkeley Square – and of mystery too. Few other songbirds are quite so difficult to see, even when one is singing at full volume, when its sound shatters through the nocturnal stillness with the force of an orchestra in a library.

What's more, the nightingale rations its appearances with all the skill of a true diva, always leaving the audience wanting more. Nightingales arrive back in Britain in the second half of April, when if you are very lucky you may catch sight of one singing in full view in broad daylight.

Most males are skulkers though, singing by night from the thickest, most impenetrable areas of scrub and coppice, intent on luring down migrating females from the dark skies above.

How to describe a song that must be heard to be believed? A rapid outpouring of liquid brilliance, deep chugging notes, piercing whistles and hair-raising crescendos, all seasoned with breathless pauses – like all great dramatists, the nightingale knows the value of silence, if only for brief moments.

If you are extremely fortunate, you may find yourself poised between two rival males, whose efforts to outdo one another can leave you stunned with admiration for their stereophonic sparring.

Another legendary duet took place in the 1920s, between the cellist Beatrice Harrison and a nightingale at the bottom of her Surrey garden. The event – transmitted on the early BBC radio network – became the very first live broadcast of any wild bird anywhere in the world, and was so popular with listeners that it was restaged every year until the Second World War.

GARDEN WARBLER

*

It is well known that the plainest birds often have the most ornate and beautiful songs, as proved by the plain brown plumage of the nightingale. The garden warbler has the distinction (if one can call it that) of being Britain's plainest bird, and indeed its only real distinguishing feature is that it has no real distinguishing features! Its plumage is what fashionistas might describe as 'taupe', the only highlights being a grey smudge on its neck and beady black eyes in an open, trusting face.

But one day in early May, as you sit in a woodland clearing, a rapid current of notes pours from a source deep within the bushes. Not for nothing is the song of the garden warbler compared to a babbling brook: it has the fluid pace of rippling water in which individual notes are hard to discern. It's often confused with the song of the closely related blackcap, but is a light, rapid contralto to the blackcap's rich soprano.

Another useful comparison when trying to tell the songs of these two apart is that while the blackcap sounds rather like a speeded-up blackbird, the garden warbler is more reminiscent of the rapid, uncontrolled outpourings of the skylark.

Garden warblers are not well named: they are rarely found in gardens (apart, perhaps, from the most rural and neglected ones), as they prefer over-grown thickets of shrubs interspersed with small trees – more characteristic of the edges of woodland and wetland habitats, especially where the trees have recently been coppiced.

They return here from Africa in April and sing until late June. After their young have fledged they depart, characteristically with little or no fanfare, filtering quietly southwards to spend the winter in the forests of West Africa.

BLACKCAP

*

The early bird catches the worm: and also wins the best breeding territory, increasing its chances of passing on its genetic material to future generations. This lesson has been put into practice by one of our commonest and most familiar warblers, the blackcap.

The male blackcap is well named: a large, greyish-brown warbler with a neat sooty cap. For his mate and youngsters, though, the name is less apt: they sport a warm, chestnut-brown cap.

Blackcaps have always been one of the earliest migrants to return to our shores, arriving back here around the time of the spring equinox, in the third week of March. That earned the species the folk-name of 'northern' or 'March' nightingale; for the song itself, while not as rich or varied as that of the true nightingale, is nevertheless tuneful and attractive.

In recent years, this spring and summer visitor has changed its travel plans – with a little help from us. Our breeding blackcaps are mostly short-distance migrants, leaving Britain in September or early October, and heading south to spend the winter around the Mediterranean basin, in Spain, Portugal or North Africa.

But since the 1960s, blackcaps breeding in central Europe – mainly southern Germany and Austria –

MAY

have begun to spend the winter in Britain. Scientists presume that juvenile blackcaps from this population have always gone astray, but that in the past they would simply have starved to death once they arrived here. Since the 1960s the long run of mainly mild winters, along with the fact that we put out food on our garden bird-tables, has allowed them not just to survive, but thrive.

These wintering blackcaps leave us in early March; just before our spring migrants arrive. By doing so, they get back to their breeding grounds a week or two before those that spend the winter around the Med. These 'early birds' secure the best territories, win the fittest females, and ultimately raise more young – each of which is programmed to migrate westwards to Britain instead of south-west to Spain.

As a result, today the vast majority of this central European population of blackcaps winters in Britain, meaning we can enjoy seeing this attractive little warbler all year round.

Incidentally, if you are browsing a bird book from the Victorian era or earlier, you will find that the name 'blackcap' can refer to a whole range of different species. Reed bunting, coal, marsh and willow tits and even the black-headed gull have been called 'blackcap' in the past; even though confusion could have been avoided simply by adopting the simple suffix 'warbler' to the blackcap's name.

GREY HERON

*

As you walk around the edge of an English or Welsh lake, a Scottish loch, or even through a central London park, you may be baffled to hear a throaty, almost prehistoric croaking from the trees above you. Its makers are often invisible and shrouded by foliage, but somewhere up there, secure in their lofty twig-nests, are broods of boggle-eyed grey herons.

It's a sound that we are hearing more and more often throughout Britain, from the Isles of Scilly in the south, to Shetland in the north, and in town and country, because our commonest native heron is on the increase.

We know this for sure, because the grey heron has been surveyed for longer than any other British bird. Back in 1928, a young ornithologist called Max Nicholson launched a project to count every heron breeding in Britain. Fortunately herons are sociable birds, nesting together in colonies known as heronries.

Following that pioneering survey, which found 4,000 nests, heronries have been visited, and the nests counted, every year. Over that time, the bird's fortunes have mainly been on the up, and today, with about 13,000 nests, there are more herons breeding in Britain than at any time in living memory.

But life's not all a bed of roses for grey herons. They are especially vulnerable during long spells of freezing winter weather, when the waterways where they hunt their prey – a diet mainly consisting of fish and frogs – become iced over. Some herons will switch diet, catching small birds, rats and even moles if they can. But nonetheless, in hard winters many perish, their slender bodies in their cloak of grey appearing even more emaciated in death than in life.

The more resourceful herons survive by heading into towns and cities, where they perform daring dawn raids on garden ponds. This doesn't endear herons to people who keep exotic fish, who protect them by placing a layer of fine netting across the surface to foil this predatory piscivore.

DARTFORD WARBLER

*

Dartford is famous for three things: its tunnel beneath the Thames, for being the childhood home of Mick Jagger and, in ornithological circles, for lending its name to one of our rarest and most enigmatic songbirds – the Dartford warbler.

Until recently, to see a Dartford warbler in Britain at all you needed to head to the far south: the furzy, heather-strewn landscapes of Dorset and Hampshire. The 'blasted heaths' of Thomas Hardy's melodramatic rural novels are classic Dartford warbler country. This tiny bird is one of only a handful of warblers that stay in Britain all year round, and so needs a constant supply of minuscule invertebrates on which to feed.

During the winter, it finds these by burrowing deep inside gorse bushes, beneath the custard-yellow flowers and inside the thickets of spiny twigs, where the insects and spiders shelter from harsh weather. Even so, in really hard winters both prey and predators struggle to survive. Following the infamous 'Big Freeze' of 1962–3, the warbler was virtually wiped out as a British breeding bird, with fewer than a dozen pairs surviving.

Come spring, the Dartford warbler grinds out its scratchy, mechanical song from a high perch on a heather-top or sprig of gorse. It can be shy and elusive, but if you do get a good look it is unmistakable: a slender little bird, greyish-brown above and the colour of deep red wine below, with a jaunty crest and long tail, often held cocked at right angles to its back. In flight, as it darts between hummocks of gorse, it looks noticeably tail-heavy.

The long trend towards milder winters since that terrible year of 1963 has allowed the Dartford warbler to bounce back. In recent years, they've increased to more than 3,000 breeding pairs, though numbers have fallen back as a result of a handful of severe winters. They have extended their range as well: westwards to Somerset, Devon and Cornwall, east to Norfolk and Suffolk, and north to the Midlands.

They're even back in Kent, although not as yet, sadly, in Dartford. Incidentally, although the folk-name of 'furze wren', or even 'gorse warbler', would be far more suitable, the name Dartford warbler has stuck – all because the very first pair ever identified were shot on Bexleyheath, near Dartford, back in 1773.

SHAG

*

At the top of a rocky cliff, three chicks squat in a nest among heaps of rotting seaweed and small pieces of driftwood bleached white by the baking summer sun. These reptilian creatures are baby shags, whose

MAY

leathery skin gives them the appearance of tiny pterodactyls: youngsters only their parents could love.

Approach too close for comfort, and the adult shag will use its relatively limited repertoire of sounds to warn you off, hissing and belching until you withdraw to a safe distance.

The shag is a rather handsome, albeit bizarre-looking, bird, more slender and delicately built than its larger relative the cormorant. It has a dark, oily-green plumage, piercing emerald eyes and a comical-looking tufted crest – which gives the bird its name.

Its more ancient names include 'scarf' and 'scart', derived from Old Norse, which mimic the shag's harsh, grating call. Another name, 'black duck', was used for a brief period during the Second World War, when food shortages led to shags being harvested in the Northern Isles and sent to London to be served in the smartest restaurants. One can only imagine the faces of the disappointed diners lifting their tureens to find this scraggy bird with fishy flesh.

In recent years, many of the shag's close relative the cormorant have moved inland to feed and breed; but shags remain true seabirds, feeding mainly on sand eels, the ubiquitous tiny fish also favoured by puffins. Scientists have put miniature cameras on diving shags, discovering that they will chase after fish in open water as well as grubbing up crabs and flatfish from the seabed. After a successful fishing trip, it's back to the nest to regurgitate its catch for the growing chick.

REED BUNTING

*

The reed bunting has been described – rather harshly – as a songbird in search of a song. Its simple, repetitive refrain – often delivered from swaying reeds or a more secure perch on top of a bush – has also been likened to a bored sound engineer: 'one … two … testing …'

But poised on top of a reed-plume, the male reed bunting atones for a lack of musical prowess with his dashing good looks. He sports a jet-black head, slashed by a snow-white moustache, streaky fawn and chestnut upperparts, and paler, greyish white below. His mate is far less conspicuous, as streaky as the reeds and sedges in which she nests, the perfect camouflage to avoid being spotted by predators. Like her mate, she sports the telltale white edges to her tail as she flies away, a useful aid to identification.

Once almost exclusively birds of marshes and fens, reed buntings have changed both their habits and their habitat since the 1960s. Today they also breed in young conifer plantations, on heathland and moorland, and even sing that hesitant song among the sulphurous sprays of oil-seed rape. But as late nesters, with chicks still in the nest well into July and even August, their young often fall victim to the blades of the combine when the rape crop is harvested in midsummer.

Outside the breeding season, they now regularly turn up in urban and suburban gardens, enjoying the bountiful supply of seeds we provide on our bird-tables. So if you see a smart little bird, looking rather like a well-scrubbed sparrow, you are probably looking at a reed bunting, always a welcome garden visitor.

WHIMBREL

*

The rippling call of a whimbrel – a rapid series of high, fluty notes – is mainly heard in the far north of Britain, as the vast majority of our small breeding population nests on Shetland, with a few scattered pairs on Orkney, the Outer Hebrides and at the northern tip of Scotland.

But whimbrels winter in southern Europe or West Africa, and so you might also hear their distinctive calls anywhere to the south. The most likely time is during late April and early May, when the birds are returning to our shores. Whimbrels often stop off to refuel at traditional sites such as the Somerset Levels, probing the damp pastures for worms and grubs, using their distinctive down-curved bills.

That bill is a clue that the whimbrel is closely related to the curlew, but you can tell them apart from their larger relatives by their smaller size, shorter bill and pale stripe along the crown. This stripe, bordered on each side by a darker band, gives the whimbrel a quite distinct appearance.

The rippling, seven-note call, which you sometimes hear from birds migrating by night, led to the whimbrel being known as the 'seven whistler'. In parts of the English Midlands, these sounds echoing through the darkness gave rise to a folk-tale about the Six Birds of Fate, which fly around the heavens seeking their lost companion. When all seven are reunited, according to the story, the world will end.

GREENFINCH

*

The greenfinch is something of a Jekyll and Hyde character. For much of the year flocks of greenfinches clamber around on our garden bird-feeders, feasting on sunflower seeds or peanuts, which they crack open with their stout bills. When joined by the dull greenish-brown youngsters in late summer, you could be forgiven for adopting the disparaging birders' slang for this species: 'grotfinch'.

But for a few short weeks each spring, you might think that an entirely new species has arrived in your backyard. For at this time of year, the male greenfinch performs his remarkable display flight.

Trilling loudly, he launches himself from the top of a tree or shrub and flaps his wings in slow motion, careering wildly around his tiny territory, looking more like a bat than a bird.

As with all courtship displays, this performance has two aims: to fend off rival males and impress the watching female. The principle is that any bird that can fly so slowly and flamboyantly, staying aloft instead of crashing ignominiously to the ground, must be fit enough to be a suitable father to her offspring.

Greenfinches don't just twitter like a canary, they also have a rather wheezy call, like a barely suppressed sneeze, a familiar sound on warm spring and summer days. Outside the breeding season, those huge and unruly Leyland cypress hedges that cause so many bitter disputes between neighbours are their favourite roosting sites, a warm, safe refuge for dozens or even hundreds of birds on a cold winter's night.

GARGANEY

*

On a fine May morning, a strange sound is emanating from the depths of a dense reedbed. It sounds like a grasshopper on steroids, but it's far too early for this insect to be singing, and the habitat doesn't fit. This noise is the call of our only summer migrant duck: the garganey. Its peculiar sound, migratory habits and small, compact size give the garganey two of its old country names, the 'cricket teal', and the 'summer teal'.

It's always worth making the effort to catch up with garganeys each spring, because the drake is one of our most handsome ducks. He uses a limited palette of browns, greys and whites to great effect, with a chocolate-brown head set off by a contrasting broad white stripe through the eye, and a pearly-grey back and flanks. Like most ducks, the female is far more muted, with a delicately marked plumage of browns, blacks and greys enabling her to stay hidden when incubating her eggs.

The garganey is one of our rarest ducks, with somewhere between fifty and a hundred pairs nesting; though during the breeding season this little duck is so secretive in its habits that some pairs may be overlooked. Garganeys also pass through Britain on the way north from their winter quarters in tropical Africa to their breeding grounds in Scandinavia. Being one of our earliest migrants, they may arrive in March or even February in some years, stopping off again in August and September on the return leg of their long journey.

Despite its scarcity in Britain, which is on the north-western edge of the species' range, globally the garganey is very common and widespread. Up to 3

million pairs breed across the temperate zones of the Old World, and winter in sub-Saharan Africa and southern Asia, where flocks of tens of thousands may be seen alongside herds of elephants and mingling with flocks of high-stepping flamingos. On their twice-yearly journey back and forth, many garganey are caught for food in the Sahel region, just south of the Sahara Desert.

REDSHANK

*

Not for nothing is the redshank called the 'warden of the marshes'. At the slightest hint of danger, a loud volley of wild, piping calls and yelps warns every bird within earshot that something is afoot. For any birder attempting to get a close view of a flock of waders on an estuary or marsh, the redshank's nervous watchfulness can be rather a nuisance.

The redshank is the default medium-sized wader: about the length of a blackbird, though with much longer legs, which are a vivid scarlet colour and give the bird its name. The species is a common presence throughout the year on freshwater marshes and coastal estuaries, and is easily identified: only the larger and scarcer spotted redshank, with its blood-red legs, and the ruff, whose legs are a paler orange in colour, are likely to cause any confusion. When redshanks fly away – as they often do, given their nervousness – the white rump and wing-panels serve as useful field-marks.

Outside the breeding season, redshanks are a rather humdrum greyish-brown shade; but in spring

they freshen up considerably, their plumage becoming darker and more vibrant. But if you thought they couldn't be more jittery than in winter, think again. Now they hoist themselves on to fence-posts, keeping a wary lookout for anything amiss, and ceaselessly chip away to inform any predators that they are guarding not just their own eggs or chicks, but also those of their fellow ground-nesting birds.

At this time of year, male redshanks perform a spectacular song-flight, yodelling to the females, and then impressing them still further by landing, spreading their wings and showing off their prowess: a display of fitness worthy of a bodybuilding contest.

Once the male has won his mate, the pair settle down to breed in damp wildflower meadows and marshes, pulling the grass blades to form a sheltering canopy over the nest. Almost as soon as the chicks have hatched, the watchful and noisy parents shepherd them to a place where they can feed and be safe – for the time being, at least.

SPOTTED CRAKE

*

It is a still, clear, May night. In a few fenny corners of Britain, the marshes and sedge-beds are echoing with a bizarre, repetitive sound, like a rapid whiplash. Spotted crakes – some of our rarest, and certainly most elusive, breeding birds – are staking out their territories.

The spotted crake is related to two of our commonest and most familiar waterbirds, the coot and moorhen. But unlike these showy species, this polka-dotted skulker is notoriously hard to find,

and even more difficult to see – only betraying its presence at all by singing (if this strange sound can be called a song); and even then, mainly under cover of darkness.

To confound us further, the spotted crake can throw its voice, often sounding much closer than it actually is, and only sings for a few weeks in late spring and early summer. It is also notoriously capricious, and may be present in a marsh or fen one year, but not the next.

Once things were very different: before the vast East Anglian fens were drained in the sixteenth and seventeenth centuries, in one of the first great acts of environmental vandalism, the spotted crake would have been both common and widespread, if not exactly easy to see. Today, even in a good year, fewer than a hundred singing males hold territory, in locations as far apart as East Anglia and the Western Isles.

Finding the nest of the spotted crake, hidden in a raised tussock of sedge amongst wet mires, is the ornithological equivalent of the Holy Grail. Most surveys rely on either hearing the call, or spotting the tiny young – which look like little balls of black soot on legs.

For most of us, the best chance of catching up with this Scarlet Pimpernel of the bird world is to wait until after the breeding season. In late summer and early autumn, especially if water levels are low around their favoured pools, you may see one emerge to creep gingerly across the mud, then scuttle back to cover between the stands of rush and reed-mace. These are often birds from much further east – probably Germany and Poland – on their way south to spend the winter in Africa.

GUILLEMOT

*

Nothing can beat the experience of sitting amid a colony of breeding seabirds, the constant sights, sounds and smells assaulting your senses from every direction. Prominent among the key players at any seabird colony are guillemots, which, with about 1 million breeding pairs, are the commonest seabird in Britain.

Lined up on the guano-streaked cliffs like brown and white skittles, guillemots spend much of their time defending their tiny territories on the narrow ledges. These are the smallest in area of any bird in the world, sometimes with a radius of only five centimetres, just enough room to accommodate their single large, speckled egg, which is laid straight on to the bare rock. This is distinctively pear-shaped to stop it from rolling off the narrow ledges and on to the rocks or sea below.

Like many seabirds, guillemots rely on small fish such as sand eels and sprats for sustenance. They dive into the water to find these, and are at once transformed from the clumsy, comical figures they are on land into the epitome of grace and speed. In determined pursuit of fish they mirror their prey's every twist, turn and sideslip, and can reach depths of up to 180 metres, the equivalent of three times the height of Nelson's Column.

When parent guillemots return with their catch to the loomery (a name for a colony of auks), they need to find their own youngster among the braying masses

of birds ranged along the rocky ledges. As its parents can carry just one fish at a time (unlike the puffin, which can bring a whole beakful), there's plenty of to-ing and fro-ing.

Once the chicks are ready to leave the cliffs – at about two weeks old – they simply launch themselves into the unknown, encouraged by the frantic calls of their parents. They plummet through the air to the sea below, a habit that has earned them the rather endearing names of 'droplings', or 'jumplings'. Each chick will then be promptly escorted away from land by its father, to make a life for itself on the high seas.

STORM PETREL

*

In Shetland, in the extreme north of the British Isles, you are closer to the Arctic Circle than you are to Manchester. So during late spring and summer the days are long, and it never really gets dark; the faint glow in the sky at night is known locally as the 'simmer dim'.

Only when light levels are at their lowest will you have any chance of hearing a phenomenon that has been compared to 'the sound of fairies being sick'. This eerie, gurgling call is that of our smallest seabird, the storm petrel, which at just sixteen centimetres long and weighing less than thirty grams (about one ounce) is only just larger than a sparrow. The birds will stay out at sea until the light has virtually disappeared, in hopes of avoiding being picked off by predatory and hungry gulls waiting by the shore.

The most famous colony of these mysterious birds is on the small island of Mousa, just off the mainland of Shetland. The storm petrels make their nest in burrows among the rocks; but also take advantage of the gaps in the walls of the ancient stone broch: a huge, conical structure memorably described by Bill Oddie as 'an Iron Age cooling-tower'.

Standing by the broch at night you may be surrounded by dozens of these tiny, fluttering birds, rather like pipistrelle bats but without the ability to echolocate, meaning that on occasion they fly straight into you. This is truly one of the most bizarre and memorable natural spectacles anywhere in Britain.

Storm petrels, of which there are about twenty species worldwide, flutter across the sea on broad, charcoal-coloured wings, flashing their distinctive white rump like marine house martins. When feeding, they often patter their feet across the surface of the waves, a behaviour that has given rise to the name 'Jesus Christ birds' for their supposed ability to walk on the water. It has been suggested that the name 'petrel' may derive from St Peter, but it is far more likely to refer to their habit of 'pitter-pattering' across the sea.

Another ancient name is 'Mother Carey's Chicken', which is thought to be a corruption either of 'Mother Mary' or the Latin 'Mata Cara'. Both refer to the Virgin Mary, whose name would have been invoked by superstitious sailors as soon as they saw these tiny birds, as their sudden appearance alongside a ship was thought to foretell a coming storm.

SEDGE WARBLER

*

Of the two common species of warbler that inhabit our reedbeds and marshes in spring and summer, the sedge warbler is undoubtedly far more assertive and extrovert than his shyer cousin the reed warbler.

As soon as the male sedge warbler returns from his winter home in western or central Africa, around the middle of April, he gets down to the serious business of defending a territory and attracting a mate. He does so in a spectacular manner: perched in full view on the top of a bush such as a bramble on the edge of a reedbed, he launches himself into the air, delivering his raucous, rapid, scratchy song before paragliding back down again.

The song itself has the style and manner of a jazz musician: an excitable improvisation around a theme, compared with the rather plodding, rhythmic song of the reed warbler. Think 'stroppy' and 'sedge' as opposed to 'regular' and 'reed'!

Sedge warblers look very different too. Both sexes are buffish-brown, with creamy white eyestripes, and are streaked above and below. They're also much less tied to reeds, and prefer to nest amid tangled vegetation alongside the water.

Before they leave our shores, sedge warblers gorge on insects – mainly plum-reed aphids, which are abundant in late summer and early autumn. The result of feeding so frantically is that sedge warblers put on a thick layer of fat and double their weight from about half an ounce to an ounce, which incredibly allows this tiny bird to fly all the way from Britain to the other side of the Sahara in a single, non-stop flight.

Nightjar
Kittiwake
Puffin
Razorbill
Goldfinch
Barn Owl
Manx Shearwater
Quail
Arctic Tern
Gannet

 # J U N E

Great Skua
Golden Oriole
Lesser Whitethroat
Cormorant
Wryneck
Little Egret
Common Sandpiper
Savi's Warbler
Marsh Warbler
Reed Warbler

JUNE IS A MONTH of plenty, when everything seems to be happening at once, as wildlife responds to the lengthening days and increasing sunshine. By now most of our migrant birds have arrived and some have already produced their first clutch of nestlings. Some birds have already fledged. At the end of June young swallows will be taking their first flights around stables and farmyards, while their parents begin planning their next family, not necessarily with each other.

In our gardens, young blackbirds, confusingly speckled in browns and russets, suddenly appear squeaking for attention, and parties of blue and great tits emerge from the gloom of their nest-holes for the first time. Whether in or out of the nest, these young birds are very demanding and so June is a month of constant activity for their harassed parents, who seem to spend all their time and energy ferrying food to insatiable fledglings.

With all this breeding activity, you might expect a reduction in song, but many birds continue to sing throughout June. Those that usually rear a single brood will stop when they no longer need to defend a territory and some birds, such as the wood warbler, nightingale and lesser whitethroat, will have fallen silent by the month's end if not sooner. However, many species, for example blackcaps, whitethroats, blackbirds and song thrushes, will continue singing as their mates produce a second clutch. Most cuckoos also fall silent by late June and some male birds may even have begun their journey south after just two months in the British Isles.

Although the dawn chorus is a little less vibrant than in May, there are special songs to listen out for. In a few fenland poplar plantations, golden orioles burble tropically among the fluttering leaves, while there's always a chance that a migrant oriole might turn up in deciduous woods anywhere this month. No June is complete without a visit to a heath at dusk where the nightjars churr like alien landing-craft. Even open farmland has a June speciality, the quail whose liquid 'wet-my-lips' notes burst above the spears of growing corn. But the star of the June chorus belongs in those tangles of nettles and willowherb that line ponds and ditches. They're rare and very local, but in a few places in the south-east of England, marsh warblers speak in tongues, imitating the songs of almost any birds from kestrels and oystercatchers to swallows and goldfinches, weaving them into a breathless babel of sound.

June is the month to visit a seabird colony because chick-rearing is in full swing. On sea-cliffs and islands puffins are ferrying beak-loads of small fish to their young hidden deep in burrows. On rocky ledges, guillemots bring sand eels to their precariously balanced chicks, while shags regurgitate all manner of seafood into the gullets of their reptilian youngsters. The constant traffic between sea and land is a visual and aural feast, and it's an olfactory one too: the smell of ripening guano under the June sunshine has to be experienced to be believed.

As elder and dog roses bloom in hedgerows and dragonflies and damselflies hunt over ponds and rivers, all the natural sights and sounds are telling us that summer is at its height. But just after Midsummer's Day, don't be surprised to see the first green and wood sandpipers on their journey south from Scandinavia. These early migrants may have failed to find a mate and so are cutting their losses and heading for their wintering areas, but the lapwings flopping lazily over the local gravel pits have reared their young much nearer home, and are leaving their nesting territories: for them, autumn has already begun.

NIGHTJAR

*

Dusk on a heath in midsummer. The warm air holds a tang of pine resin, as moths blunder past and the first bats hawk around the treetops. As daylight condenses and shapes begin to blur, songbirds surrender to the dark. In this brief interlude of stillness, it begins: a strange mechanical churring sound, which you feel as much as hear. Nightjars – half branch, half bird – are stirring.

Warm summer evenings are the best time to encounter a nightjar, whose surreal song is most often heard between late May and late July. Our medieval ancestors called it the 'fern owl', because it spends the daylight hours roosting in bracken, its bark-like plumage giving almost total camouflage. They also believed that nightjars sucked the milk from nanny goats – hence the folk-name 'goatsucker' – which only goes to prove that ancient wisdom is not always as reliable as we might assume.

The churring sound, delivered from a static perch on a branch or treetop, has a rather unworldly, machine-like quality. Like the song of another mysterious British bird, the grasshopper warbler, it seems to go on for ever, varying marginally in tone and pitch as the bird turns its head towards or away from the human listener.

Only when it stops do you have a chance of seeing this enigmatic bird, whose appearance may be announced with a brusque clapping of its long, slender

wings. Especially under the light of the moon, the snow-white patches near the male nightjar's wingtips reveal the bird to its rivals and audience alike.

Country folk have long known that twirling a couple of white handkerchiefs in the air, like an over-enthusiastic Morris dancer, will attract nightjars. But diverting the birds in this manner seems unfair when the summer nights are so short, giving them only a brief window of opportunity to feed.

The nightjar hunts like a giant bat, manoeuvring itself through the air with its long tail. A series of bristles around the edge of its mouth alerts it to the presence of flying insects; and as soon as the signal is received, the bill snaps shut.

Somewhere beneath him, among the heather or bracken, his mate is incubating her clutch of two off-white eggs, marbled with grey and brown. Later she will join the male, hunting insects in the dark, until a pastel glow in the east signals approaching dawn, and these masters of camouflage once again become one with the heath on which they live.

KITTIWAKE

*

As salt-spray from the crashing waves whirls around the clifftop where you stand, so do the cries of our most ocean-going gull, shouting its name from the ledges below.

Like the cuckoo and chiffchaff, the kittiwake's name is a human representation of its call, which echoes around the vertiginous sea-cliffs in a constant chorus.

Unlike other gulls, which tend to stay close to the coast, or live inland, the kittiwake is a true seafarer. Kittiwakes spend much of their time on the high seas, where they follow fishing trawlers, plucking morsels of food from the surface. But like other seabirds, at the start of the breeding season they return to land, where they build untidy nests out of seaweed, vegetation and other marine debris, cemented together with mud and the birds' own droppings.

The vast majority of kittiwakes nest on narrow cliff-ledges to avoid land-based predators. But one colony has chosen a very different home. On the River Tyne between Newcastle and Gateshead, the birds nest on the window ledges of buildings, and even on the rigid metal structure of the Tyne Bridge itself. This is the furthest inland kittiwake colony in the world, and the most urban one. Yet despite being more than five miles from the sea, the birds here are thriving: perhaps because the young are sheltered from storms. Local people mostly welcome these birds, though there have been some complaints about their mess and noise – ironic when you consider that Newcastle city centre is famous for its rowdy nightlife.

It is easy to dismiss all gulls as looking the same. But kittiwakes have a delicacy about them that few other gulls can match. They are neat, innocent-looking birds, with a snow-white head and body set off with pearl-grey wings, jet-black legs and feet, and a citrus-yellow bill. In flight, their jet-black wingtips look as if they have been dipped in ink. Young birds, with their black collars and prominent dark zigzag pattern across their wings, almost look like a different species.

Kittiwakes generally lay two eggs, and feed their fluffy chicks on small fish – especially sand eels – that they often travel long distances to catch. Sand eels themselves feed on tiny plankton, which means that kittiwakes are very vulnerable to shifts in the distribution of plankton caused by variations in sea temperature, in turn the result of global climate change.

In some kittiwake colonies this has led to sharp declines, but elsewhere in Britain new colonies have been established, as the birds adapt to nesting on man-made structures such as piers. So these charismatic gulls remain one of the classic sights around our coastline, and a colony in full cry is still one of the most stirring of all our natural sounds.

PUFFIN

*

As you tread carefully between rabbit burrows on a tiny island, you may be surprised to hear the squawks of E.T., the alien extra-terrestrial, coming from beneath your feet. These strange groans are definitely of this planet, though, and come from a bird we all know, even if we've never seen one: the puffin.

'Sea parrot', 'coulter neb', and 'clown of the sea': all these folk-names refer either to its remarkable multicoloured bill, its comical, penguin-like waddle – or both. Waddling through clumps of pink thrift and sea-campion, the puffin may look ungainly on land, but this is a true seabird, which spends much of its life on the open ocean, far out of sight of land. Like its relatives the guillemots and razorbills, it only comes ashore because it must: not even the puffin can lay its eggs on the surface of the sea.

Puffins are comical in flight too, frantically flapping their wings as if they fear dropping out of the sky at any moment. Only when they enter the water does their body shape reveal its true grace and efficiency.

They are superb divers, flying underwater to seize tiny sand eels. Their triangular bills with serrated edges enable them to grab a new fish without losing those they have already caught. This allows them to carry up to a dozen fish in their bill at any one time – vital if they are to bring enough food back to feed their hungry chick, deep in the darkness of its burrow.

There may be more than a million puffins breeding in Britain, but why so few people have seen a real, live one is that they nest on offshore islands and remote headlands, to minimize the risk of their eggs and chicks falling victim to foxes or rats.

Safe in its subterranean cell, the solitary, soot-coloured chick fattens up on fish all summer. After five or six weeks, once it has reached its full size and acquired its adult plumage (though not, for the moment, that gaudy bill which appears the following spring), the young puffin will emerge under cover of darkness and launch itself from the top of the nearest cliff. It may then spend up to five years at sea, until it finally returns to its birthplace to begin breeding. Meanwhile its parents have long gone, shedding their brightly coloured bill-plates to reveal a much drabber sea-going version beneath.

It has recently been shown definitively that puffins spend over half the year in the open ocean, circumnavigating the Atlantic during the stormy autumn and winter, because scientists are now able to fit tiny geolocators on to the birds. When the puffins return to land, these can be read to reveal the exact location where they have spent the winter, and the route they have taken on their journey there and back.

RAZORBILL

*

As smart as a dinner-jacketed waiter, and with a deep, blunt beak resembling an old-fashioned razor, the razorbill is a vision in black and white: a graphic designer's favourite. This compensates for its rather grating voice, which sounds quite like the grumbling of an old man with a hangover.

Like the guillemot and puffin, the razorbill is a member of the auk family: a group of rather stocky seabirds, clumsy on land and comical in flight, but with a balletic grace few of us are privileged to see once chasing a fish beneath the waves.

Like all auks, razorbills have a mainly pelagic lifestyle, only coming to land for a few months in spring and summer to breed on headlands and islands around our coasts. But unlike guillemots, which lay their eggs on narrow ledges, or puffins, which breed in old rabbit burrows, razorbills like nothing better than a rocky niche or crevice sheltered from the sea-spray, away from the hurly-burly of the main seabird colonies.

He may not be renowned for his skills as an aviator, but the male razorbill does have one special talent to impress his potential mate. He performs a remarkable slow flapping 'butterfly flight' out from the nesting cliffs near his territory, which demands a great deal of energy. It is as if he is saying 'Look at me ... if I can fly this slowly I must be super-fit, and worth investing in as a partner ...'

If this strategy works, and he finds a mate, she will lay just one egg, but this is a true whopper: the equivalent in size to a human female giving birth to a baby weighing about twenty pounds.

The razorbill chick grows rapidly, fuelled by a constant diet of fish supplied by both parents. Eventually the male entices it down to the sea by calling constantly until the youngster finally takes the plunge, to begin its new way of life as a true seabird.

GOLDFINCH

*

The tinkling of a group of goldfinches as they tease out tiny seeds from hanks of thistledown is one of the most evocative sounds made by any songbird; small wonder that a goldfinch flock is often called a 'charm'. Happily, it's a sound you are far more likely to hear today than a generation or more ago.

The song of the goldfinch is a fluid series of high-pitched whistles, twitters and tweets, with a delicate quality, like the music of ice on winter ponds, and is audible even above the drone of city traffic. The birds are equally attractive visually, with their bright yellow wing flashes and faces feathered in black, white and red. The crimson circlet around the bill is said to be because a goldfinch took pity on the crucified Christ, and pulled the thorns from his crown. Goldfinches are also sometimes known as 'King Harry redcaps', a reference to the flamboyantly dressed monarch Henry VIII.

However the goldfinch's combination of physical and aural appeal almost led to its downfall. In Victorian times it was much in demand as a cagebird. The finches were caught by the thousand using nets, twigs coated with a sticky birdlime concocted from mistletoe berries, and 'chardonneret traps' – named after the French word for goldfinch.

As a result of this wholesale trapping, by the 1890s the goldfinch had become an endangered species. Fortunately the newly formed Society for the Protection of Birds (later to become the RSPB) made the recovery of the goldfinch one of its main priorities, and at the eleventh hour the bird was saved.

For most of the twentieth century the goldfinch remained a fairly common bird; but in the past decade or two its numbers have soared – and this is mainly down to us. As more and more people feed garden birds, and offer a more varied menu, more goldfinches survive hard winters. Peanuts aren't their bag though: they are particularly fond of the tiny black seeds known as nyger, which they prise from the feeders using their sharp, tweezer-like bills. Now the tinkling, crystalline song of the goldfinch is the soundtrack to many of our gardens and even city streets throughout the year.

BARN OWL

*

If you find yourself at dusk scanning rolling farmland, young forestry plantations or bleak saltmarshes, the glimpse of a distant, pale, moth-like creature fanning along a ditch or hedgerow never fails to quicken the blood, and set the pulse racing.

Barn owls often live alongside us in old or disused buildings, and their piercing screech echoing through the darkness near a ruined castle or church tower can test even the most rational. When an angelic white bird appears at a window ledge, and floats silently off into the night, you can understand why our more credulous ancestors might have believed they had seen a ghost.

The screeching spectre is almost invariably a barn owl, with its ominous, ear-piercing wail, as Lady Macbeth points out:

> *Hark! Peace!*
> *It was the owl that shrieked, the fatal bellman*
> *Which gives the stern'st goodnight . . .*

Barn owls are usually nocturnal, but sometimes fly at dawn and dusk, especially when food is hard to come by. They are supremely adapted to hunting, quartering the ground effortlessly on rounded, silent wings, whose fringed feathers absorb any sound made by the passing wind.

The owl's head-shape too is crucial: the concave, heart-shaped face concentrates the minute squeaks and tiny footfalls of voles and mice, focusing them towards the bird's ears. The ears themselves are placed asymmetrically on the sides of the owl's head, one slightly higher than the other. This enables it to pinpoint the exact location of its unseen prey, before plunging down into the long grass below and seizing the unfortunate rodent in its sharp talons. This combination of features explains how barn owls can hunt even on moonless nights, in almost total darkness.

They need to be efficient hunters: they have to catch more than a thousand small rodents a year to feed themselves and their hungry offspring. But barn owls do have an Achilles heel: when it rains, those soft feathers become waterlogged, and the birds are unable to hunt. So in wet summers they sometimes fail to raise any young at all.

Because their food supply is governed both by the weather and the natural rises and falls in rodent populations, barn owls have one further trick up their sleeve. Unlike many birds, which wait until their whole clutch is ready until they begin incubating, barn owls start to sit on their eggs as soon as they are laid, meaning that a single brood contains youngsters of very different sizes. In good years all will survive; but in lean years the older chicks will sometimes feed on their younger siblings, this cannibalism ensuring their survival.

Barn owls may have a specialized lifestyle, but they are one of the world's most widespread birds, found on six of the world's seven continents (the exception, of course, being Antarctica), and on many offshore islands. But they are mainly confined to warmer latitudes, so those in Scotland have the distinction of being the northernmost population found anywhere in the world.

MANX SHEARWATER

*

An island, just off Britain's western coastline. As dusk falls, the yelping of gulls fades away and, after a brief period of silence, is replaced by an altogether more bizarre sound: the diabolical shrieks of the Manx shearwater.

Shearwaters don't make this blood-curdling sound for fun: they do so to try to relocate their single chick, deep inside its burrow on the grassy clifftop. The adult has been out at sea for days, possibly weeks

on end, and has now returned under cover of darkness to avoid being picked off by predatory great black-backed gulls. The long-winged shearwater, black above and white below, is remarkably streamlined as it glides over the waves, but is clumsy and awkward when on land.

Its belly is full of food, which it will regurgitate to feed its hungry offspring. But first it has to find it. Even though thousands of shearwaters may be screeching at the same time, the chick is able to recognize its parent's call and respond, allowing the adult to locate the nest.

Named after a small breeding colony at the southern tip of the Isle of Man, Manx shearwaters also nest in vast numbers on other offshore islands: notably Rum in the Hebrides, and Skomer and Skokholm off the south-west coast of Wales.

Incredibly, Britain and Ireland are home to more than 75 per cent of the world population of this enigmatic seabird – about 350,000 pairs. But its ocean-going lifestyle means they are rarely seen except by keen birders, who are willing to watch from a windblown headland or take to the seas in a small boat.

Manxies, as they are affectionately known, are among the world's greatest avian travellers, migrating twice a year between their island homes around the British Isles and the coasts of South America, a round trip of almost 20,000 kilometres. They are also exceptional navigators: when, in the 1930s, the pioneering ornithologist Ronald Lockley took a shearwater from Wales all the way to Venice and released it, the bird arrived home in just fourteen days.

Like many other seabirds, they are also incredibly long-lived: one bird from Bardsey Island in Wales lived for over fifty years. During its lifetime it was estimated to have clocked up 8 million kilometres in flight – ten times the distance to the moon and back.

QUAIL

*

We don't usually think of birds as ventriloquists, but some are; and few are so adept at using this trick to conceal themselves from human sight as the quail. Our smallest game bird, about the size of a plump thrush, it rivals the spotted crake for the title of Britain's most elusive breeding bird.

It's a sound guaranteed to stop us in our tracks: a liquid three-note call, often described as 'wet-my-lips', with the stress on the first syllable. On a hot summer's day, somewhere in the vastness of a thousand hectares of cereal lurks the bird itself, its notes rising above the cornstalks and seeming almost to evaporate in the heat. The call carries far and, if heard at close quarters, is preceded by a strange growling sound.

If you're lucky enough to catch sight of a quail, as it whirrs low over the corn, it looks remarkably like a miniature partridge: plump and rounded, and streaked in shades of brown and cream to blend in with its surroundings.

Quails are unpredictable summer visitors to Britain, much commoner in some years than others. They spend the winter in Africa or southern Europe, and often migrate in flocks. Evidence suggests that they must once have been more prevalent than today: the Old Testament Book of Exodus refers to them falling from the sky in huge numbers, providing a welcome source of protein for Moses and his hungry followers in the desert.

In some 'quail years' there is a fresh influx of breeding birds in late summer. Remarkably, some of these may have been born earlier in the season, further to the south, as young quail are sexually precocious, able to breed at the age of just twelve weeks. This 'leapfrogging' of different generations breeding in different locations is a very unusual breeding strategy, one more closely associated with butterflies such as the painted lady than with a game bird.

ARCTIC TERN

*

If you are planning to visit an Arctic tern colony, make sure you wear a hard hat, or, failing that, carry a stick above your head. That's because as you walk through the areas where the birds nest, you'll find yourself running the gauntlet of a relentless aerial bombardment.

Should you fail to defend yourself, you will soon discover that the blood-red bill of this graceful, pale bluish-grey-and-white seabird is not merely for decoration: its sharp, pointed tip can actually draw blood. The terns don't just attack humans: in the high Arctic, these feisty little birds are not afraid to dive-bomb passing polar bears.

The attack itself is usually preceded by a salvo of raucous, ear-splitting screeches, at odds with the bird's apparent fragility and physical elegance. These calls – and the aerial attacks – are in deadly earnest: the tern is trying to drive you away from its nest sites on the ground, to protect its well-camouflaged eggs or fluffy chicks from being destroyed. Like many other

seabirds, Arctic terns lay only one or two eggs, and if these fail to hatch they will have no opportunity to breed again for another twelve months.

During that time, they will undertake a longer journey, and see more daylight, than any other living creature on the planet. Their migration takes them from the northern hemisphere, across the tropics and Equator, to the furthest reaches of the southern oceans around Antarctica – a round trip of a staggering 72,000 kilometres.

Arctic terns tagged in the Netherlands have recently been shown to fly to the coasts of eastern Australia and New Zealand on their way to the Antarctic Ocean – as if their voyage wasn't already epic enough. This is all the more remarkable given their flimsy appearance: their slender shape and long tail-feathers have earned them the name 'sea-swallows'.

Arctic terns return to Britain in April, sometimes stopping off at inland reservoirs and wetlands before reaching their breeding colonies in Scotland. One of the best places to see them at close quarters is the Farne Islands off the Northumberland coast – just don't forget the hard hat.

GANNET

*

Even if you've never visited a gannetry, it's not hard to imagine the sight of thousands of these huge seabirds, and the grating clamour of the colony. What you might not be prepared for, though, is the smell.

Gannets live up to their reputation as gluttons by consuming huge quantities of fish, and the result is tons of guano with a pungent aroma, which assails your nostrils from the moment you set foot ashore.

The North Atlantic is the global stronghold of this, our largest seabird. The gannet has a wingspan of nearly two metres, and the bird's grandeur is enhanced by its rather haughty, remorseless gaze and long, dagger-like bill.

The gannet's scientific name, *Morus bassanus*, comes from our best-known colony, just outside Edinburgh on the Bass Rock in the Firth of Forth. Other spectacular colonies can be found on the northern tip of Shetland at Hermaness, on the Welsh island of Grassholm, and on the cliffs of Boreray, part of the group of islands known as St Kilda. With about 50,000 pairs, this is one of the largest gannet colonies anywhere in the world. The sole English colony is, conveniently for birdwatchers, on the mainland: at Bempton Cliffs in Yorkshire.

Among all our seabirds, gannets are the ultimate exhibitionists. To watch them fold back their wings and plunge like an arrow into the sea, at speeds of almost 100 kilometres per hour, is a truly exhilarating experience; especially when you discover that beneath the waves they can reach depths of twenty metres. They will also fly long distances in search of fish to feed their single youngster – several hundred kilometres in a single outing if necessary.

Like all our seabirds, gannets are strictly protected by law, with one notable exception. Each year, the men of Ness, a tiny community on the northern tip of the Isle of Lewis in the Outer Hebrides, take part in the 'guga hunt'.

The guga is the Scottish Gaelic name for young gannets, and to catch them, the islanders head out in flimsy boats to the remote, rocky island of Sula Sgeir. Once there, they harvest the young gannets, which are then plucked, smoked and boiled in milk as a delicacy – memorably described by the Hebridean author Donald Murray as having the taste and texture of 'smoked-mackerel-flavoured chicken', or, less appetizingly, 'chamois leather dipped in oil'.

GREAT SKUA

*

Imagine a buzzard crossed with a gull, and you have that formidable predator of the northern seas: the great skua. Great skuas are also known by their local Shetland name of 'bonxie', which somehow suggests imminent collision, as you will soon discover if you have the misfortune to stray into their breeding colony.

Just like Arctic terns, great skuas will attack any large creature – human or not – that threatens their young. And they do so not with the rapid darting movements of the terns, but lumbering out of the sky like a Second World War bomber, before giving you a hefty clout with their mighty wings.

Attack is second nature to bonxies. Like other skuas, they are kleptoparasites, chasing down smaller seabirds until they drop their precious fishy catch, and then grabbing it before it hits the sea below. They are also opportunistic scavengers and fearsome predators, able to wreak havoc on seabird colonies, killing birds as big as gannets and herons with their powerful talons and thick, hooked beak.

Great skuas do have a softer side, though. They sometimes gather to bathe on one of the many lochans that dot their Shetland home (more than half the world's bonxies breed on our most northerly archipelago), fastidiously twisting and turning their bodies in the water to make sure their plumage gets a thorough wash.

Globally, great skuas are one of the scarcest of all Britain's breeding birds, with a world population of just 16,000 pairs. Fortunately they have recently enjoyed a boom in numbers, thanks partly to an increase in fish discarded from trawlers, which the skuas are able to pick up from the surface of the sea.

Away from their northern summer homes, great skuas can often be seen migrating along our coasts, when their dark brown plumage makes them look rather like dark, short-winged young gulls. The telltale white flashes on their wings should help you identify them, even at a distance.

They come closer inshore during stormy weather, and in the teeth of an autumn gale their flight can seem lumbering. But if they spot a potential victim, they are capable of impressive bursts of speed.

GOLDEN ORIOLE

*

Large stands of poplar trees lend a continental air to parts of the English countryside, reminiscent of long, tree-lined, canal-side roads in northern France. In a very few places in East Anglia, these plantations echo to a sound with a sunny, almost tropical quality: the fluting song of the golden oriole.

Even the name has an exotic flavour, and the bird certainly lives up to its billing. About the size of a song thrush, the male oriole is a wonderfully golden yellow in hue, with contrasting black wings and a reddish bill. Few other birds match it for sheer elegance and beauty.

But for all its ostentation, the golden oriole simply vanishes among the fluttering poplar leaves, and can be extremely hard to see unless it flies between two stands of trees. That's why the 'weel-a-wee-oo' song, and the harsh cat-like call, are the best ways of locating this elusive bird.

Until the late 1960s, golden orioles were scarce passage migrants here in Britain, with a handful of these stunning birds stopping off in spring and autumn on their way between continental Europe and Africa. But as we began to grow plantations of poplar trees, to provide wood to make matches, the birds found an ideal home.

Breeding orioles like airy, open woods. They live high in the canopy where the shy, greenish-coloured females can blend in with the trembling leaves, and where, in angled forks between the branches, they build their cup-shaped nest. Poplars provide plenty of nesting places and, as a bonus, are the foodplant of many caterpillars and other large insects.

Although there were as many as thirty pairs breeding in their fen heartland towards the end of the twentieth century, the fortunes of English golden orioles are now in the balance. Matches are no longer made from poplar wood in Britain, and as these plantations reach maturity they are harvested without being replaced, so oriole numbers have fallen.

Conservationists are beginning to replant poplar trees to try to halt this decline, but with only one or two pairs remaining, it may be too late to save this glorious creature. In future, our best hope of seeing or hearing this flamboyant songster may rest with the migrating birds that pass through Britain each May or June.

LESSER
WHITETHROAT

*

When hawthorns foam with blossom and dog roses begin to bloom, it's time to listen for the song of the lesser whitethroat. A loud rattle from deep within the thickest roadside hedge or patch of scrub is often the first sign that one of our most skulking summer visitors is back from its African winter home. Lesser white-throats have a fairly simple song for a warbler: a soft, almost apologetic mumble followed by a more strident series of notes, reminiscent of the yellowhammer's more famous song.

Lesser whitethroats are smaller – and much shyer – than their relative, the common whitethroat, so are easily overlooked. When you do get a glimpse of one, perched momentarily on a flowering spray of hawthorn, the combination of grey above and white below (sometimes with a blush of pink), set off with a black bandit mask, gives them a rather dapper appearance.

As well as singing, the male lesser whitethroat also builds more than one partial nest to attract a mate. When he finally succeeds in doing so he will stop singing and devote his energies to building the real nest, often in the thickest part of a thorny hedge, where the eggs and chicks will be safe from predators.

Apart from the occasional burst of song through the summer, the next you will see of these little birds is usually just before they leave our shores. In late August and early September lesser whitethroats feast on the berries of bushy plants, especially elder and bramble, and on the insects attracted by these soft, purple fruits. Watch closely and you may see them darting in and out of the foliage like fish taking refuge on a coral reef, some with their snow-white underparts stained purple from the elderberry or bramble juice.

This hedonism has a purpose. It is vital that the birds fatten up, because unusually for a British warbler, migrating lesser whitethroats don't take the most direct route south to Africa. Instead they fly eastwards, around the Mediterranean Sea and through the Middle East, before trickling down into the scrubby dry country south of the Sahara Desert – a far cry from their summer home, the lush hedgerows of the British countryside.

CORMORANT

*

The classic image of a cormorant is a large, dark, rather clumsy-looking seabird, its wings outstretched in a heraldic posture, on a wave-washed rock by the sea. The famous Liver Birds, towering over the banks of the Mersey in Liverpool, have the typical wing-drying pose of cormorants.

But this marine connection is only part of the picture. In twenty-first-century Britain, cormorants are increasingly choosing to live inland, assembling their guano-streaked stick-nests in trees, and fishing not in the 'briny', but in freshwater lakes, rivers and gravel pits. Here you'll see them, periscoping serpentine necks above the surface or digesting their catch while perching incongruously on electricity pylons and, with unconscious irony, on 'No Fishing' signs.

This change of habits and habitat may well be due to an increase in inland lakes and gravel pits, but it has also brought the cormorant into direct conflict with anglers, resentful of the bird's ability to catch fish rather better than they can. In the water, any clumsiness disappears, as it twists and turns in pursuit of its fishy prey. Calls for culls of cormorants have been met with stiff resistance from conservationists, but even so these birds are regularly killed.

When you look carefully, cormorants aren't the sombre, all-black bird they appear from a distance. In the breeding season they sport white patches on their thighs, and silvery feathers (known as filoplumes) on their heads, which make them look rather dashing.

Outside the breeding season cormorants gather in dramatic communal roosts, often in waterside trees, and sometimes involving hundreds of birds. As they glide in dark squadrons across the winter skyline they have a primeval look: a memorable, if somewhat incongruous spectacle on our inland waterways.

WRYNECK

*

Once the orchards of southern England would have rung with the high-pitched, falcon-like calls of wrynecks. Now, these strange, cryptically coloured birds are virtually extinct as a British breeding species.

The wryneck's decline began sometime in the early decades of the twentieth century: slowly at first,

but then accelerating, until the bird finally disappeared. The reasons for its demise are not altogether clear, but it may have been associated with a period of cool summers, which reduced the availability of ants, the species' main food.

Wrynecks are members of the woodpecker family, but look nothing like the more striking great spotted and green woodpeckers we see in our woods and gardens. A wryneck's plumage is a subtle and finely vermiculated pattern, hatched in bars and stripes of lichen grey, brown, black and buff, which combine to make the bird look like an animated fragment of tree-bark.

But why the unusual name? It derives from the wryneck's peculiar habit, unique among British birds, of twisting and turning its head around at seemingly impossible angles, often hissing while doing so. Such serpentine behaviour, which evolved to deter predators from raiding its nest in a hole in a tree, suggested erotic associations to our ancestors.

In ancient Greece and Rome it was believed that if you bound a wryneck to a spinning wheel, known as an 'iynx', this would lure a potential partner or lost sweetheart. To this day, the scientific name for the bird is *Jynx torquilla*, the word 'jinx' now suggesting a curse, with *torquilla* meaning 'little twister', from that curious head-turning habit.

In summer there's a remote possibility that you might hear the wryneck's call at the opposite end of the country from where it used to be found, in the Highlands of Scotland. In recent years a handful of pairs have bred there, almost certainly birds originally bound for Scandinavia.

But your best chance of an encounter with this bizarre bird is on an autumn morning on the east coast. Suddenly, what seems to be a large, long-tailed, grey warbler appears around a bend in the path. Approaching with care, you see an intricately patterned bird, belly to the ground and probing the turf for ants with a long pink tongue. You've found a wryneck.

LITTLE EGRET

*

A walk alongside a river or wetland in southern Britain is enlivened by the appearance of an elegant, Persil-white bird, floating along on broad wings, or hunting stealthily for its prey: a little egret.

Not so long ago, well within many birders' memories, we would only have encountered little egrets when on holiday around the Mediterranean. Indeed this elegant small heron somehow typified the exotic birdlife of southern Europe, in sharp contrast with the more pedestrian birdlife of our own country.

Then within a decade or so, from the end of the 1980s to the turn of the millennium, all that changed: possibly as a result of global climate change. Little egrets had always been an occasional visitor to our shores, sometimes turning up in twos or threes, but no one was prepared for a mass invasion of these charming birds – flocks of a score or more on our south coast estuaries, delicately stalking small fish and stabbing at them with their slender, black, rapier-like bill.

By the mid-1990s, little egrets had begun to breed here: nesting, like grey herons, in colonies at the tops of trees. Within a few years they were everywhere – at least in southern Britain – on rivers, creeks, ponds and lakes. They soon spread northwards into Wales and the Midlands, and are now forging ahead into northern England and even Scotland, though they have yet to breed north of the border.

There are now almost a thousand pairs of little egrets nesting in Britain, and they have recently been joined by their much larger and even more elegant cousin, the great white egret. Even today, though, it is hard to take them for granted; surely such an exotic-looking creature doesn't really belong here . . .

COMMON SANDPIPER

*

A high-pitched whistle, cutting through the conversation of a fast-flowing upland river, is a sure sign that a common sandpiper is around. Like other birds of this specialized habitat, the sandpiper's high frequency call evolved so that they can hear each other above the white noise made by the rushing water.

A moment or two later, it arrives on frantically whirring wings: a dapper little wader about the size of a starling, white below and olive brown above, with a brown head and upper breast.

Common sandpipers are, like the grey wagtail and dipper, intimately connected with upland streams and rivers and the sides of Scottish lochs, where they bob up and down in a characteristically endearing manner, before flying off with a sudden flick of those bowed wings.

So it comes as something of a surprise to discover that these small waders migrate to West Africa for the winter, where they wander among elephants, hippos and zebras as they drink and bathe at muddy

waterholes. The Victorians, who knew at least some of their global wanderings, called them 'summer snipe'.

Given their favoured habitats, common sandpipers breed mainly in the north and west of Britain. They hide their nest among the dense waterside plants, and, once hatched, the young feed on the insects attracted by the water.

But wherever you live, we all have the chance to see common sandpipers as they migrate south or north, because they will stop off at pools, canals and small streams in the lowlands, teetering on the muddy margins to snap up insects. A handful choose to spend the winter with us, usually around the edge of river creeks and estuaries in the milder south-west of Britain, where they enliven the winter scene with their piercing calls.

SAVI'S
WARBLER

*

If you hear the buzzing song of a Savi's warbler you should count yourself very lucky indeed, for this skulking reedbed-dweller is one of our rarest breeding birds, a cousin of the commoner, more widespread, but no less elusive grasshopper warbler. Both belong to the genus *Locustella*, meaning 'little locust', and the song does indeed sound more like that of an insect than a bird.

Both species remind the listener of a fishing reel being unwound: a long, sustained buzzing sound, which at a distance can also be confused with the static from an electricity cable. The Savi's warbler's song is subtly different from that of the grasshopper warbler: lower in pitch, though also persisting for several minutes without a break.

The bird delivers its song from halfway up a reed-stem, often deep in the densest part of a vast reedbed, making it almost impossible to see. Occasionally, especially at dawn and dusk, the singer will clamber higher up the reed and reveal himself. This can be something of an anticlimax, as Savi's warblers look remarkably like a slightly larger, more uniformly coloured version of a reed warbler, but with a more rounded tail. For the dedicated birder though, the glamour of the bird lies in its scarcity: a singing Savi's is always something to celebrate.

Like most warblers, Savi's (named, incidentally, after a nineteenth-century Italian naturalist) are migrants to Britain from Africa. Just a handful turn up each spring or early summer, mainly in the south and east, with a few more regular haunts in Norfolk, Suffolk and Kent. But although they nest only a stone's throw away in the Netherlands, they have not yet managed to establish more than a toehold as a British breeding bird.

MARSH
WARBLER

*

Early on a fine morning in early June, as you walk alongside a wetland in south-east England, you hear the song of a blue tit coming from a small bush by the side of the path. Nothing unusual there. But moments later, it is followed by the sound of a reed warbler, then a nightingale, a skylark, an oystercatcher, a kestrel and a weird burst of song you can't place at all – a tropical sound more reminiscent of Africa than Kent or Sussex.

But there isn't a full orchestra of birds in that bush – just one: a marsh warbler. For this unprepossessing little bird is an ornithological jukebox, able to imitate dozens of different species, seemingly in a single outburst of sound.

Overall, marsh warblers have been found to mimic the songs of about a hundred kinds of European birds, and even more African ones: over 200 species in all. They learn these on their breeding territories, and also on their wintering grounds in south-east Africa, where a whole new suite of species comes into earshot.

How this modest-looking small bird came to acquire such an astonishing skill puzzled scientists for a long time. They now believe that it developed as a kind of 'arms race' between rival males, where the best and most varied performers would win the best territories and attract the fittest females. They would then pass on their skills as a mimic to their offspring, through the process of natural selection. The marsh warbler's remarkable sonic repertoire is in some ways the aural equivalent of the peacock's tail, and just as amazing.

When they are not singing, marsh warblers can be really hard to identify, as they look very similar to their much commoner relative the reed warbler. Perhaps the best indication that they are something

different – apart, of course, from that incredible song – is their choice of habitat.

Whereas reed warblers tend to prefer reeds, marsh warblers usually nest in tall, thick vegetation alongside water. Stands of willowherb and nettle beds are favoured spots where the birds weave their nests with 'basket handles' to secure them to the stalks of plants.

Until the late twentieth century, small numbers of marsh warblers bred in south Worcestershire, along the river valleys of the Severn and Avon. Sadly they have now vanished from this part of the country, and only a few pairs nest in the extreme south-east of England, close to much larger populations on the near Continent. But in June, marsh warblers can and do turn up elsewhere, so listen out for that extraordinary song – an entire dawn chorus condensed into a single bird.

REED
WARBLER

*

A rhythmic, repetitive chatter coming from deep inside a reedbed may be the only indication that a shy, retiring bird has returned from its African winter quarters: the aptly named reed warbler.

Unlike many other long-distance migrant birds, reed warblers are doing rather well, perhaps because we are creating more suitable reedbed habitats in gravel pits and nature reserves. They are spreading north too, and now regularly breed in southern Scotland.

You could easily confuse the song of the reed warbler with that of its close relative the sedge warbler. But while the reed warbler is repetitive and rhythmic, the sedge warbler is jazzy and excitable. Sedge warblers often launch themselves into the air to sing, something no self-respecting reed warbler would ever contemplate.

If you do glimpse a singing reed warbler, it's a small, slender bird with a rather drab brown plumage, paler buff below: a classic LBJ, birders' parlance for a 'little brown job'. You may, however, admire its ability to grip on to the vertical stems of the *Phragmites* – or common reed – often straddling two stems at a time while reaching up to pluck an insect from a nearby leaf-blade.

Reeds and reed warblers go together like birders and binoculars, and it's among these swaying stems that the birds nest. They rival the African weaverbirds for their tailoring ability, creating a neat basket from woven grasses supported by several reed stems, into which the female lays up to six blotched, greenish-white eggs.

What better way to deter predators such as mink, which find it impossible to climb up the delicate reed stems to reach their quarry? But one bird is able to foil the reed warbler, and fool it too.

The cuckoo lays a single egg inside the nests of up to twenty different reed warblers, each egg like a ticking time bomb. Once the baby cuckoo hatches, it ruthlessly elbows any reed warbler chicks or unhatched eggs from the nest, which then drop below to a watery grave.

The reed warblers then devote the rest of their precious time to raising the huge cuckoo chick, frantically racing to obtain enough insect food to keep it alive. By the time it fledges, almost three weeks after hatching, this vast incumbent has far outgrown the warblers' tiny nest, hanging over the edges like a Sumo wrestler squeezed into a bathtub.

Those reed warbler broods that do not fall victim to the parasitic cuckoo fledge a couple of weeks after hatching, and clamber around the reedbed like awkward teenagers, rhythmically chuntering to themselves in a pale imitation of their father's song. They then rapidly boost their weight by feeding avidly on aphids, before undertaking the long and perilous journey south to Africa.

Corn Bunting
Yellowhammer
Turtle Dove
Sandwich Tern
Buzzard
Osprey
Corncrake
House Martin
Coal Tit
Tree Pipit
Herring Gull
Kingfisher

 JULY

Cirl Bunting
Spotted Flycatcher
Lesser Black-backed Gull
Sparrowhawk
Dotterel
Red-necked Phalarope
Black-browed Albatross
Whinchat
Kestrel
Little Tern
Red-backed Shrike

INTRODUCTION

IN JULY the ornithological year begins to tilt on its axis. Most birds (whether migrant or resident) have reared at least one brood or are still feeding their young in the nest. Meanwhile, the first signs of autumn are beginning to appear, as early migrants depart while others pass through Britain on their way south to the Mediterranean or Africa.

For some late starters such as the buntings, the breeding cycle is only just getting under way. Among the ripening crops, male yellowhammers, corn buntings and cirl buntings are still singing out in the midday sun, while their mates – and for the corn bunting there may be a dozen or more – are incubating their eggs or feeding tiny nestlings.

High in the trees, in abandoned crows' nests, hobbies have timed their breeding perfectly to coincide with the bonanza of young swallows and martins on the wing, for the young birds are easier to catch than their wary parents. On heaths and in glades tree pipits perform their paper-dart song-flights, even in the hottest weather. By night, the same heaths vibrate with the whirring of nightjars and the 'squeaky-gate' calls of begging long-eared owlets. True song is on the wane, though wrens, dunnocks and some of the warblers will continue to sing persistently until the end of the month.

It's far from quiet, though, if you know where to look. The woods are full of small birds roaming through the undergrowth in mixed flocks, sometimes of over a hundred strong, which reduces the risk of being caught by a sparrowhawk. If you stand in a clearing and wait for them to pass, you're likely to see and hear long-tailed, blue, coal and great tits, with a scattering of goldcrests, chiffchaffs and other warblers. With treecreepers and nuthatches also joining the throng, these flocks are a good measure of how successful the breeding season has been.

In suburban gardens, young blackbirds chuckle from the undergrowth, while overhead, parties of screaming swifts celebrate summer by racing in mobs through the streets, feeding in flocks on high-flying insects and ballooning spiders. From now on, the young swifts may not touch land for eighteen months or more, and by the end of July, many will already be well on their way to their ancestral home in Africa. Around our homes house martins, whose gritty calls are the soundtrack to a midsummer day, feed their growing chicks; the essence of Africa under our eaves.

In the vast seabird colonies around our rocky northern and western coasts, departures are being plotted. On midsummer evenings, many a guillemot mother is persuading her single chick to plunge off its ledge and on to the water below, where its father is waiting to escort it out to sea for the rest of the year.

Strange plumages begin to appear in July. Young blue tits and great tits look like washed-out versions of the adults, while immature robins are speckled, and lack the orange breast feathers that will appear when they first moult in September.

Starlings in particular can look very confusing. When the brownish youngsters feed on the lawn with their glossy parents, they appear to be a completely different species. From city rooftops, muddy-brown gull chicks launch themselves on their maiden flights and wheel overhead with thin, wheedling cries as they beg to be fed, though from now on they're on their own. Sometimes you can see starlings and gulls performing an aerial ballet over town, a sign that ants are swarming. These myriads of airborne insects are an irresistible target, but they do tax the young gulls' flying skills to the limit.

After the earliest hint of wader passage in late June, July sees the beginning of migration in earnest. It's well worth casting an eye over your local marsh or gravel pit for southbound birds, often those that have failed to find a mate on their northern breeding grounds. The triple call of a greenshank is a sign that autumn is on its way, even though for us summer is still in full swing. They're not alone: young willow warblers and whinchats are also heading south, the first in what will soon become a flood of songbird migrants heading towards Africa.

CORN BUNTING

*

A dot on a distant telegraph wire and a skirl of brittle song floating across the ripening crops tells you that a corn bunting is defending his territory against his rival males. Few birds sing among the rolling acres of cereals that make up much of our lowland landscape in midsummer, but the corn bunting – once known as the fat bird of the barley – is in his element here.

For hours on end he delivers his parched phrases, which have been likened to the jangling of a bunch of keys, and also have more than a hint of a freewheeling bicycle wheel about them. From a prominent perch – a tree in the middle of a hedgerow, a fence-post, or a tall plant – he sings on even through the midday sun.

The corn bunting's jangling song continues to ring out across the ripening crops each summer, mostly in arable areas of southern and eastern England, from Wiltshire to Norfolk. But this portly, plain brown bunting, looking rather like a sparrow on steroids, has fallen silent in many of his former haunts, including large swathes of northern and western Britain. Industrial farming methods, designed to squeeze the highest yields per acre, have wrought havoc with the complex family life of this bird.

Like its relative the yellowhammer, the corn bunting breeds late, and frequently has young chicks in the nest well into July or even August. So in fine summers, when the crops are harvested early, the

buntings' nests are often destroyed by the merciless blades of the combine.

Things are no better in autumn and winter. The shift towards producing crops all year round leaves little or no waste seed on the ground, and stubble fields are now a thing of the past across much of this bird's range.

Corn buntings may look rather drab and clumsy as they flutter around, legs dangling beneath them, but the male is a true Lothario of the bird world, and can have up to eighteen different partners in a single breeding season.

His females build their nests among the cornstalks or in the undergrowth at the edge of the field, weaving together blades of grass into a small, neat cup, into which they lay up to five streaky-brown eggs. Where the buntings still thrive, the male birds need to sing loud and long, for they have their work cut out to defend their harems against rival males.

YELLOWHAMMER

*

The song of the yellowhammer – famously interpreted as 'a little bit of bread and no cheeeeese!' – is as much a part of the British summer as strawberries and cream, the thwack of leather on willow, and bank holiday traffic jams.

If you hear the yellowhammer's song, you may wish to ascribe your own mnemonic to help you remember it. Bill Oddie famously likened it to a reluctant country milkmaid being wooed by an amorous farmhand: 'No-no-no-no-no pleeeeease . . .'

Incidentally, the 'hammer' has nothing to do with the percussive tone of the yellowhammer's song – it simply derives from the German word *ammer*, meaning 'bunting'.

Take a closer look at the male, and you could be forgiven for assuming you are looking at an escaped canary. He sings from a hedgerow perch, his brilliant sulphur-yellow head thrown back, in vivid contrast with his streaky brown and black body.

His mate is more self-effacing, with yellow tinges to her brownish-olive plumage, but like her partner has a rust coloured rump, which she reveals in flight.

Female yellowhammers build their nests from woven grass at the bottom of hedgerows or in shrubby thickets, to avoid predators. The eggs are camouflaged with a series of fine, wobbly lines, which led our ancestors to give this species the folk-names 'writing lark' and 'scribble lark'.

To observers in Wales, these markings apparently suggested serpents, hence the Welsh name which translates as 'servant of the snake', from the erroneous belief that yellowhammers warn snakes of impending danger.

TURTLE DOVE

*

Of all the sounds that conjure up an image of lazy, hazy summer days, perhaps the most evocative of all is the soporific purring of the turtle dove. The turtle dove's soothing song was one of the first bird sounds mentioned in the Bible, in the Old Testament Song of Solomon: 'The time of the singing of the birds is come. And the voice of the turtle is heard in our land.'

Around the Mediterranean basin, turtle doves are real harbingers of spring, but by the time they reach Britain, that season is well under way. May blossom covers the high, thick hedgerows that turtle doves often choose for singing: cocooned by flowers and foliage, the bird itself is often invisible, so it's the all-pervading song that hijacks the senses.

Sometimes they will perch on telegraph wires, allowing a closer look at our smallest dove. It is not much larger than a blackbird, with fine terracotta and black scaling on its back, and contrasting black and white stripes across the side of its neck, rather like the gill slits of a shark. When it flies, jinking from side to side more like a wader than a dove, you see blue-grey wing-patches and striking white tips to its dark tail-feathers.

Turtle doves are happiest on weedy farmland with tall hedges, in scrub, or on the edges of heathland. Sadly, though, the voice of the turtle dove is no longer being heard across much of Britain. This once common and widespread farmland bird is declining faster than any other species: down by more than 90 per cent since 1970, and still falling sharply. At this rate the turtle dove is predicted to disappear from our countryside completely, soon after the year 2020.

Even more worryingly, the freefall in the turtle dove population is being mirrored across much of the rest of its breeding range in Europe and western Asia. That's because the species is being hit by a triple whammy of habitat loss here in Britain, drought on its wintering grounds south of the Sahara, and wholesale slaughter on its migration routes to and from Africa.

JULY

Every spring and autumn, the rapidly dwindling cohort of European turtle doves must run the gauntlet of thousands of shotguns as they cross the Mediterranean Sea on their migratory journeys. Over places such as Malta and Sicily, huge numbers of migrant birds are killed each year, and turtle doves, which fly fast but low, have been hit harder than most.

The species has already been described as 'Europe's passenger pigeon', which is a dire prediction about its possible fate. At the eleventh hour, efforts are now being made to stop this senseless slaughter; but, sadly, for the turtle dove it may already be too late.

SANDWICH TERN

*

A visit to the seaside on a summer's day may be rewarded with the sight – and sound – of our largest breeding tern. Even from afar, it has the distinctive look of a brilliant-white gull with long, pointed wings. The sharp double 'kirr-ick' call leaves little doubt that you're watching a Sandwich tern.

Like most members of their family, Sandwich terns are primarily a bird of the coast, nesting in noisy, crowded colonies among sand dunes, on shingle beaches and on offshore islands. These charismatic seabirds keep up their raucous din from dawn to dusk, as they go about raising their families. Close to, they are handsome birds indeed: snow white beneath and pearl grey above, with a shaggy black crest and sharp, stiletto-like bill, jet black with a yellow tip.

Having returned early in March from their winter home in West Africa, mainly along the coast of Ghana

and Senegal, Sandwich terns lay one or two eggs, which hatch into fluffy chicks. Their speckled downy plumage makes a perfect camouflage against attack by aerial predators such as the larger gulls and crows, or danger on the ground from stoats, rats and foxes.

Their rather unusual name comes from the seaside town of Sandwich in east Kent. Here, in 1784, the bird was first shot by a Kentish surgeon and amateur ornithologist named William Boys, and identified as a new species to science by his colleague Dr John Latham. Along with two other species – Dartford warbler and Kentish plover – it is among the few birds to be named after a place in Britain; as it happens, all from the same county.

Nowadays, the name seems rather parochial for this global wanderer, which can be found on both sides of the Atlantic and in five of the world's seven continents.

BUZZARD

*

Above a wooded Welsh valley, wings held in a shallow V, a buzzard is circling, head lowered as it scans the bracken-covered slopes for its prey. Until recently that was the typical view of a bird we used to associate with remote upland regions of Britain. But in one of the most dramatic recoveries of any British species, this stocky raptor has returned

to reoccupy the lowlands. In just two decades or so since the last BTO Atlas survey, the buzzard has spread south and eastwards to colonize every county in England.

With as many as 75,000 breeding pairs, it has even overtaken the kestrel and sparrowhawk to become our commonest bird of prey. Its plaintive, mewing call – rather a weak sound for such a large, robust bird – is increasingly familiar in the countryside.

Buzzards are also now regularly seen in built-up areas, and you'll often notice them hunched on telegraph poles or fences as they watch for the movements of small mammals, or scan for roadkill. They're great opportunists with a varied diet, and will waddle behind the plough in search of earthworms, or wait patiently for moles to emerge from their burrows. They are most often seen in flight, as they wheel and soar over their territories on wings that can be a metre or more across. On clear days, these broad wings harness the rising thermal air currents as buzzards advertise their territories.

The reason for this rapid turnaround in fortunes is simple: buzzards are no longer being poisoned by agricultural chemicals such as DDT, which massively reduced numbers during the 1950s and 1960s. This decline was compounded by the short-sighted introduction of myxomatosis to control the population of rabbits, a major part of the buzzard's diet. They are also no longer routinely shot and poisoned by farmers and gamekeepers.

But the buzzard's return is now attracting attention from some pheasant breeders who regard them as a threat to their game birds, and there have been requests to issue licences to control breeding buzzards in some areas to protect pheasant chicks.

In Scotland, where buzzards have always been a fairly common sight, the species is known as the 'tourist eagle', because visitors from the south have traditionally confused it with the much larger and more majestic golden eagle.

OSPREY

*

The sight of an osprey plunging its talons into the waters of a Scottish loch, to emerge amid a glittering shower of spray, carrying a salmon, is a truly breathtaking spectacle. Most birds of prey kill and eat mammals or other birds, but this raptor is a true piscivore and is well equipped for the job. Its feet have coarse scales and a reversible outer toe to allow it to grip slippery prey when in flight. The birds also waterproof their feathers by oiling them with secretions from a preen gland, in preparation for those spectacular dives.

Ospreys are undeniably handsome: dark brown above and white below, with long wings that make them look rather gull-like from a distance. Closer to, you'll see the dark face-mask and white head. It is ironic – given the osprey's fishy diet – that its name derives from the Latin word *ossifraga*, meaning 'bone-breaker'. A more appropriate name is one rarely heard nowadays: 'fish-hawk'.

These striking raptors are now firmly part of the British scene, yet they only returned to breed here just over half a century ago.

Ospreys and people have always had an uneasy relationship, ever since these impressive birds used to raid fishponds in medieval times. But during the nineteenth century, like all other birds of prey, they were ruthlessly persecuted. Then, once their numbers dwindled, they and their eggs were targeted by collectors, keen to display a stuffed osprey and its clutch to their friends.

By the early twentieth century the osprey had been eliminated as a British breeding bird, with only a few migrants passing through each spring and autumn on their way from Africa to Scandinavia and back. But in the spring of 1954 a pair stopped off in the Scottish Highlands, at Loch Garten in Speyside, and settled down to breed.

The osprey was back – but not, perhaps, for long. Egg-collectors continued to target the new colonists, and so in 1959 the RSPB set up 'Operation Osprey', a military-style operation to guard the nest and its precious eggs. Slowly but surely, the ospreys began to thrive, and spread out to other sites. Today there are more than 200 breeding pairs in Scotland, and the species now nests in Wales and England as well. The osprey has also been given a helping hand by a reintroduction programme at Rutland Water, in the heart of England's smallest county.

As well as saving a threatened species, Operation Osprey also became one of the first examples of successful wildlife tourism anywhere in the world, attracting almost 3 million visitors since it first began. The original template – inviting people to come and see a rare bird at its nest – has been copied all over Britain and elsewhere in the world, encouraging many people to engage in conservation.

Once they have bred, ospreys migrate south to spend the winter months in West Africa. Until recently the actual route they took was something of a mystery, but thanks to new miniaturized transmitters we can now follow the birds' progress in real time, as they head south across the Bay of Biscay, Spain and the Sahara Desert in autumn and return here the following spring.

CORNCRAKE
*

It is almost impossible to imagine nowadays, but not all that long ago the monotonous and grating call of the corncrake was one of the most familiar sounds of the British countryside.

Writing in the early years of the nineteenth century, the poet John Clare referred to what he called the land rail, 'a summer noise among the meadow hay'. In Clare's native Northamptonshire – as in the rest of lowland Britain – the corncrake was a regular summer visitor, whose call, repeated throughout the day and night, became a constant soundtrack throughout the harvest season.

Not that this elusive bird was any easier to see, even when it was common. Clare summed up its elusive omnipresence in this couplet:

> *Tis like a fancy everywhere*
> *A sort of living doubt*
> *We know tis something but it ne'er*
> *Will blab the secret out*

Your best chance of seeing a corncrake nowadays is to visit islands in the Inner and Outer Hebrides, where they lurk among the green swords of iris leaves or skulk in nettle-patches on crofts. On the Isle of Iona, off the western end of Mull, their ceaseless summer rasping resounds from the abbey walls. If you're lucky enough to see one, it is usually in flight: looking like a slim, brown moorhen with rusty-coloured wings. They fly so feebly, it's hard to believe that they migrate here from sub-Saharan Africa, but they do.

The corncrake was the first victim of modern farming methods, which began to work against nature rather than with it, as traditional farming always had done. Mechanical mowing destroyed the nests spared by hand-cutting the hay, while agricultural chemicals reduced the amount of insect food needed by the young.

By the start of the Second World War the corncrake had vanished from most of rural England and Wales; and by the millennium it could only be found in the far north and west of Scotland, where crofters carried on haymaking in the time-honoured, traditional way.

At one point the population fell below 500 pairs, and it looked as if the corncrake might be doomed as a British breeding bird. But a partnership between conservationists and crofters has reaped benefits, and today there are more than 1,200 males in Scotland, each capable of calling up to 20,000 times in a single night.

For those living in the south, far away from the corncrake's Scottish refuge, there is now fresh hope. A consortium of conservationists has reintroduced the species into the Nene Washes near Peterborough, and so far the scheme is going to plan. It may take a few years, but there is now a good chance that this mysterious 'summer noise' will once again echo across the East Anglian fens, not very far from where John Clare listened to it two centuries earlier.

HOUSE MARTIN

*

Patterned like a miniature killer whale, the house martin swoops through the clear blue skies in search of small flying insects, which it catches with a sudden snap of its bill. Its flight is accompanied by the martin's gritty call, a sound that is the essence of a summer's day, and which is often used to add a bucolic atmosphere to radio and television dramas.

House martins are often confused with their cousins the swallows, but they are noticeably smaller and dumpier, without the long tail-streamers. They're dark bluish-black above and white below, with a neat white rump and snowy feathers around their feet.

Like swallows, they build their nests with tiny pellets of mud, which they collect from puddles or the sides of ponds and lakes. They cement these together, a beakful at a time, under the eaves of our houses. This produces a cup-shaped, gravity-defying nest sheltering up to five rapidly growing youngsters, which by the point of fledging can barely squeeze into their cramped home.

To some people, it is an honour to see these youngsters gaping for food like pied froglets from their nest under the eaves; others, perhaps understandably, object to the messy droppings and loud calls that the martins produce.

Of course they haven't always relied on us. Long before humans arrived, martins nested on natural cliffs, both inland and on the coast. A few pairs still exploit this ancient habitat, despite the ample availability of houses in modern Britain.

Some martins have grander ambitions than a suburban semi, and nest on ancient stone bridges, country mansions and even castles, as William Shakespeare noted in *Macbeth*, where Banquo observes that:

JULY

No jutty, frieze, buttress nor coign of vantage, but this bird
Hath made his pendant bed and procreant cradle.
Where they most breed and haunt, I have observed
The air is delicate.

House martins may be familiar to us, but they hold one big secret: we don't yet know where in Africa their main wintering grounds are. Ornithologists believe that they may feed on insects high over the Congolese rainforests, but until we can design a transmitter small enough to fit on this tiny bird – and that will surely happen soon – we can't be sure. It's intriguing that a bird with which we share our homes can still be such a mystery to us.

COAL TIT

*

If you hear a sound like a squeaky toy coming from the depths of a yew, pine or other evergreen tree, it's probably a coal tit. Higher-pitched and thinner than the song of the great tit, and more rhythmic than that of the chiffchaff, it comes from the smallest member of the tit family in Britain: the adult coal tit weighs just nine grams.

Cloaked by curtains of conifer needles, coal tits are often best located by their squeaks; but a better look will reveal a smart and attractive bird, though less colourful than its relatives. Instead of the great and blue tits' striking blues, greens and yellows, the coal tit is mainly black, buff and brown, with white cheeks and a white patch on its nape, a useful way of telling it apart from marsh and willow tits. There are also two white

bars on its wings, which stand out surprisingly well at a distance.

Being so small, coal tits are not very high up the pecking order on the average bird-table. So, unlike the large and bulky great tit, or the small but feisty blue tit, they tend to swoop in as quickly as they can, pausing only momentarily to grab a seed or peanut before guiltily dashing off.

They are also taking some food away to eat later. Coal tits like to stockpile items of food, a habit known as 'caching'. As long as they remember where they've stashed their morsels, they can be sure of having something to eat if the weather turns bad, and ice and snow cover up their usual food sources.

Coal tits prefer conifers partly because their thin bills are well suited to probing for insects among pine and spruce needles. They may also make their nests in holes in the trunk or among hollows in the roots, laying up to ten tiny, pale eggs. By July the trees resound to the querulous squeaks of newly fledged broods of coal tits as they rove through the canopy in search of food. No matter how hard you search for them though, they are almost impossible to see amid the dense, dark green foliage.

As the summer turns to autumn, and then winter, coal tits often join mixed flocks of blue and great tits, nuthatches and treecreepers. The principle is simple: more pairs of eyes to find food, and to keep a lookout for predators such as sparrowhawks.

TREE PIPIT

*

At noon on a fine midsummer's day, a patch of gorse- and heather-strewn heathland shimmers in the heat haze. The intense heat of the midday sun makes the blackened gorse-pods pop loudly, firing seeds away from the bush like tiny bullets. By this time of day, and at this time of year, most birds have stopped singing and are either resting or foraging for food. But one species is still serenading its mate and proclaiming its territory: the tree pipit.

HERRING GULL

*

He does so in pretty spectacular fashion: launching himself into the air and delivering a crescendo of song, then parachuting downwards like a spiralling paper dart, back to his perch on top of a scrawny tree or bush. This combination of the distinctive song and the bird's habit of using a tree as a perch rather than returning to the ground enables you to tell the tree pipit apart from his very similar relative the meadow pipit.

Writing in 1773, the celebrated naturalist Gilbert White said that tree pipits, which he called titlarks, 'Not only sing sweetly as they sit on trees, but also as they play and toy about on the wing . . .'

If you do get a close view, you will see that both sexes are slender brown birds, streaked like the grass in which they make their nest. Their favourite breeding areas are heaths, woodland clearings and young plantations. While tree pipits are feeding young you will often see them perched nervously on a branch nearby, with their bill full of insects.

When they migrate south, if you're sharp-eared, you might hear their buzzing call as they fly overhead. By late August many have already gone, winging their way across the Sahara to spend the winter in Africa's savannah woodlands.

One of the most evocative natural sounds heard in the British Isles, the raucous yet haunting call of the herring gull, conjures up childhood memories of summer holidays at the seaside: ice-cream cones, saucy postcards and kiss-me-quick hats.

So it may come as a surprise to discover two things about the herring gull. First, that its population has plummeted so rapidly in recent years that it is now on the Red List of birds under threat in Britain; and second, that most herring gulls no longer live by the sea at all.

The story begins with the Clean Air Act of 1956. This was passed to put an end to those terrible smogs that blighted London and other British towns and cities in the post-war years, caused by a combination of coal fires and the burning of domestic refuse. But by insisting that our rubbish must be dumped in landfill sites, rather than burned, the Act's supporters inadvertently provided a free breakfast, lunch, tea and dinner for herring gulls and their relatives.

At the same time, we were building reservoirs that could be conveniently used as safe night-time roosts, and tall buildings with flat roofs on which the birds could nest, safe from predators such as foxes. We were also reducing the amount of food for gulls around our shores, by changing fishing practices, which meant that fish were now no longer gutted onshore, but out at sea. Together with other pressures, this reduced numbers nesting on the coast.

As a result of this perfect storm of unrelated factors, many herring gulls have simply forsaken the seaside and made a new life inland, in our city centres. Nowadays, the urban dawn chorus has a new soloist: the accompanist to the theme tune of *Desert Island Discs* is now a member of the city orchestra, its call echoing across the city skyline like a muezzin calling the faithful to prayer.

So new generations of city dwellers are learning to live with this large and feisty bird – despite its antisocial habits. Herring gulls are intelligent and adaptable, and have rapidly learned to raid litterbins, steal chips from unwary nocturnal revellers, and even snatch ice creams from the hands of small children.

This makes them unpopular with many, who think that the herring gull should have stayed where it belongs, at the seaside. But in spite of calls for a cull of urban gulls, they are here to stay – and instead of condemning them, we should perhaps learn to admire their resourcefulness and guile.

KINGFISHER

*

A sharp, metallic whistle by a lake or river is a cue to scan the water's surface and surrounding bushes for its maker. More brightly coloured than any bird deserves to be, kingfishers are nevertheless usually given away by their call, which is followed by what looks like a

missile whizzing by, wings whirring as it goes. They are so quick they are like a radar trace against the poolside willows, so bright their after-image feels seared on the retina.

Few birds fly quite as straight as the kingfisher; and none shares this combination of beauty and brilliance in miniature. For it is a tiny bird: no bigger than a starling, with a stump of a tail, an outsize head and a dagger of a bill, which always looks too big for the bird to carry.

If you can approach closely enough, a kingfisher shimmers with aquamarine and turquoise above, set off perfectly by a white throat and rusty-orange cheeks and underparts, reflecting the dappled movements of the river below it.

Kingfishers are well and truly tied to water, building their nest in a burrow deep in a sandy riverbank, and bringing in more than a hundred fish every day to feed their hungry brood. The resulting accumulation of bones and fish offal produces a stench that is somewhat at odds with the bird's smart appearance.

Kingfishers always seem as if they are in a hurry – and they are. They rarely live longer than a year or so, and are very vulnerable to the weather: droughts, floods, snow and ice can all reduce their chances of survival. So to compensate, each have up to three broods of half a dozen chicks in a single season, the young rapidly gaining independence as soon as they leave the nest.

The ancient Greeks called the bird the 'halcyon' and believed that the female built her nest on the waves, calming the seas while she brooded her eggs. This gave rise to the expression 'halcyon days', which we now use to describe a time of calm and tranquillity. But for many of us, our reaction to that all-too-brief flash of colour and movement is anything but tranquil.

CIRL BUNTING

*

As you wander alongside an overgrown hedgerow in the far south-west of England, you hear a dry rattle, sounding rather like a yellowhammer that has forgotten to finish off its song. This is the sound of one of our scarcest and most localized breeding birds: the cirl bunting.

Cirl buntings – the unusual name derives from an Italian word meaning 'to chirp' – are closely related to the yellowhammer, and can look very similar. On closer inspection, though, the male cirl bunting has an obvious black and yellow face and a greenish chest-band, which in combination with his streaky brown plumage gives him a rather odd appearance, as if he has been put together by a committee. Females are much plainer, and both sexes have grey-olive rumps, unlike the rusty-red rumps of yellowhammers.

Once known as the 'French yellowhammer', the cirl bunting is indeed mainly a bird of continental Europe, the Mediterranean and North Africa, more at home in sunny olive groves than chilly English fields. Here in Britain, on the very north-western edge of its breeding range, the cirl bunting's fortunes have changed in the past few decades.

At the end of the Second World War the species could be found in farmland across a wide swathe of our southern counties. But the cirl bunting needs just the right combination of insect-rich hedgerows where it nests in spring and summer, and weedy fields where it can forage for seeds in autumn and winter.

Sadly most of the countryside in southern Britain has been homogenized by industrial farming methods.

Deprived of weedy stubble fields and large insects, the cirl bunting population went into freefall, eventually retreating to a last refuge in the ancient farmed landscape of south Devon.

But now, at last, there is some good news. Hard work by conservationists has raised the population from a low point of fewer than 120 pairs in 1989 to almost 1,000 pairs today. They succeeded by encouraging farmers to leave stubble over winter to provide seeds for the birds, and to create field margins for insects in summer. The recovery project has been a resounding success, so much so that cirl buntings have now been reintroduced into neighbouring Cornwall.

In winter, cirl buntings regularly visit bird-tables; so local people have also become involved in the species' comeback. However, being one of our most sedentary species, progress is necessarily slow, and it will be a very long time, if ever, before this attractive little seed-eater returns to its former range.

SPOTTED FLYCATCHER

*

A country churchyard, full of ancient, lichen-encrusted gravestones. A small bird flits into view, highlighted by a ray of sun across an ancient monument, where it perches momentarily. It is a spotted flycatcher: an unexceptional-looking, dull grey-brown bird perhaps, but a spark of irrepressible life amid this place of stillness and contemplation.

Of all the migrants that visit us each summer, the spotted flycatcher is surely the perkiest, with a charm all of its own. It is also one of the latest to arrive, in mid-May. The first sighting is often a pale shape darting from a tree and plucking an unsuspecting fly out of mid-air with an audible snap of its bill, before returning to its perch. Its calls and song are minimal to say the least: a series of spitting squeaks and a sharp 'zee-tuk-tuk' to alert you to its presence high in the treetops.

It is easy to watch this bird all day long; its balletic grace is breathtaking as it follows every twist and turn of its prey. Between these feeding flights, the flycatcher sits ramrod straight, like a sergeant major on parade, keeping a beady black eye out for the next passing insect.

When making their nest, spotted flycatchers choose nooks and crannies behind the bark of a tree, or deep inside the foliage of a climbing shrub. Like robins, they also sometimes choose more unconventional sites: one enterprising pair was discovered nesting inside an empty baked-bean can.

Late in the summer, when the youngsters leave the safety of their nest, you can finally see how the species acquired the first part of its name. Unlike their parents, young spotted flycatchers have pale spots across their back. These disappear thousands of miles away when they moult into their breeding plumage, in the middle of an African forest, somewhere south of the Equator during the British winter.

LESSER BLACK-BACKED GULL

*

The year of Elizabeth II's coronation, 1953, saw fewer than 200 lesser black-backed gulls winter in Britain. Sixty years later, when the nation celebrated the Diamond Jubilee, more than 100,000 did so.

The reason? Not some loyal attachment to the monarchy, but simply because we have made the lesser black-backed gull's life about as easy as it could be. Why bother to migrate all the way to Spain or North Africa when a constant buffet is available, all year round, at landfill sites? After all, birds only migrate if they must, because food is scarce. So if a new food source comes on tap, birds soon change their habits to take advantage of it.

Charcoal grey above, alabaster white below, lesser black-backs are smart birds, perfectly complementing their slightly larger, paler and altogether more aggressive-looking cousin the herring gull. Like them, they can be found throughout Britain, not just on the coast. They are equally at home on school playing-fields or in city squares as they are by the seaside, in contrast to their larger relative the great black-backed gull, which rarely ventures inland.

Like herring gulls, lesser black-backed gulls have also taken to nesting on flat roofs. As a result they have become phenomenally successful, often raising all three of their downy young to fledging stage and beyond. Urban gulls make a basic nest of twigs and grasses, and it seems that almost any flat surface will do. One motorist returned to his vehicle after work one day to find a nest of twigs on the roof – complete with an egg in it – created in less than three hours.

SPARROWHAWK

*

A flurry of wings around the bird-table and a sudden silence among the diners means that a sparrowhawk is hunting. It's a male bird: blue-grey above and orange below, with broad, blunt wings and a long, barred tail. Its yellow legs, no thicker than knitting needles, stretch out to seize a dunnock that's dashed for cover. This time the hawk is unsuccessful and flies off, gaining height with brief bursts of flapping and gliding.

Sparrowhawks have the biggest size difference between the sexes of any British bird, the males being up to one-third smaller than the browner females. This adaptation enables the pair to exploit a wide range of different-sized prey, with the male hunting smaller songbirds while the female can take down a pigeon.

It's a privilege to see this master-predator hunting in the suburbs, but few birds – apart, of course, from the notorious magpie – arouse quite so much passion and fury as the sparrowhawk. Its inconvenient habit of feeding on small songbirds has placed it firmly in the pantheon of rogues and villains, especially among the millions of people who enjoy feeding birds in their garden.

When a sparrowhawk shoots through the scene, scattering blue tits this way and that before grabbing one in its razor-sharp talons, it can feel as if this intruder has spilt blood on our living-room carpet.

Yet sparrowhawks, like any other bird, are simply doing what they have evolved to do: catch and kill their prey. Just as blue tits are the caterpillar's mortal enemy, and blackbirds would win no fan mail from earthworms, so these charismatic predators follow their basic instincts.

Whatever your view, it's hard not to be impressed by the sparrowhawk's hunting skills. They use bushes, hedgerows and fences as cover, slaloming up, over and around them to perform the perfect ambush. This strategy works particularly well in hard winters, when songbirds are too busy finding food to eat to worry about predators; and in late summer, when there are plenty of naïve and unwary youngsters for the bird to target.

But songbirds are always alert to the danger, and have evolved a battery of ways to avoid being caught. Listen out for a rally of high-pitched alarm calls, and you'll know a sparrowhawk is lurking close by; the sharp 'pik pik' calls of starlings are a particularly reliable indicator of its presence.

You may also hear the sparrowhawk's call: it's rather like the yaffling of the green woodpecker, but more piercing in tone. Today, you can often hear it above our tree-lined suburban streets, which have become the modern equivalent of forest glades for this sylvan bird. But had you been walking the same streets fifty years ago, you would not have heard it in town or, indeed, in most of the countryside. Then sparrowhawks were in big trouble, following the boom in the use of agricultural pesticides in the years after the Second World War. These deadly chemicals passed from prey to predator, and soon built up to dangerous levels in the sparrowhawks' bodies. As well as poisoning the birds themselves, pesticides made their eggshells wafer-thin, so when the hen sat on the eggs to incubate they simply broke. As a result, during the late 1950s and 1960s sparrowhawk numbers went into freefall.

Once these pesticides were finally banned, sparrowhawks recovered rapidly, and they are now widespread across much of Britain, constantly on the lookout for prey with their unblinking, lemon-yellow eyes.

DOTTEREL

*

Waders are, in general, shy and flighty birds. But high on the arctic-alpine plateau of Britain's last great wilderness, the Cairngorm Mountains, one wader is the exception that proves the rule. The dotterel is one of the tamest and most approachable of all British birds. Indeed the name itself suggests stupidity – as in 'dotard' – and the Gaelic name for the species translates as 'peat-bog fool'. Even the bird's scientific name, *morinellus*, translates as 'dim' or 'foolish'.

Our Victorian ancestors took full advantage of the dotterel's obliging habits, collecting their eggs and catching the birds themselves, which were reputed to be very good to eat.

The dotterel may have a reputation for stupidity, but no one can deny that it is a truly handsome bird. Similar to a golden plover in shape and structure, with a plump body and short, stubby bill, the dotterel is chestnut-orange beneath, with scalloped brown upper-parts. Its most noticeable field-marks are a white band across the chest and a broad white stripe above each eye, meeting at the back of the head.

The great Scottish ornithologist Desmond Nethersole-Thompson, who spent many hours studying the birds of the high mountaintops, memorably described dotterels as wearing 'brown-rimmed tam o'shanters'.

The dotterel certainly appealed to early collectors, but they would surely have been shocked if they had

known what we do today about the dotterel's unusual approach to family life. In a clear affront to 'Victorian values', female dotterels are not only more brightly coloured than their mate, but also take the lead in the business of courtship and breeding.

Once the female has laid her clutch of two or three eggs, she leaves her mate to incubate them and rear the chicks alone, often going off to find another partner and repeating the process over again. More incredibly still, about four out of five female dotterels that nest in Scotland then go on to Scandinavia or Russia, where they attempt to breed once more.

Because of their British breeding habitat, we tend to think of dotterels as birds of the mountains. Yet they are far more adaptable than we might think: in the Netherlands they nest on reclaimed land known as polders, several metres below sea level. And on their journeys to and from Africa, parties of dotterels (known as 'trips') often spend a day or two at favoured stopover points in the south of Britain, including the ridges of ploughed fields, where they can hide from observers surprisingly easily in the furrows.

RED-NECKED PHALAROPE

*

A boggy lochan fringed with sedges in the extreme north of the British Isles is one of the few places in this country where you can guarantee seeing a red-necked phalarope, at least during the summer months. This charming little wader, even smaller than a starling, is more or less confined as a British breeding bird to the island groups of Shetland and the Outer Hebrides, with fewer than thirty breeding pairs in total.

That's because red-necked phalaropes are truly Arctic birds, on the very southern edge of their range here. Further north they can be found in their millions across the tundra, where they take advantage of the summer boom in tiny insects to breed.

They then head south to spend the winter out at sea, in such far-flung locations as off the coast of Arabia, and among the islands of South-East Asia and the vast Pacific Ocean. One bird tracked from Shetland did a round trip of more than 25,000 kilometres, via Greenland and the Caribbean, to reach its winter home off Peru. Sometimes migrating birds will stop off inland where, dwarfed by mallards and other ducks, they quietly feed before moving on.

Unlike other European waders, red-necked phalaropes are keen swimmers, with tiny flaps known as lobes around their toes to help them – the derivation of their strange name, which means 'coot-footed' in Latin. When feeding, a phalarope spins around on the water to create a mini-whirlpool, thus stirring up prey beneath the surface, which the bird can then pick off with its needle-sharp bill.

Like the dotterel, phalaropes can be remarkably trusting, often allowing you to approach within a foot or two. They also share another characteristic with that species: the females are more brightly coloured, take the lead in courtship, and after laying the eggs leave the male to do all the hard work of raising the tiny chicks.

BLACK-BROWED ALBATROSS

*

Remember the 'Summer of Love' – the heady days of 1967, when the Beatles ruled the charts and Swinging London was the centre of the world? It was in May that

year that a huge, ungainly bird turned up in the colony of gannets on the Bass Rock in the Firth of Forth.

This unusual arrival was a black-browed albatross, a huge, wandering seabird from the vast southern oceans, which had somehow crossed over the area of calm seas around the Equator known as the Doldrums, and into the northern hemisphere. Alone and unable to find a mate, he settled for the next best thing: our own largest seabird, the gannet, which he attempted to woo by prancing back and forth and uttering his braying, donkey-like call.

Soon christened Albert (short for Albert Ross), this particular individual returned to the Bass Rock for the following two seasons. Then he disappeared; but just three years later he – or perhaps another black-browed albatross – was discovered in the gannet colony at Britain's most northerly point, Hermaness on Shetland. This bird remained there almost every spring and summer for more than twenty years, making his final appearance in the summer of 1995. Sadly, Albert never managed to find a mate.

But the story doesn't end there. Recently another – or perhaps the same – albatross turned up on the remote Scottish outcrop of Sula Sgeir, again among a colony of gannets. It may seem far-fetched to suggest that this could be the same individual as that on Hermaness and the Bass Rock, but albatrosses are among the world's longest-lived birds, and have been known to survive for more than fifty years.

Of the twenty or so species of albatross, the black-browed is by far the most abundant, with more than 1 million individuals. The Falkland Islands are home to almost three-quarters of all breeding black-browed albatrosses, which after nesting range far and wide across the oceans of the southern hemisphere in search of food from fishing trawlers.

As with other albatrosses, many black-brows fall victim to the barbaric practice of 'longlining', in which baited hooks to catch fish attract the birds, which then suffer a painful and lingering death. Conservationists and fishermen are now working together to change fishing methods and hopefully save these magnificent seabirds.

WHINCHAT

*

On a windswept moor, a small, robin-sized bird perches on top of a gorse bush, singing a wistful song: a whinchat. Its very name evokes the vegetation of its habitat, too. 'Whin' is the Scottish name for gorse, whose coconut-scented yellow flowers are commonest on heaths and moorland; other folk-names for this perky little bird include 'gorse chat', 'furze chat' and 'gorse hopper'.

Whinchats are long-distance migrants, spending the winter months in Africa south of the Sahara. As soon as the male returns he chooses a prominent song-perch and sets about attracting a mate. This is when he's at his most colourful: rusty orange beneath and scaly brown above, his dark head slashed by a brilliant white stripe, which is creamier and less prominent in the female.

Perched on their spiky surveillance points, whinchats are ever vigilant, and if you approach will give a soft, warning call followed by the sound of two stones being tapped together, gentler than the more percussive call of the stonechat.

Not so long ago, whinchats used to breed in river meadows and open areas with plenty of perches, but they have disappeared from many of these places in the last few decades, for reasons that aren't fully understood. Now you are most likely to find them on higher ground in the north and west of Britain.

On migration, though, whinchats can turn up in almost any suitable open space, including fields with hedgerows or haystacks from which they can survey their temporary home. In autumn, many of these southbound migrants are not British breeders, but have crossed the North Sea from Scandinavia, giving us all the chance to admire this sprightly and attractive little bird.

KESTREL

*

The Victorian poet Gerard Manley Hopkins, a keen observer of the natural world, wrote about the kestrel in one of his best-known poems, *The Windhover*:

I caught this morning morning's minion, king-dom of daylight's dauphin, dapple-dawn-drawn Falcon …

Windhover is the perfect name for a bird with such breathtaking aerial control. Watch a kestrel

hovering over a roadside verge, and you can only marvel at the precision of its movements. Its habit of hunting along roadside verges has also earned it the less glamorous nickname 'motorway hawk'.

Facing into the wind, it barely needs to beat its wings, making minute adjustments with its tail to hold itself stationary. The key is to keep its head completely motionless, allowing the falcon to pinpoint the presence of small mammals such as mice and voles in the grass below.

The kestrel also has a secret weapon up its sleeve. It can see the wavelength of ultraviolet light, which allows the bird to trace the movements of these tiny rodents from the trails of urine they leave behind them – invisible to our own eyes, but to a kestrel, the equivalent of luminous signposts.

Kestrels are unmistakable when you get a good view of them: mainly chestnut above, though the slightly smaller males have a blue-grey head and tail. In flight the tail looks long in proportion to the wings, giving them a rakish and less compact appearance than our other falcons.

Until recently, the kestrel was not only our commonest bird of prey, but also the only raptor species we would regularly encounter, especially in lowland Britain. But in the past decade or so the species has been overtaken by the buzzard and sparrowhawk, and is now declining in some areas. We are not sure why, though a shortage of rough grassland habitat for its rodent prey may be one reason for the kestrel's decline.

The kestrel's ubiquity and familiarity mean that our ancestors placed it firmly at the bottom of the falconry pecking order. According to the fifteenth-century *Book of St Albans*, a guide to how gentlemen of the period should live, the hierarchy of ownership went from an eagle for an emperor, via a peregrine for a prince, and ended with a kestrel for a knave. That last phrase is now best known as the original title of Barry Hines's gritty tale of northern boyhood, featuring a kestrel called Kes, later made into a classic British film.

LITTLE TERN

*

For a noisy, hectic colony of our smallest tern, life's a beach . . .

Little terns are truly tiny – about the size of a song thrush – and can easily be picked out from other terns by their smaller size, white forehead, and yellow bill with a black tip, as well as their faster wingbeats and altogether more frantic flight action. They are usually seen patrolling just offshore, as they scan the shallow waters for small fish, which they plunge down into the water to grab.

Move too close to their breeding colony, though, and you'll unleash a tirade of grating shrieks, followed by continuous dive-bombing swoops, as they try to intimidate you into leaving their territory. Their fear is palpable and justified: little terns lay their eggs on shingle beaches, where they are perfectly camouflaged – and very easy to tread on and destroy in error.

For this reason, nesting in a colony makes perfect sense: little terns rely on safety in numbers. All the birds are constantly alert for danger, which can come from the air as well as on the ground. Foxes, stoats, gulls, crows and even kestrels can take a heavy toll of chicks and eggs.

Because people also share beaches with little terns, dog-walkers, joggers and holidaymakers can inadvertently wreak havoc; thus many known colonies are now protected behind electric fences and guarded by wardens. Even so, the little tern is at risk, with fewer than 1,500 pairs in about fifty colonies scattered around our coasts, mostly between Lincolnshire and Hampshire.

RED-BACKED
SHRIKE

*

For a fierce-looking, hook-billed predator, known as the 'butcher-bird' for its habit of impaling its prey on thorn bushes, the red-backed shrike has a surprisingly musical song – a series of scratchy, warbling notes rather like a sedge warbler in tone.

A century ago, this sound would have been heard over wide areas of England and Wales, as red-backed shrikes were regular summer visitors to scrubby hillsides and heathery heaths and commons.

They've always been connoisseurs' birds, and understandably so. Male red-backs are truly handsome, and sport pearl-grey heads, foxy mantles and white-with-a-hint-of-pink underparts. But it's their black bandit mask that is most obvious, and gives them the appearance of a pantomime villain. The females and juveniles have a brownish mask and are less eye-catching, but have a subtle beauty of their own.

However, seeing the red-backed shrike in Britain is now quite a challenge. Throughout the twentieth century the species underwent a steady decline, and by the late 1980s only a single pair remained, breeding on heathland on the Norfolk Brecks. Birders made a pilgrimage there to see the last of the shrikes, until one year they failed to return, and were declared extinct as a British breeding bird.

The reason the red-backed shrike declined so rapidly remains something of a mystery, but is likely to be a result of a series of cooler, wetter summers and the indiscriminate use of agricultural pesticides, which reduced the availability of large insects on which they feed their young. Habitat loss – shrikes prefer scrub, heath and traditionally farmed landscapes with plenty of hedgerows and small fields – may also have contributed to their demise.

The good news is that after sporadic breeding in Scotland and Wales, the red-backed shrike has recently returned to a site in Devon, where a handful of pairs have nested successfully for the past few years. A twenty-four-hour watch from conservationists and volunteers during the breeding season guards the shrikes from the unwelcome attention of egg-collectors, and there may yet be hope that the butcher-bird will once again be seen and heard in its former haunts.

Stonechat

House Sparrow

Woodpigeon

Ringed Plover

Great Black-backed Gull

Oystercatcher

Long-tailed Tit

Redstart

Bullfinch

Rock Pipit

Arctic Skua

❋ AUGUST ❋

Yellow Wagtail

Icterine Warbler

Northern Wheatear

White Stork

Honey-buzzard

Common Tern

Common Gull

Spotted Redshank

Golden Eagle

White-tailed Eagle

Barred Warbler

INTRODUCTION

FOR MOST BIRDS, August is a time to move on or moult. It's easy to be distracted by the butterflies feeding busily on the buddleia in our gardens and then suddenly wonder where all the birds have gone. Blackbirds and song thrushes vanish apparently without trace. Dunnocks, wrens and tits are harder to find too, though robins are at least easy to hear as they begin their autumn song.

But in most cases these birds haven't gone anywhere – they're simply lying low. The reason for this subterfuge is that after the rigours of the breeding season, many birds' feathers have suffered wear and tear, and they need time to shed the old ones and grow the new. Although our songbirds stagger their moult, so they don't lose the power of flight, they are more vulnerable at this time to predators such as cats and sparrowhawks, and thus sensibly disappear from view.

Other birds lose many of their flight feathers simultaneously. You may wonder why there are no drake mallards in your local park; and where those smart black and white tufted ducks on the local gravel pit have gone. They all seem to have been replaced by brownish females and youngsters.

That's because after the breeding season, the drakes of most of our duck species lose their colourful plumage and look superficially much more like the females. These new feathers are known as 'eclipse plumage' and although both sexes moult, it's the drakes that show the most dramatic colour changes. For ducks such as mallards, it can be a risky business, because while they grow their new feathers they are temporarily flightless, so it pays to be as inconspicuous as possible to avoid attracting predators. Eclipse lasts for about a month or six weeks and by autumn they have resumed their familiar features. On the park lake, they're often joined by returning black-headed gulls, which are now losing their chocolate (not black) hoods.

However some birds are hard to find because they genuinely are no longer around. By the middle of the month the guillemots, razorbills and puffins have left their breeding cliffs and grassy islands to spend the winter way out on the open ocean. Shags and cormorants are still in evidence because many of them remain around their breeding areas for most of the year. Manx shearwaters also begin to move south as the month progresses, joining a trickle of northern seabirds such as skuas, storm petrels and Arctic terns, some of which will winter way down into the southern hemisphere.

Most of the swifts have gone too from our towns and cities, the adults often leaving before their chicks, which are left to find their way to Africa unsupervised. You'll still see them, though, in high-flying groups scudding south or pausing over a ripening field of crops to feed on swarms of flying insects.

There's plenty to see in August, nonetheless, as many land migrants are on the move. As they filter south, leaving more specialized breeding places such as moorlands and western oak woods, they will often grace more humdrum habitats for a short while. Sheltered hedgerows almost anywhere are worth scanning for redstarts, which you may hear before you see them. Listen for a crisp 'hoo-it' call and look for a flash of orange or a tail-quivering silhouette. On rough ground, it's worth scanning fence-posts and taller plant-stems for whinchats.

Spotted flycatchers are also on the move, especially at woodland edges or along river corridors, where you may see a family group, the youngsters as agile as their parents as they snap up flies. There are young warblers everywhere now, usually brighter and neater looking than their parents. Chiffchaffs and willow warblers often pass quietly through our gardens and allotments along with blackcaps and whitethroats, as they stop to feed on the juicy berries they need to give them the energy to migrate.

It's always worth visiting a local marsh for wandering waders. Green and common sandpipers are the standard, but very welcome fare, seasoned by occasional wood sandpipers and spotted redshanks. Even if they're not around, you can enjoy the dragonflies: August is an excellent month to watch aerobatic hawkers and darters skimming through the warm summer air.

While all this movement is going on, though, some species are still busy raising a family. Swallows may be feeding their second or even third broods. On farmland, corn buntings and yellowhammers are ferrying beakfuls of insects to their growing chicks, a risky business as combine harvesters surge remorselessly through the crops that they nest among. On moors and commons, newly fledged young stonechats are being fed by their parents in a landscape turned mauve by the mass flowering of heather, as we all await the turning of the calendar to autumn.

STONECHAT

*

If you hear a sharp, tapping sound when walking across moorland, it's either someone working on a dry-stone wall, or a stonechat is calling.

Few birds are as well named as the stonechat, whose call sounds uncannily like two pebbles being repeatedly struck together. The Scottish poet Norman MacCaig captured it perfectly when he wrote:

> *A flint-on-flint ticking – and there he is,*
> *Trim and dandy – in square miles of bracken*
> *And bogs and boulders, a tiny work of art ...*

And a work of art the stonechat certainly is: especially the neat, richly coloured male. You'll see him centre stage, ostentatiously flicking his wings and tail on the topmost sprig of a gorse bush. He's a plump, robin-sized bird with a black head, white collar and bright orange chest, with white flashes on each dark wing.

His mate, who needs camouflage when incubating the eggs in her hidden nest, is less showy, and a more washed-out, softer shade of brown with hints of orange. Their presence in this open landscape adds something to their surroundings – no heath, moor or common is complete without a perky pair of stonechats.

Stonechats build their nest either on the ground or low in a gorse bush, from whose apex the male delivers his distinctive song, flicking the white in his wings to draw attention to his performance. There are usually five or six pale greenish-blue eggs, speckled with reddish brown.

Like many small birds, stonechats live short lives, which they compensate for by having two or even three broods in a single season. They need to be prolific because they feed mainly on insects and other tiny invertebrates, a diet that makes them very vulnerable to cold winters, especially when ice and snow cover up their food sources. When a cold snap is prolonged, up to 90 per cent of stonechats can starve to death, as happened in the infamous winter of 1962–3.

Although they don't travel as far as their cousin the whinchat, which winters south of the Sahara, some British stonechats do migrate, heading either to the coast or hopping across the Channel to spend the winter in Spain and Portugal. Others remain in Britain, moving from heaths to waste ground, marshes or unkempt corners on farmland, where the unexpected appearance of these tawny little birds brightens a dull winter's day.

HOUSE SPARROW

*

One bird sound has been a close accompaniment to our lives for thousands of years – maybe longer than that of any other British bird. Its call may not be particularly melodic, or tuneful, but nonetheless evokes a familiar sense of pleasure every time we hear it: the companionable chirp of the house sparrow.

House sparrows are one of only two representatives of a mainly tropical African and Asian family to have made the long journey north with our prehistoric ancestors, and still live alongside us today. But whereas the tree sparrow, in Britain at least, is a creature of rural fields and hedgerows, the house sparrow is very definitely at home in the built environment. Like another bird that nests on buildings, the house martin, its success is unquestionably linked with our own.

House sparrows lived alongside the very first farmers, who 10,000 years ago began to stay in their chosen area and cultivate crops for food. Sparrows eat seeds and grain, so rapidly became both a neighbour and a pest to these early settlers, for their habit of stealing precious grain. Our relationship with sparrows has been rather uneasy ever since: we admire their cheekiness and adaptability – it's no accident that east Londoners still refer to themselves as 'cockney sparrers' – while at the same time resenting their thieving habits and denigrating their humdrum appearance.

Not that the male house sparrow is dull: a closer look reveals a rather handsome bird whose combination of chestnut, grey and black makes for a pleasing whole. The female, it is true, is much less striking; but has a quiet charm of her own.

When Bede compared a man's life to the swift flight of a sparrow through a banqueting hall on a winter's day, he was deliberately calling up an image that would have been familiar to his eighth-century audience. But the way that house sparrows have adapted to live in such a range of buildings is truly remarkable. We are used to them sharing our homes, but one small colony lived completely indoors, inside a terminal at Heathrow, one of the world's busiest airports. They roosted in the lighting recesses in the ceiling and survived – indeed thrived – by eating waste food from the airport restaurants and snack bars.

Even more enterprising were the house sparrows that successfully bred over 600 metres below ground in a working coalmine at Frickley Colliery in Yorkshire. Two birds entered through a shaft in 1975 and were later followed by a third. The three sparrows lived underground in a small area lit by artificial lighting,

surviving on food and water provided by the miners. They even produced youngsters, but when they could not find enough insects so far underground, the fledglings sadly died.

Although they are so adaptable, house sparrows have nevertheless vanished from many of their former haunts. Even in places where they do survive, numbers are much lower than they used to be.

Just why they've declined isn't certain, but there are several potential causes. Sparrows feed on seeds and grains left in stubble fields in the countryside in autumn and winter and these are much less common now. Our towns and cities contain fewer nest sites, and insecticides may be reducing the numbers of insects the growing chicks need. Even exhaust fumes have been suggested as a problem, as they appear to affect the very sedentary sparrow more than other species.

Whatever the cause, we certainly no longer take sparrows for granted, and even perhaps feel a greater affection for them now they are threatened. Where they do manage to hang on, they are welcome neighbours, filling the air with their chattering calls.

WOODPIGEON
*

Few bird sounds evoke the sense of lazy, hazy summer days quite so well as the repetitive crooning of the woodpigeon; a sound immortalized by Alfred, Lord Tennyson as 'the moan of doves in immemorial elms'.

Sadly those elms have long since vanished from the English countryside, but the soundtrack of summer continues: a deep, rhythmic song penetrating through the thick August heat.

The woodpigeon's five-note lullaby, with its stress on the second and third syllables, has variously been likened to 'Take two cows, Taffy', or 'My toe is bleeding'. But however you choose to remember it, there's no shortage of chances to hear this universal chorus.

Woodpigeons are now among our most successful birds. Once mainly concentrated in rural areas, they can still be found throughout our countryside. But in recent years woodpigeons have come to town, building their flimsy nests in trees in our suburbs and city centres, and even waddling among the sunbathers in busy urban parks.

Not everyone welcomes the sight of a woodpigeon in their garden, because they do deter other birds from the bird-table, and because a lot of the food we put out on our bird-tables ends up in the gullets of squabs, young woodpigeons. Along with seeds and green foliage, woodpigeons feed their chicks with 'pigeon milk' – a secretion from their stomach lining – a practice shared with only a few other species of bird.

So this familiar bird has some unusual habits. It is also rather an attractive creature. The woodpigeon's plumage may appear grey from a distance, but it sports several striking features, including a bright white slash across the neck. The celebrated Scottish bird artist Donald Watson summed it up perfectly when he described woodpigeons among wet beech leaves as 'rose-grey, like china in a cool room'.

RINGED PLOVER

*

As we take to the beaches in our summer hordes, we may not notice some of their natural inhabitants. Out in the open, the ringed plover is a striking bird, so it's odd that you can stare at one without actually seeing it. That's because although on a mudflat or sandy beach its contrasting brown and white plumage and black mask stand out like the proverbial sore thumb, on shingle it can easily fade into the background, only revealing itself when it chooses to move. Usually it will give away its presence by emitting a soft, clear, two-note whistle.

Camouflage is crucial to ringed plovers because they lay their eggs among the pebbles and shingle on an open beach, where their clutch of four eggs is almost perfectly hidden. The young chicks are also speckled like their gravelly environment and freeze completely when a predator such as a crow or gull passes overhead.

The female ringed plover is more obvious, especially when disturbed from her crouching position to reveal brilliant white underparts. But she has a trick up her sleeve – or rather, under her wing. Instead of trying to hide, she makes herself as obvious as possible, stumbling away from the nest while stretching out a wing and dragging it along the ground, as if it is broken.

This 'broken-wing display' enables her to distract attention from her precious eggs or chicks. It is a risky strategy, as she is in danger of being killed herself. But instinct tells her when to call time; as soon as she thinks she has lured the predator far enough away from the nest, she miraculously 'recovers' and flies back to guard her young.

GREAT
BLACK-BACKED
GULL

*

A summer's day on a rocky coastline, somewhere in the north or west of the British Isles. Above the familiar cries of herring gulls comes a deep, gruff barking – a sound that says that the owner means business. It comes from the largest British gull, and indeed the largest of all the world's fifty or so members of its family: the great black-backed gull.

When it comes to heavyweights, this is a true champion. Bulky and muscular, with a charcoal back and snow-white underparts, a bill the colour of spilled egg-yolk and a cold, penetrating gaze, it's a bird without equal for exuding an air of menace. Unlike some other majestic birds, which have a rather weedy voice (the buzzard is one example), the great black-backed gull's call matches its bulk: no other British gull can quite match it for bass and depth of tone.

Great black-backed gulls are the most marine of our larger gulls, rarely venturing far inland, though they can be seen along the tidal parts of river systems not far from the coast and will scavenge on rubbish tips in small numbers. In spring and summer, you'll often see them on a rocky crag or island, where they perch on eminences to survey their territory, always on the lookout for something to eat.

Like most gulls, great black-backs are highly adaptable: they scavenge for fish or offal, steal food from other birds, and will also kill with ruthless efficiency, preying mainly on their fellow seabirds.

On fine summer evenings they stand guard at dusk on islands off the coast of Wales, waiting for Manx shearwaters to emerge from their burrows. As the ocean-going shearwaters struggle to take off from their land-based breeding site, the gulls simply grab them, toss them into the air and swallow them whole: which is a shock for anyone watching, but a very effective strategy.

OYSTERCATCHER

*

Waders are known for their strident, piercing calls, but for sheer gusto few can match the piping sound of the oystercatcher. Should a predator appear – or indeed should you approach too close to their territory – the piping increases in intensity and volume until it reaches fever pitch. This ear-splitting cacophony is matched by the extraordinary behaviour of the birds themselves, striding around as if they are about to burst.

Many waders are grey or brown in colour, but oystercatchers have an appearance to match their vocal powers. Jet black and brilliant white, with pink legs and a long, thick, orange bill looking as if someone has stuck a carrot in their face, they used to be called the 'sea-pie'.

This is a far more appropriate name than the current one: for oystercatchers do not feed on oysters, but on mussels – hence the north-eastern nickname

'mussel cracker'. It seems that the erroneous name was originally given by an eighteenth-century ornithologist, Mark Catesby, to the American oyster-catcher, a different species from ours; and then crossed the Atlantic and was adopted over here.

Oystercatchers prise open or hammer mussel shells with those powerful bills, and probe for cockles in estuaries at low tide. They also use their beaks to extract worms and insect larvae from mud. With such a varied diet, they are able to breed inland as well as on the coast, laying two or three well-camouflaged eggs on the shingle banks of rivers, around gravel pits and even in ploughed fields. In recent years they have taken to nesting on flat roofs of buildings, where their eggs and chicks are safer from predators such as foxes.

Once the young have hatched, these feisty birds are quick to defend them against any perceived danger, and will unleash their volley of voluble calls on people, sheep or cattle that have wandered innocently into their territory.

LONG-TAILED TIT

*

As you walk along a hedgerow or woodland ride, it's the volley of sneezes and splutters interwoven with high-pitched needling cries that you hear first. The sounds grow louder as one, then another, and then another small flying lollipop shoots across a gap in a hedgerow. A family party of long-tailed tits is on the move.

Long-tailed tits – known locally as 'bumbarrels' or 'mumruffins' – are arguably our most endearing bird. They're uniquely patterned for a British species, in pink, black and white, with very long tails that look as if they've been stuck on as an afterthought.

Up close, they are very trusting birds, almost oblivious of us as they forage for insects, giving you the chance to look at the detail of their appearance, down to the delicate red rims around their eyes. But their behaviour is equally fascinating. The flocks you see streaming along a late summer hedgerow are made up of relatives: sons and daughters, brothers and sisters, and aunts and uncles. Should one pair of long-tailed tits lose their clutch of eggs or brood of chicks to a predator, or to bad weather, these birds will often help a related pair to raise their own family.

Co-operative breeding such as this is rare in the bird world, but makes sense for this sedentary species, where many birds in the same area are siblings or cousins. And long-tailed tits take this neighbourliness still further: they travel and feed together from summer onwards, and roost together at night, huddling up against each other on the same branch to keep warm – a strategy that saves lives during cold winters.

In spring, the females break away from their extended family to join another group and find a new partner. Together, the pair will then build one of the most elaborate nests of any British bird: a tight little ball about the size and shape of a grapefruit, interwoven from moss, lichen, animal hair, spider's webs and feathers.

A single nest can include up to two thousand different feathers. To collect them, long-tailed tits set aside their charming nature and plunder the remains of birds killed by predators – a method both grisly and effective.

REDSTART

*

A crisp 'hoo-it' and a flash of orange along an August hedgerow is a sure sign that redstarts are on the move. These stunning birds are summer visitors to Britain, arriving in April and heading south in August and September to spend the winter in the Sahel Zone, a strip of land running across the width of Africa immediately south of the Sahara Desert.

The male redstart – the name 'start', incidentally, derives from an Anglo-Saxon word for tail – is one of our most handsome and striking breeding birds. It is about the size of a robin, but looks slimmer, with a black mask, white forehead, grey head and a constantly quivering orange tail. It was this colour and habit of tail-trembling that gave the redstart one of its many folk-names: 'firetail'.

To see them at their best, go to the airy oak woods of western England, Wales and Scotland, where the plainer females brood their sky-blue clutches in holes in trees or walls. When the male arrives back from Africa he sings loudly from April to June. The song begins with several strident phrases, but never quite delivers on its initial promise, and quickly fades away in a jumbled farrago of notes. The Victorian naturalist W.H. Hudson summed it up when he wrote: 'Its strain is only the prelude of a song, a promise never performed.'

Hudson may have thought that the redstart's song was short and unfulfilled, but it was a very welcome spring sound to the soldier, poet and ornithologist John Buxton, who was captured in the ill-fated Norway campaign of 1940, and held prisoner in Germany for the remaining five years of the Second World War.

One April morning he observed a pair of redstarts flitting in and out of his POW camp, and decided to watch their movements on a daily basis throughout the coming breeding season. Enlisting his fellow inmates as observers, he built up the most detailed portrait of nesting behaviour ever achieved, obtaining fascinating insights into these little birds' lives, which after the war he published in his masterful monograph of the species.

More importantly, perhaps, Buxton and his fellow 'prison-camp ornithologists' also discovered that watching birds was a key way of maintaining morale and sanity while incarcerated. We can still share his wonder: in late summer, as redstarts filter south along the sunlit networks of hedgerows, we too can savour this fleeting sense of connection as our paths cross theirs.

BULLFINCH

*

A flash of white as it disappears along a hedgerow, accompanied by a soft, almost childlike whistle, is often all you will see and hear of a bullfinch. The contrast between this shyness and the male's gaudy colours makes the bullfinch a bird it is always a privilege to see.

The male bullfinch is a stunning bird, its bright rose-pink breast contrasting with a black cap, face and tail, grey back and snow-white rump. The female is a duller pinkish grey, while both males and females have a rather thickset appearance that perhaps led to the species' somewhat odd name.

A more appropriate name would be 'budfinch', for in spring bullfinches feed voraciously on the newly emerging buds of trees and shrubs, especially fruit trees. In the past bullfinches were very unpopular indeed with fruit growers: so much so, that in many parts of Britain there was a price on their heads.

Accounts of parish expenditure from the seventeenth and eighteenth centuries note that a bounty of one old penny a bird was paid for the killing of 'malps, hoops and nopps' as bullfinches were known back then. Almost 7,000 were killed in thirty-six years in a single Cheshire parish, with as many as 452 being taken in a single year.

The birds continued to be regarded as pests all the way into the second half of the twentieth century: the 1954 Protection of Birds Act, which gave legal protection to almost all species, still allowed bullfinches to be killed in the important fruit-growing areas of Kent and the Vale of Evesham. Even as late as the 1980s men were employed full-time on one farm to shoot bullfinches – not for a bounty of an old penny a head, but for one pound: 240 times the original sum. However, after a long decline, bullfinches now rarely occur in flocks large enough to damage a whole orchard.

ROCK PIPIT

*

To deal with the rigours of living on the British coast, a bird needs to be tough. Rocky shorelines may provide a breeding fortress but, battered by wind and waves, they are one of the harshest and most challenging environments of all. Many of the birds breeding here are true seabirds such as petrels and shearwaters, along with more coastal species such as gulls. But there is one, often unsung songbird, that braves these conditions throughout the year: the rock pipit.

Rock pipits are closely related to meadow pipits, but are more robust. Between a sparrow and a starling in size, they are easy to miss as they bob across seaweed-covered rocks or forage on wave-spattered overhangs, well camouflaged by their smoky plumage. Even their legs are dark grey, and it's often easier to pick up their short breathless whistle as they fly between boulders: for such a high-pitched call, it carries above the loudest winter breakers. The pipit's distribution in Britain clings to the rocky coasts of the north and west, as opposed to the softer, southern and eastern shores, which the breeding birds shun.

In August, rock pipits are often travelling *en famille*, as they probe with their fledglings for insects and small crustaceans among the flotsam and jetsam. They are especially fond of the tiny sandhoppers that leap into the air like manic fleas whenever you turn over a clump of seaweed.

Usually each pair has two broods of chicks, so some young birds can still be in the nest in August, huddled together in the shelter of a rocky niche, or hidden by cushions of thrift or sea campion, while holidaymakers cavort unaware on the nearby beach. Most birds will spend the whole year here, though some rock pipits do occasionally turn up inland at gravel pits and reservoirs.

ARCTIC SKUA

*

You don't have to travel the high seas or visit your local multiplex to watch pirates in action: a trip north to Shetland to see Arctic skuas will do just as well.

Arctic skuas are the bandits of the seabird world, chasing down hapless kittiwakes or terns until the panicked victim eventually regurgitates and drops its fishy catch, allowing the chasing skua to grab a free lunch in mid-air. Technically this behaviour is known as 'kleptoparasitism', from two Greek words meaning 'to steal' and 'to live off another', but to the casual observer the term piracy fits just as well. The North American name for the species, parasitic jaeger, also refers to this behaviour: jaeger derives from the German word for hunter.

Despite their antisocial habits, Arctic skuas are elegant birds, with long, angular wings, projecting central tail-feathers and a fearsome hooked bill – giving them the appearance of a gull with attitude. They're the falcons of the sea and as agile as those raptors in flight, shadowing every move of their victim as they close in to relieve it of its catch. As their name suggests, you need to head north to see Arctic skuas in Britain, with the vast majority of breeding birds found in Orkney and Shetland, although they do breed as far south as Argyll.

Skuas have a dense layer of feathers and rapid metabolism, useful adaptations for living in the far north; but which probably prevent them from breeding further south where it is too warm.

Arctic skuas come in two separate forms – pale phase and dark phase – which are so distinct they can appear to be completely different species. Nevertheless birds of the two phases happily pair up, despite the fact that one bird sports dark chocolate-brown plumage, while the other is pale creamy white beneath with a primrose-yellow collar. Pale phase birds are far more common the further north you go: those in Spitsbergen are almost all pale, while only about one-quarter of the birds in Shetland are.

Like many seabirds, Arctic skuas are global wanderers. Once they have finished breeding they head south, wintering off the coasts of South America, Africa and even as far as south-east Australia. As they travel south along our coasts in autumn, look out for their dark rakish forms, powering over stormy seas or harrying an unsuspecting gull.

YELLOW WAGTAIL

*

A loud 'sweep' call overhead is the signal to look up, to trace the bounding course of a flyover yellow wagtail. In late summer and autumn you can hear birds on the move over both town and country. Even with a quick view, you can see they're well named. The adult birds are slender with a long tail, and the male is bright canary yellow, like a rather elegant flying lemon. Females are much less bright, while the youngsters are brownish and can look almost like pipits.

Yellow wagtails are summer visitors to Britain from their winter quarters in tropical and equatorial Africa, and breed in wet meadows, running the risk of flooding, or of having their nest trampled by grazing cattle. Livestock attracts insects though, and it's worth inspecting pony paddocks and cattle fields where the wagtails dance attendance on the beasts, darting between their hooves to catch beetles and flies.

Unfortunately, many of the water meadows and marshes that provide cover and food for nesting wagtails have been lost over the past fifty years or so, owing to drainage and 'improvement' for intensive farming. As a result the yellow wagtail is one of our fastest declining birds, numbers having dropped by up to 90 per cent in the past few decades.

Some yellow wagtails have adapted to breeding elsewhere on farmland, notably in potato fields where they build their nest on the ridges among the plants, and use the furrows to hide from predators. The male cannot, however, resist showing off: often singing from a prominent perch on a fence-post – if singing is the right word for such a simple, repetitive ditty.

Globally, the yellow wagtail can be found throughout temperate Europe and Asia, from the Atlantic in the west to central Siberia in the east. But the species is made up of about eighteen different races, some of which are so distinctive they may indeed turn out to be separate species. The race breeding in Britain is known as 'flavissima', from the Latin meaning 'yellowest of all'. But whatever their colours, they all live up to their name by wagging their tails constantly.

ICTERINE WARBLER

*

If you are among a crowd of birders, somewhere on the east coast in late August or early September, you may hear an excited cry of 'I've found a hippo!' The creature in question is not the well-known African mammal, but a chunky warbler with a long, stout bill: a member of the genus *Hippolais*.

Moments later, the finder confirms the bird's identity: 'It's an icky!' This is another piece of birders'

shorthand, referring to an icterine warbler, distinguished from its very similar-looking cousin the melodious warbler by its longer wings.

The reason for all this excitement is that the icterine warbler is an infrequent visitor to Britain, mainly turning up in late summer or early autumn, when birds that have bred in northern Europe and Scandinavia head south and west on their journey to Africa.

Given the right weather conditions (ideally easterly winds with some cloud and rain), some icterine warblers drift off course and end up on our east coast, anywhere from Shetland to Kent. They are most often seen where birders gather in large flocks at bird observatories such as Fair Isle, or well-known migration watchpoints such as Blakeney Point in Norfolk.

The name icterine derives from *ikteros*, an ancient Greek word for jaundice, which perfectly describes the spring adult's rather washed-out, brownish-yellow plumage. But in autumn, the youngsters we're likely to see are much greyer, so identifying them can be pretty tricky – especially without their song to help you out.

Icterine warblers have occasionally bred in Britain, in Strathspey and Orkney for example, giving us a rare chance to hear their lively and varied song. They are accomplished mimics, often including snatches of notes or phrases from other songbirds. Their preferred habitat on the Continent is woodland edges, parks and large, wooded gardens, with plenty of bushes and trees where they can nest.

NORTHERN WHEATEAR

*

A call that clatters around a hillside like the sound of falling stones is an appropriate accompaniment to a walk on the wild and windswept moors. The sound comes from one of our smartest and most charismatic song-birds: the wheatear. Up it bounds, straight as a soldier on parade, to scold you from a lichen-covered boulder. Every movement is crisp and economical; wheatears don't fidget or fuss like dunnocks and warblers.

'Our' species is known officially as the 'northern wheatear', to distinguish it from the many other species in its family, and is the only wheatear to breed in the temperate zones of northern Europe; the others are mainly found in the rocky deserts of North Africa and the Middle East.

With its black mask, white belly, grey back and apricot chest, the male wheatear is a supremely handsome bird. What you will probably spot first, though, is its white rump, which shines like a beacon as it flits away from you along the path, and is especially visible on dull, misty days on moors and mountains.

It is the rump that gives the wheatear its name, which has nothing to do with cereal crops, but is a polite version of the Anglo-Saxon meaning 'white arse'. Female and young wheatears also have a white rump, but are paler and sandier in colour.

Wheatears are early arrivals in Britain, returning from Africa in March, often when their favourite grassy slopes are still streaked with winter snows. They raise one or two broods in a crevice between boulders or an old rabbit burrow, and then from early August begin their long journey back south. Fortunately they don't seem to be in much of a hurry, and often stop off to feed along the way, turning up in ploughed fields, heaths and commons and on sports pitches; they've even been seen at Lord's Cricket Ground, while play was in progress.

The sheer scale of the voyage undertaken by these fly-by-night migrants, which flirt briefly with us before moving on, is epic. Some of the birds you see in late summer or autumn on your local common or playing-field have travelled from as far afield as Greenland, or even Arctic Canada. With practice you can pick out these larger, bulkier birds, which may travel more than 11,000 kilometres en route to Africa, the longest regular journey made by any of the world's songbirds.

WHITE STORK

*

Finding out which birds bred in Britain many centuries ago can take a lot of detective work; but occasionally a record turns up that leaves no doubt as to the bird's identity. That is the case with the only successful breeding record of the white stork, which nested on St Giles' Cathedral, Edinburgh, in 1416.

It took almost six centuries before these magnificent waterbirds tried to breed again in Britain, when in 2004 a pair of white storks was seen carrying nesting material on to an electricity pylon in West Yorkshire. Unfortunately the site was deemed too dangerous, and when the nest was moved to an artificial platform nearby, the birds gave up their breeding attempt.

The classic image of white storks is of a pair feeding chicks in their massive nest, a bundle of sticks perched on red-pantiled continental rooftops. But several white storks turn up in Britain every year, mostly between spring and autumn. They're often very mobile, however, and without a realistic prospect of a mate soon catch the nearest thermal and float off to more promising pastures.

Across the Channel, white storks are on the increase, and are usually made welcome, though in some cases their nests and accompanying droppings are tolerated rather than encouraged. In many places, having a pair nesting on your home is seen as a sign of good luck, and also marks the coming of spring in countries such as Poland.

In particular, storks are linked with fertility, perhaps because of the rather phallic, upright nature of the bird itself. When meeting at the nest, the male and female engage in a peculiar form of pair bonding: clattering their bills together in a noisy yet intimate display of mutual affection.

White storks are large birds, standing over a metre tall and with a wingspan of more than two metres. Each year, they make an epic journey between Europe and Africa. Because they struggle to fly across large expanses of open water, they gather at key crossover points such as the Straits of Gibraltar and the Bosphorus in Turkey, where flocks of tens of thousands may sometimes be seen passing overhead – one of the most spectacular sights anywhere in the natural world.

HONEY-BUZZARD

*

'What's the point of wasps?' is a question we often ask ourselves on late summer days, as these pesky insects buzz around us and frighten our children. Of course, wasps do have an important role in the ecosystem, but birders should welcome them with open arms because their grubs are food for one of our rarest and most elusive raptors, the honey-buzzard.

Honey-buzzards are summer visitors to Britain, and although they are fairly common and widespread in continental Europe, they've always been scarce here and so are guaranteed to quicken the pulse of any birder. Part of their mystique is that they look very similar to common buzzards, even though they are not closely related. Both species have broad wings, but if the bird soaring low over your local wood has long wings, which it holds flat or slightly down-curved, a long, thin tail and a small and protruding head, then it could be the real thing.

Another clue is where you see it. The fifty or so pairs of breeding honey-buzzards in Britain occur in just a handful of woods scattered throughout the British Isles, and even if you have picked the right place to look, you still need to be very patient. They rarely spend much time aloft in the sky, preferring to stay amid the forest canopy as they scan the forest floor for wasps' and bees' nests.

August is a good time to search for honey-buzzards because that's when the young birds occasionally soar with the adults over their nesting woods. They're larger but less bulky than common buzzards and have a looser, more elastic flight action.

When it finds a nest, the honey-buzzard does not actually eat the honey. Instead it digs out the honeycomb using its powerful talons, and then breaks into it using its long, hooked bill to feast on the tasty grubs. It seems oblivious to the angry response from the creatures whose home it is destroying; fortunately the honey-buzzard has specially thickened skin and stout bristles around its face to protect it from the stinging insects.

COMMON TERN

*

Think of a tern, and the image you conjure up is usually of an elegant bird plunging into seaside surf; no wonder that an alternative name for terns is 'sea-swallows'. Spot one wafting over streams of juggernauts on a major road, and you might think it has lost its way. But nothing could be further from the truth. One species, the common tern, has embraced the inland life and now even breeds in the very heart of our towns and cities.

The common tern is, as its name suggests, the most numerous and widespread of our five breeding species of tern. It has an elegant, buoyant flight, bobbing and floating in the air on long, slender wings, while its deeply forked tail with long streamers trails behind.

The nature writer Simon Barnes memorably described a common tern as 'a gull that's died and gone to heaven', and this image of grace and beauty is only slightly tarnished by the bird's raucous call, which cuts through the sound of city traffic very effectively indeed.

Although many common terns continue to nest on the coast, inland birds now commonly breed on lakes and gravel pits. They often nest on small islands, but are also quick to colonize artificial rafts placed there by conservationists.

Some birds are happy to lay their eggs in open wire-mesh cages on these rafts, where they can raise their small, fluffy chicks safe from danger. Should a predator appear, it will usually be deterred by the parents' sharp bills and screeching attacks. The young are fed on a selection of small fish caught in nearby lakes, rivers and canals, and fledge by late summer. Then they are ready to begin the long journey south to their wintering areas off the coast of West Africa.

COMMON GULL

*

Don't be fooled by its name, for the common gull is by no means as common or widespread as several other species in its family. The species was (mis) named by the eighteenth-century ornithologist Thomas Pennant, who described it as the most numerous of its genus. He might, of course, have seen a colony of these birds alongside a Scottish loch, where certainly they are common.

Alternatively, perhaps, the species could have been named after its habitat, since common gulls do often gather on open, grassy areas such as playing-fields or, indeed, commons. Perhaps a more suitable name is that used in North America: mew gull, so called because of its mewing, cat-like calls.

Although they do breed on the coast, common gulls are really birds of the uplands, where they nest in colonies on islands in lakes, or among the rushes and cotton grass on wet moorland, where predatory mammals are less of a threat. Although their colonies are often remote, they are great lay-by loiterers and in Scotland often hijack passing tourists heading for the Highlands.

Towards the end of summer, adults and young birds head south to forage in open fields on farmland. Many also visit urban areas, where they scavenge worms from parks and playing-fields – the goalpost gull would be a better name in winter – and join the blizzards of gulls squabbling over waste food at landfill sites.

With practice they can easily be told apart from the other gulls: they are larger and plumper than black-headed gulls, and look like they would be better to eat, as one observer wryly noted. They're noticeably smaller and more delicate than herring gulls, and have darker grey wings with black tips showing white 'mirrors', greenish legs and a citrus-yellow bill. But it's that high, wheedling call that really singles them out: a wild and evocative sound, bringing a welcome flavour of the moorlands of Scotland to our grey suburban landscapes.

SPOTTED REDSHANK

*

The loud, cheery whistle of a spotted redshank sounds, in the words of writer and naturalist Richard Mabey, 'like a porter hailing a taxi'. Another way of remembering the call is that it has two syllables, rather than the common redshank's three or more: it is often rendered as 'chew-*it*', with the emphasis on the second note.

Spotted redshanks are real 'birder's birds', long-legged waders that don't breed in Britain, but pass through in good numbers in spring and autumn. These birds are stopping off on coastal marshes to refuel on their long journey between their summer home in the marshes of Scandinavia and Siberia, and their wintering grounds in the tropics of Africa. A few spotted redshanks do stay here in winter, usually on estuaries in southern England, where the milder climate enables them to find enough food.

In August and September especially, there's a quiet satisfaction in being able to pick out their more slender shapes among the more common resident redshanks. They are almost as long-legged as a godwit, and so often venture into deeper water than most waders to feed, snapping up small fish and invertebrates with their long, blood-red bills. When feeding they bob their head rhythmically up and down, which gives them an automated quality rather like a sewing machine.

In autumn and winter, spotted redshanks are pale, almost pearly grey in colour. But birds heading north in May to breed are resplendent in their breeding plumage, sooty black with contrasting silvery-white spangles on their backs, hence their name. In this finery, they are one of the smartest and most distinctive of all the world's waders.

GOLDEN EAGLE

*

Eagles have a central place in our folklore and culture, and have symbolized power and majesty since civilization first began. So although we may not see these magnificent birds every day, their influence is all around us: in advertising, company logos and even in the typeface of this book. The lower-case version of the modern letter 'a' is based on the shape of a perched eagle, a throwback to ancient Egyptian hieroglyphs adopted by the Phoenicians when they developed the first alphabet.

Golden eagles are pretty impressive birds in reality too. When you see one at a distance, soaring effortlessly over a Scottish glen, it can be hard to appreciate the sheer size of the bird against this vast, mountainous backdrop. But this is a very big bird indeed. With a wingspan of over two metres their courtship displays are dramatic affairs, involving spectacular aerobatics during which the birds will soar, plummet and perform switchback rides over their huge territories.

A hunting eagle can dive down on to its quarry at great speed, using its ultra-sharp talons to grab and dispatch its unsuspecting prey: ptarmigan, red grouse and mountain hare. But golden eagles are also scavengers, feeding on the carcasses of deer, especially in winter.

Eagles that mainly feed on hares tend to build their huge nest of sticks and branches – known as an eyrie – lower down the mountainside than those that prey on the lighter grouse or ptarmigan; in this way they avoid wasting energy carrying the heavy carcass right up the mountain.

Life in the nest can be harsh for young eagles. Although golden eagles usually lay two eggs, from which two eaglets hatch, sometimes the older chick will attack and kill the younger bird. This behaviour is known as Cainism, or Cain and Abel Syndrome, from the biblical story in which Adam and Eve's son Cain killed his brother Abel.

The theory behind this grisly act is that it happens when food supplies are short and the parents aren't able to bring enough prey to the nest; but sometimes the younger chick dies anyway, even when there is plenty to eat, as the older sibling will keep the lion's share of the food to itself.

WHITE-TAILED EAGLE

*

Often described as a 'flying barn door', the white-tailed or sea eagle is an incredible sight. Our largest bird of prey – even larger and more bulky than the golden eagle – this hulk of a raptor is one of the most memorable of all British wild creatures.

Hunched on the ground, it bears a passing resemblance to a large mammal: brown and shaggy with a pale head and huge, buttercup-yellow bill. In flight the adult eagles reveal their most obvious feature: a snow-white, diamond-shaped tail, which contrasts with the massive, dark, rectangular wings; they really do deserve that 'barn-door' description.

AUGUST

Yet for a long period from the First World War to the 1970s, you could not see white-tailed eagles in Britain at all; apart perhaps from the occasional very rare vagrant that managed to cross the North Sea from Scandinavia. That's because we drove the species to extinction as a British breeding bird during the Victorian and Edwardian eras, the last pair nesting on the Isle of Skye in 1916.

In the late 1960s attempts were made to reintroduce white-tailed eagles on to Fair Isle, between Orkney and Shetland. When the scheme failed important lessons were learned, and from the mid-1970s birds were released on the Isle of Rum in the Inner Hebrides.

After a slow start, during which the eagles were sometimes persecuted by local farmers and landowners, the population finally took hold. Today, there are more than fifty breeding pairs in western Scotland, and a re-introduction project on the east coast bore fruit in 2013, when a pair nested in Fife.

The Isle of Mull has taken the eagles to its heart: local schoolchildren named two chicks that appeared regularly on the BBC's *Springwatch* Itchy and Scratchy, after cartoon characters in *The Simpsons*. The eagles have rewarded their affection, bringing up to £5 million every year into the island's economy, a fine example of the benefits of wildlife tourism to far-flung communities.

But not everyone welcomes these birds. A scheme to reintroduce them into East Anglia foundered when the government was persuaded to call a halt, on the debatable grounds that the eagles would kill livestock. So if you want to enjoy the sight of a pair of majestic white-tailed eagles displaying over the marshes of southern Britain, you may have to wait a long time.

BARRED WARBLER

*

With its glaring yellow eyes, grey back, finely scalloped underparts and long, white-tipped tail, the barred warbler is always an exciting sight. But you are very unlikely to hear one singing in Britain, as it is a scarce passage migrant, hardly ever seen in spring. The birds that turn up in late summer and autumn are nearly all youngsters, which are much plainer, but still a welcome discovery.

These rather bulky warblers, slightly larger than a house sparrow, are related to our more familiar blackcaps and whitethroats, and breed in the temperate zone running from central Europe, east through Russia, all the way to Kazakhstan and Mongolia. Although they are skulkers for most of the year, during the breeding season the males launch into song-flights, ascending to a height of about ten metres before gliding down to land on a nearby bush, making a distinctive wing-clapping sound as they do so.

Most of the young barred warblers that turn up in Britain have accidentally drifted off course and crossed the North Sea as they head south to winter in East Africa, in a relatively small area from South Sudan to Tanzania. They are usually found in scrub on the north and east coasts, and will generally manage to reorient themselves and continue their journey south.

Although these hulking birds are less nimble than their smaller, slimmer relatives, they are nevertheless very elusive, which can be frustrating if you are hoping to get good views of one. Often their presence is only discovered when bird-ringers put out mist-nets to trap migrating birds, and a barred warbler blunders into the mesh.

However, unlike some scarce migrants, the numbers of barred warblers seen here appears to be falling, possibly reflecting a decline in their breeding areas to the east of Britain.

Swallow
Roseate Tern
Greenshank
Red Grouse
Meadow Pipit
Green Sandpiper
Wood Sandpiper
Great Shearwater
Hobby

✳ SEPTEMBER ✳

Turnstone
Thrush Nightingale
Jay
Bluethroat
Aquatic Warbler
Melodious Warbler
Great Reed Warbler
Tawny Pipit
Serin

✳ INTRODUCTION ✳

IN OUR WORLD, September is a time of change, as following the long summer holidays we go back to work and school. In terms of weather, it can be a glorious month – Keats's famous 'season of mists and mellow fruitfulness' – as summer comes to an end and autumn begins.

For much of our wildlife, September is a month of quiet withdrawal. Flowers are fewer now and bumblebee colonies are dwindling. Many species of butterflies are no longer on the wing and the rest are mostly past their peak.

For birds and their watchers, this is a pulse-quickening time: as winds change, sparking rumours of rare or unexpected migrants. Many birders are drawn inexorably towards far-flung observatories where they unfurl mist-nets to catch birds for ringing, hang around huge wire-mesh traps, or loiter near likely bushes in the hope of connecting with a hapless migrant. Those in the know whisper of 'Sibes' and 'Yanks', birds from northern Russia or North America, which have been blown off course or betrayed their genes by migrating in the wrong direction.

September is the first of two important migration months and the excitement isn't just about rarity: it can be about quantity too. Migrants travelling south along the edges of the North Sea can be forced down by weather systems, with heavy rain or strong winds. When this happens, large numbers of migrants suddenly appear on our eastern coasts. These 'falls', as they're known, will include warblers, chats, thrushes and flycatchers and there's always the hope of seeing something rarer such as a bluethroat, wryneck or ortolan bunting.

But you don't need to live on the coast to see migration in action. Simply get out in the garden or pick a vantage point from where you can scan the skies, and you'll soon pick up birds moving purposefully overhead. One of the first

signs of September passage is often early in the month, when meadow
pipits begin to fly south from their upland breeding areas.

If you live in the lowlands where meadow pipits are scarce in summer,
the first thin 'seep, seep' overhead will instantly tell you that autumn is on
its way. Look up and you'll see one or more tiny dots struggling against the
breeze as the pipits fly over city or country on their way to the grassy fields
and saltmarshes where they spend the winter.

Along with the pipits you might see small groups of skylarks or parties
of chaffinches. Choose a good viewpoint and this visible migration-watching
can soon become addictive. In September there's always the chance that
something really special will fly over: an osprey en route for West Africa or
a southbound honey-buzzard that could have been chewing wasp grubs in a
Scandinavian forest just a week earlier.

Swallows and martins will certainly show up and one of the bittersweet
delights of September sky-watching is witnessing their purposeful passage
south – not a desertion but just a temporary departure until next spring.
Swallows from continental Europe also join our breeding birds and will mingle
in reedbeds or willow scrub roosts en route. Martins and swallows are the
favourite prey of young hobbies, which have just fledged and are now cashing
in on the bounty, before they too head south on the long journey to Africa.

After flying through the night, as dawn breaks many migrants will
pitch down for a few hours to feed, so will be around one day, gone the next.
Scan your local playing-field or any area of open grass and you might see a
wheatear flitting across the turf, flashing its white rump as it flies. Not all
migrants are as easy to see, but lurking near a bramble clump or a fruiting
elder bush, you may well see tiny warblers darting among the trusses of
deep blackish-purple berries. These could be blackcaps, garden warblers,
whitethroats or even neat lesser whitethroats, whose pure white chests are
likely to be stained with purple juice from the berries. Fattening up is important
with such a long journey ahead.

While departure is September's strong theme, we should not forget
that many birds are arriving too. From Iceland pink-footed geese make landfall
in Scotland and northern England, the prelude to a wildfowl bonanza that
makes our islands resound with cackles, honks and whistles throughout the
winter months. In our gardens, resident robins sing loudly on September
mornings, establishing their territories before the arrival of continental
interlopers in the great October rush.

✻ SEPTEMBER ✻

SWALLOW

*

Strung out like musical notes on a stave, swallows are twittering as they gather on telegraph wires. As summer turns inexorably into autumn, and insect numbers rapidly dwindle, they are busy preparing for their long journey south. The swallow may weigh barely twenty grams – less than an ounce – yet this resourceful bird travels further than almost all our summer visitors. Some venture as far as the Cape of Good Hope, at the southern tip of Africa – a round trip of almost 20,000 kilometres.

Adult swallows are one of the smartest and most elegant birds, with a long, forked tail, shining blue back and wings, and a brick-coloured throat patch. Some males have tail-streamers longer than their peers, and we now know that female swallows find this attractive, and are more likely to mate with longer-tailed suitors.

On a fine September day, look out for this summer's youngsters among the gathering flocks of birds; they have much shorter tails, duller throats and a less glossy plumage than their parents. Some have only just left the safety of their nest in a barn or shed: a female swallow regularly rears two broods of young each year, and if the weather has been hot and sunny, with plenty of flying insects, she may even manage a third.

When the young birds leave the nest, they assemble with other swallows, and sometimes house and sand martins, before beginning their epic journey. During this period they seem restless, flying around and twittering incessantly to one another before landing again – almost as if daring each other to take

the plunge and finally head south. We don't have a word in English for this pre-migratory restlessness, but the Germans do: *Zugunruhe*.

Sometimes you may see a single swallow land on a wire and begin twittering. Within a minute or two, a second has arrived, then another and another, until dozens have congregated together. But these aren't necessarily local birds: they often include swallows that have bred across the North Sea in Scandinavia, mingling with our birds before embarking on that incredible voyage over the Mediterranean Sea and Sahara Desert, then down to the very tip of Africa.

ROSEATE TERN

*

One of the rarest and most sought-after of our breeding seabirds, roseate terns are exquisitely graceful, yet their loud, raucous calls sound incongruous compared with their elegant appearance. The word roseate means 'flushed with pink', and seen close to, this bird does have a faint pale pink wash across its chest during the summer breeding season.

From a distance, though, the best way to distinguish the roseate from its relatives is the brilliant, freshly laundered whiteness of its back and wings, which stands out among the greyer tone of the common and Arctic terns. If you get a closer look, you'll also notice that its bill is all black instead of the others' red. However, in September, when many young birds move south, they often slip by

unnoticed, as they are remarkably similar to their cousins.

In the British Isles roseate terns only breed in a few places, tending to prefer small islands, such as Coquet Island off the coast of Northumberland. They also nest on the Welsh island of Anglesey, but their main colony is across the Irish Sea, at Rockabill, a few miles up the coast from the bustling city of Dublin.

The roseate tern has a large global range, being found in six of the world's seven continents. Its stronghold is in the western Pacific Ocean, from Japan and Taiwan south to Australia, but there are also large colonies in East Africa and the Indian Ocean, and smaller ones in the eastern United States and the Caribbean.

Back in western Europe, roseate tern numbers have fallen sharply since the 1960s, almost certainly because of persecution in their winter homes. Off the coast of West Africa, the terns were regularly caught using baited hooks, for food and sport and to obtain the leg rings that western scientists use to monitor the bird's movements, but which also can be turned into attractive bracelets and necklaces. Conservationists have been working successfully with local communities in countries such as Ghana to draw attention to the roseate tern's plight through education. Together with the improving economic situation in the region, this may now be contributing to a rosier future for this stylish seabird.

GREENSHANK

✳

As you walk along the edge of an estuary in autumn, the air rings with the calls of waders: the shrill piping of oystercatchers, the haunting cries of curlews, and the yelps of redshanks – known as the sentinels of the marshes for their constant vigilance.

Then another sound cuts through the chorus: a ringing, three-note call, very similar to that of the redshank, but somehow more tuneful and pleasing to the ear. When the bird pitches down and bobs nervously at the bend of a creek, you can see that it's a tall, elegant wader with a pale, ghostly appearance: a greenshank.

As you might expect from its name, this excitable extrovert has greenish legs, and is mottled lichen grey above and pure white below. When it flies, the dazzling white rump gleams like a beacon, especially on dull autumn days. The rich fluting call, which has the extraordinary power of harnessing the acoustics of any location to maximize its effect, is a sure sign that autumn migration is well under way.

The birds that we see around lowland pools and estuaries have travelled from their breeding grounds in Scandinavia or northern Scotland, where greenshanks are on the very western edge of their global breeding range. Here they nest in the remote bogs and mires of the Flow Country of Caithness and Sutherland, in the far north of the Scottish mainland.

On their breeding territories, among bogs and peaty moorlands studded with lochans and tiny pools, the male greenshanks sing as they perform elaborate display flights to attract the watching females. After pairing up, the female will quietly brood her clutch of four buff-coloured eggs, mottled with brown to conceal them among the grasses and lichens.

In autumn, both young and adult birds will head back south, to winter in southern Europe or Africa. Others remain closer to home, on the smaller estuaries of our southern and western coasts, their stirring calls echoing around the marshy creeks.

RED GROUSE

*

A bizarre clucking sound travelling over a wild, windswept moor is clear evidence that red grouse are in residence. Scan the hummocks of flowering heather and you may see their dumpy reddish-brown shapes creeping across a patch of burned ground, or pick out the telltale scarlet wattle of a male bird among the mauve spikes.

But it's the almost human-sounding 'go-back, go-back' call that grabs our attention, followed by the sight of a small flock skimming the moor on bowed wings. It's an experience that symbolizes the very places in which this feisty game bird lives: a true image of wildness and wilderness.

Except that most grouse moors are about as artificial a habitat as it is possible to imagine. As for the red grouse's supposed wildness, no other native British bird is quite so carefully managed and cosseted, almost from the moment they are born to when they meet their maker on the 'Glorious Twelfth'.

Red grouse are fussy birds, which need a combination of young heather to eat and older, tougher clumps where they can find shelter from predators and severe weather. This mix is provided by an army of gamekeepers dedicated to giving the grouse everything they could possibly need.

Of course this isn't done out of altruism. Red grouse are effectively the most expensive farmed animal in Britain: nurtured and safeguarded in order to sustain the multimillion-pound industry of grouse shooting,

for which its aficionados are prepared to pay several thousand pounds per day.

Grouse shooting undoubtedly brings valuable economic benefits to deprived areas of the Scottish and northern English uplands. But that comes at a price: in this case, the virtual elimination of hen harriers and other predators from much of the red grouse's range. Despite being illegal, the ruthless persecution of raptors continues, and is now the most serious area of conflict between landowners and conservationists in Britain.

The paradox is that without shooting and moorland management, red grouse would be at the very least endangered in Britain, and possibly even extinct. That would matter not just because it is a beautiful bird, but also because this distinctive race of the willow ptarmigan (formerly willow grouse) is only found in Britain and Ireland.

With an estimated population of a quarter of a million pairs, red grouse both thrive and perish on our watch. But because of the controversy surrounding the species, there's a danger of losing sight of them as unique and fascinating birds, which have evolved to cope with one of the harshest of all our environments.

MEADOW PIPIT

*

Some birds immediately grab your attention: the call of the cuckoo, the brilliance of the kingfisher, or the exotic plumage of the ring-necked parakeet. Others, like the meadow pipit, are more modest, revealing their virtues in a less showy manner.

Yet even more so than the swallow and the cuckoo, in some ways the meadow pipit embodies the changing of the seasons here in Britain. Found in almost every habitat, from windswept coasts to rural farmland, and high on a remote hillside or the middle of a bustling metropolis, the meadow pipit's thin, distinctive call is a constant reminder of its presence. At the key turning points of the year, when summer gives way to autumn, or winter merges into spring, this little songbird can often be heard overhead.

In autumn, when there are fewer insects about in their upland homes, meadow pipits head down to the lowlands. Those of us who live outside the pipits' breeding range are, on a September morning, reminded that the year is turning by a reedy 'seep, seep' call coming from the skies above. Look up and you'll see small groups of the birds struggling purposefully against the breeze as they trickle south. On the ground they are almost anonymous, but have a quiet charm as they waddle jerkily between tufts of grass.

In winter you'll see them on farmland, by saltmarshes and on rough grassland and commons almost anywhere in lowland Britain. In spring and summer, though, they are wedded to mountains, moorland and grassy plains, the males rising and falling like marionettes as they deliver their tuneful song. At first sight, the meadow pipit is the classic 'little brown job' – like a slimline sparrow but with a more slender bill. But a closer look reveals subtle shades of buff, olive and ochre, and a chest streaked with darker spots and lines.

They build their nests among clumps of grass or heather, but despite their attempts at concealment, these are often discovered by cuckoos. Meadow pipits are one of the three main hosts in Britain for this parasitic bird, and many a pipit pair ends up spending every daylight hour stuffing insects into the beak of a cuckoo chick much larger than either of them.

GREEN SANDPIPER

✳

With its glaring white rump, contrasting with a dark back and wings, a green sandpiper looks like a giant house martin as it flashes up from a pool, calling loudly. That wonderful yodelling sound is usually the first sign of this unpredictable and slightly hysterical autumn migrant, which hides in the smallest of ponds and the narrowest of ditches, before leaping up from its feeding place and dashing away into the distance.

This is a shy bird best seen from a hide as it patters around muddy pools. Its legs are a dark olive, but other than that, it's really greenish-black above with white below, and a white eye-ring. When it flies, you'll be dazzled by the white rump and enchanted by the gorgeous fluting call.

By September, most green sandpipers have already passed through Britain on their way south, for this elegant little wader is one of the earliest of our autumn passage migrants. The first birds may appear in early July or even late June; autumn starts early for some birds. They prefer freshwater habitats, where like their smaller cousin the common sandpiper they bob up and down while feeding on tiny aquatic invertebrates and small fish.

These birds, the first in the vanguard of autumn migrants, have already bred in the vast forests of Scandinavia, and are now heading down to Africa for the winter. On their breeding grounds, the males deliver their surprisingly tuneful song from the top of a fir tree, but that's not their biggest surprise. The female green sandpiper lays her eggs not on the ground, like most waders, but in a tree. She often chooses the disused nest of another bird or the drey of a squirrel, where she incubates her clutch among a forest of protective needles.

When the chicks hatch, they tumble to the ground and, unharmed, are escorted to safe feeding places by their parents, until ready to head south on their first long migratory journey. A handful of pairs nest here in Britain too: but since they were first found in the Scottish Highlands in the late 1950s they have not managed to establish a permanent breeding population, unlike their close relative the wood sandpiper.

WOOD SANDPIPER

*

On a blustery September day a sound like an old penny-whistle echoes across a freshwater marsh along our windswept east coast. It is a new arrival from the north-east: a wood sandpiper, one of our most elegant medium-sized waders.

Wood sandpipers break their journey south at pools and marshes here in Britain, usually appearing between July and late September. Many of these passage migrants are young birds, born earlier in the year. These have a neat plumage: spotted and flecked above, and like the adults have yellowish legs. It's that shrill call, however, that alerts you to their presence.

The wood sandpiper nests in the forests and bogs of northern Scandinavia, though a small but elusive population of a dozen or so pairs does also breed in the far north of Scotland. They prefer remote boggy places, usually nesting on the ground among tall grasses or heather, laying a clutch of four mottled greenish-brown eggs. However, they will also use the abandoned nests of other birds, including song thrush, fieldfare and magpie. Once the young hatch, they are cared for by their parents for a few days, but after that have to fend for themselves as the adults begin to head south.

The contrast between the wood sandpiper's two worlds could hardly be greater: they spend the other half of the year around lakes and waterholes in Africa, darting daintily between the legs of flamingos, or catching flies right in front of the noses of drinking wildebeest.

GREAT SHEARWATER

*

You need patience, good sea legs and a strong stomach to go looking for great shearwaters. Few other regular British birds are quite so hard to see as these charismatic wanderers of the open ocean; and few have travelled quite so far to be here.

The usual place to see a great shearwater is the heaving deck of a passenger ship, way out beyond the

Isles of Scilly, in the Western Approaches of the Atlantic Ocean. As the sun beats down (the peak time to see shearwaters is late summer and early autumn), hordes of seabirds are tempted close to the vessel by means of buckets of 'chum', an oily concoction of putrid fish guts guaranteed to make even the most experienced seafarer queasy.

Among the commoner gulls and gannets are swirling clouds of tiny storm petrels, a piratical skua and a token tern or two. Then, without fanfare, a larger, darker and altogether sleeker bird swoops in, with all the authority of an airborne shark: a great shearwater, lured in by the reek of the rotting fish.

With a wingspan of more than a metre, the great shearwater dwarfs its smaller and commoner relative the Manx shearwater. Brown above with darker wingtips, and white below, it also has a dark cap contrasting with white cheeks, and a distinctive, stiff-winged appearance.

Timing is everything if you want to see these impressive birds. They don't breed in Britain and Europe, or indeed anywhere in the northern hemisphere. Instead their main colony, numbering about 5 million pairs, is in the middle of the South Atlantic on the remote volcanic island group of Tristan da Cunha, where the birds nest deep in underground burrows.

After breeding, great shearwaters disperse widely, many following fish and squid shoals northwards. This takes them in a long arc around the North Atlantic, past the east coast of North America before they turn and head back south, a route that passes close by the south-western coasts of Britain and Ireland. Numbers vary from year to year, with thousands passing one autumn, but far fewer the next, depending on the prevailing winds and weather conditions.

If chum and choppy waters don't appeal, you could try looking for great shearwaters from a Cornish or Irish headland, using a powerful telescope to gaze across the wavecrests. But for close encounters with these global wanderers, by far your best option is an autumnal voyage out into the Atlantic.

HOBBY

*

With its sickle-shaped wings, brick-red trousers and black moustache, the hobby is a strikingly beautiful falcon. It's also a heartwarming success story: back in the 1970s there were barely a hundred pairs of hobbies breeding in Britain, mainly in the New Forest and Salisbury Plain, where they were often targeted by unscrupulous egg thieves. But since then, for reasons not entirely clear, the bird's fortunes have taken a turn for the better, and now almost 3,000 pairs breed here, as far north as Strathspey in the Highlands of Scotland.

Early autumn is a good time to look for these elegant falcons over lakes, marshes and farmland, as newly fledged birds try out their skills on swallows, martins and dragonflies. Hobbies can be remarkably delicate hunters, plucking insects as small as crane-flies rising through the still September air, smoothly de-winging them with their beaks then swallowing the bodies.

Young hobbies often stay with their parents well into September, hunting birds and insects in family groups, the youngsters presumably learning from the more skilled adults. You can pick them out from the resident kestrels even in silhouette: hobbies have a looser, more elastic flight action, where leisurely soaring intersperses with madcap chases after prey. They have shorter tails and look more taut and compact than kestrels, and unlike them they don't hover.

By early October, most are gone, hot on the tail of the southbound swallows. British hobbies spend our winter over the savannah grasslands of central and East

Africa, returning here in spring, arriving in late April or early May. After their long journey they gather in flocks of up to fifty over wetlands in southern Britain, once again feeding on swallows, martins and dragonflies.

They then disperse and become more elusive as they settle down to breed, often in disused crow's nests. In the quest for food for their growing chicks, hobbies will even chase down swifts in breathtaking aerial manoeuvres.

Incidentally their name 'hobby' comes from the Old French word *hober*, meaning 'to jump about', presumably a reference to its aerial expertise. Even if you're not a birder, you may be familiar with the bird's scientific name, *subbuteo*, as in the famous tabletop football game played by generations of children and adults.

Peter Adolph, the inventor of the game, originally wanted to call it 'Hobby', but the powers that be refused to allow this as a trademark. Being a keen birder, he simply adopted the Latin name – which means 'small buzzard' – instead.

TURNSTONE

*

As the tide goes out on an autumn day, herring and great black-backed gulls swoop down to grab anything edible revealed by the receding waters. But a flock of smaller birds is there too, their dappled brown plumage blending in with the glistening rocks as they quietly go about their business. These are turnstones.

Turnstones are stocky little waders which, as you'd expect from their name, flip over stones and pebbles and probe behind seaweed curtains in search of small shellfish and crustaceans, which they dispatch and dismember with their short, stout bills.

These unprepossessing beachside waders are one of the great global voyagers. They travel from their breeding grounds in the high Arctic to their winter quarters on coastlines all around the world, from Europe to South Africa, the USA to South America, and Thailand to Australia. Some pass through Britain on their way south, while others spend the whole winter here.

The turnstone's rather drab winter plumage is nothing to write home about; but in spring and summer it is as intricately patterned as a tortoiseshell cat: a fusion of vivid chestnuts, blacks and whites that transform it into a truly beautiful bird.

Perhaps because they nest in such remote places, they seem unafraid of people, often living cheek by jowl with holidaymakers in coastal resorts. They have been spied foraging for food in the rainwater gutters of a Cornish warehouse, and even using a passenger ferry service to cross a river.

But it's the turnstone's diet that has attracted most attention. Unusually for waders they have catholic tastes and will sample just about anything they come across. One ghoulish feeding incident has become a classic of ornithological observation.

A correspondent to the journal *British Birds* reported that, while walking along a beach in Anglesey in February 1966, he saw five turnstones feeding on what he assumed to be a drowned pig on the tideline, tearing small shreds of flesh away from the facial muscles and the neck. Approaching more closely, he was horrified to discover that they were picnicking on a human corpse.

THRUSH NIGHTINGALE

*

If you are lucky enough to come across a nightingale on the east coast in autumn, at a time when most of our breeding birds have long departed on their journey south to Africa, then take a closer look. For if the bird has a pattern of subtle, thrush-like spots on its upper breast, it may well be the common nightingale's northern – and much rarer – cousin: the thrush nightingale.

Thrush nightingales replace their close relative the nightingale to the north and east of Britain: in southern Sweden, Finland and eastern Europe, where their song is a feature of leafy parks in Prague, Moscow and Budapest each spring. If you see one, its plain colour and cocked tail make it immediately recognizable as 'a' nightingale, but it is subtly different from 'the' nightingale that breeds in Britain and the south and west of Europe.

As well as its breast feathers having a thrush-like pattern, and being a little greyer and less rufous than its cousin, the thrush nightingale's song has hints of song thrush to it, as both birds repeat their phrases several times. Overall, its repertoire of whistles, rattles and croaks is not as varied as that of the common nightingale, with fewer crescendos, and is delivered at a more leisurely pace and at a slightly lower pitch. Both species, though, like the same habitat of dense,

scrubby thickets and are often very hard to see as they sing from deep cover.

The handful of thrush nightingales that skim our coasts each spring and autumn are equally elusive and many more must go undetected skulking in seaside scrub. Most move on quickly, heading south to winter in eastern and southern Africa.

JAY

*

The silence of an autumn wood is broken every now and then by the plaintive song of a robin. Then, a harsh screech like the amplified tearing of linen shatters the peace: the call of one of the most colourful yet shyest of all Britain's birds, the jay. No wonder that in Wales the bird is known as 'the screamer of the woods', and in Somerset as the 'devil scritch'.

Jays are flamboyant members of the generally black crow family, and have all the panache and swagger – and forensic intelligence – of their tribe. But when breeding they can be remarkably secretive for such a large bird, disappearing into the woodlands where they build their untidy twig nest, usually in a fork between branches.

When you catch sight of a jay flying away, as they often do, the bird's brilliant white rump shows up like a light bulb among the dark trees. They're strikingly coloured too: mainly pinkish brown, with a neat black throat, dark streaking on the crown, and black, white and with a vivid patch of blue on the wings. These blue wing-feathers, fringed with jet

black, are particularly prized by anglers for making artificial flies to catch trout.

Jays and oak trees have an unusual symbiotic relationship. In September and October jays become more conspicuous and you'll often see them flying between woods or over open countryside with their bills and throats crammed with acorns. In this autumn glut there are far too many for the bird to eat, so it buries the surplus in an underground cache for the winter. One study has estimated that a single bird hid about 5,000 acorns each day.

But even this highly intelligent bird can't remember where it buried every acorn, and so many germinate and grow into young oaks, making the jay a tree-planter on a national scale. And by burying the acorns in higher ground than the original tree, jays even help oak woodlands move uphill.

In autumn our native population of jays is sometimes boosted by huge invasions from mainland Europe. Should the continental acorn crop fail, thousands of jays – sometimes in flocks of several hundred strong – cross the North Sea to forage here for the rest of the autumn and winter, turning the cold air even bluer with their profane screeches.

BLUETHROAT

*

We like to think of the robin, with its orange-red breast, as one of the most beautiful of all our small songbirds. But it is outdone by one of its close relatives, a scarce visitor to our shores: the perfectly named bluethroat.

Nothing quite prepares you for your first male bluethroat. From behind, he is indeed rather robin-like, with a plump body, greyish-brown back and permanently cocked tail. Then he turns to face you, to reveal a shimmering sapphire bib, with a red or white spot in the centre. If you're extremely lucky, and he's a singing male, then his sequence of buzzes, clucks and ringing notes might remind you of a novice nightingale.

Occasionally male bluethroats establish a territory and sing for a few days or weeks; in 1968 one pair actually bred in Scotland, though the eggs never hatched. Later breeding attempts during the 1980s and 1990s were successful, and involved both red-spotted and white-spotted males. Given how close it breeds to Britain, it would not be surprising if this beautiful bird were to become a permanent colonist some time in the near future.

Bluethroats are summer migrants, wintering in Africa and breeding in marshes, woods and damp thickets from the Atlantic coast of France, eastwards and northwards across the European continent and throughout much of Asia, all the way over to the Bering Strait.

We see them mainly as they clip the corners of the UK in spring and autumn on their journey to and from breeding grounds. In spring the resplendent males are easy to identify, but autumn youngsters and some females can be puzzling because they have no blue in their plumage. To recognize them you need to look for the creamy eyestripe and rusty patch on either side of the tail.

AQUATIC WARBLER

*

Some birds are easy to see on migration: swallows, for instance, which gather to feed in noisy, chattering flocks en route. But others are like the

Scarlet Pimpernel: so skulking and mysterious that they are rarely seen at all. The latter category includes the only globally threatened European songbird, which passes through southern England in small numbers every autumn: the aquatic warbler.

The aquatic warbler lives up to its name, breeding in soggy sedge meadows in eastern Europe, with a tiny range extending from north-east Germany and Poland in the west, through Lithuania and Belarus, to Ukraine in the east. The entire world population of this streaky brown warbler now numbers as few as 11,000 singing males, making it very vulnerable to threats such as the drainage of its watery habitat for intensive farming. The population dropped by 95 per cent during the twentieth century, and this decline continues.

Most species of eastern European migrants take a direct route south in autumn, so do not pass through Britain. But the aquatic warbler is a notable exception: after breeding, they head westwards, a route that takes some of them along our south coast before they turn southwards and head through Iberia to winter in Africa.

Almost all aquatic warblers in Britain are discovered by bird-ringers, when they come across these elusive songbirds in their mist-nets. But every year a few do reveal themselves at well-known sites such as Marazion Marsh in Cornwall.

Adult aquatic warblers are remarkably similar to their much commoner relative the sedge warbler:

streaky buff and black above and pale below. Fortunately most birds seen on passage in Britain are juveniles, which buck the usual trend by being far brighter and more noticeable than their parents. Watch out for a small, active warbler that looks like an old-fashioned humbug: with alternate brownish-black and yellow-buff stripes, two 'tramlines' down the back, and a clear creamy stripe across the crown.

Until recently we didn't know exactly where aquatic warblers spent the winter, but thanks to some detective work by BirdLife International and the RSPB, the mystery has now been solved. The chemical composition of rainwater varies around the world and is incorporated into a bird's tissue by the food that bird eats. Scientists took feather samples from birds newly arrived on their European breeding grounds and compared these with isotope maps of West Africa. They located a crucial wintering site in north-west Senegal, which holds between 5,000 and 10,000 aquatic warblers and is clearly a vital focus for the bird's conservation in future.

MELODIOUS WARBLER

*

If you enjoy summer holidays in the south of France or Spain, you'll have ample opportunity to savour the song of this well-named bird: the melodious warbler. Its repertoire is tuneful and varied: speeding up, then slowing down, with a breathless tone as if it is trying to keep up with itself, and the occasional less

melodious, nasal, chattering phrase rather reminiscent
of a house sparrow.

Melodious warblers aren't showy songsters,
but they do occasionally perch in full view, giving us
a chance to take a good look at them. They're medium-
sized warblers, a little smaller than the blackcap,
moss green above and pale yellow below, with the
heavy bill characteristic of their group – the *Hippolais*
warblers, known to birders as 'hippos'. The specific
name, *polyglotta*, derives from the Greek for 'having
many voices'.

Melodious warblers are summer visitors to
western Europe, where they breed in olive groves,
large parks and gardens from Belgium through France,
Italy, Switzerland and Spain, to the tip of north-west
Africa. They winter in West Africa, from Senegal
south to Cameroon.

You might wonder why a southern European
bird is appearing in a book about British birds.
But as a migrant, it cocks a snook at our artificial
national boundaries, and so an average of about thirty
melodious warblers spill on to our shores every year,
often in late summer or autumn, and usually in the
south-west of Britain, as you might expect given its
breeding range.

If you are lucky enough to come across what you
suspect is a melodious warbler, you need to take great
care to distinguish it from its sibling species, the icterine
warbler. The best way to do so is to look at the largest
feathers in its wing, which are clearly shorter than those
of the icterine, because the melodious warbler does not
travel as far on migration.

It's a mystery why the melodious warbler breeds
so close to us on the Continent but shuns the British
Isles. However, in June 2013 one male did hold territory
in Nottinghamshire, singing for several days, but
sadly failed to attract a female. Nevertheless, with the
species gradually extending its range northwards and
eastwards, there is a good chance that the melodious
warbler will breed in Britain in the next decade or two.

GREAT
REED WARBLER

*

A warbler the size of a thrush, but with a voice like
a frog armed with a megaphone, is well worth seeing
and hearing. As its name suggest, the great reed
warbler looks – and sounds – like a reed warbler on
steroids. Weighing in at thirty-three grams, and twenty
centimetres long, it's a true giant among European
warblers, almost double the size and well over twice
the weight of the reed warbler.

In September and October, those peak months
for bird movements, young great reed warblers from
continental Europe sometimes blunder into mist-nets
set to catch migrants here in Britain, and never fail to
impress and astound their finders.

Great reed warblers also turn up here every
spring and sometimes hold territory for a few days.
The male's vocal powers are as extraordinary as his
size, echoing across the reeds and being audible at
least 500 metres away, allowing him to establish his
territory, fend off rival males and attract a mate.

The song is a rhythmic but rambling collection
of croaks, rattles and loud squeaks, which may not
sound much to the human ear, but which scientists

have shown is crucial to attracting the female. The more complex the male's song, the better he turns out to be at raising a brood of chicks. This link is so strong that a female great reed warbler can sometimes be lured away from her existing partner by a more accomplished singer, and go on to raise a second brood of chicks in the same breeding season.

The great reed warbler has a huge range across continental Europe, North Africa and Asia, from Portugal in the west to Japan in the east, and as far north as Sweden and Finland. But strangely it remains a scarce visitor to Britain. So male birds holding territory in the UK belt out their extraordinary song in the slim hope that a passing female may hear it, and be tempted to stay and breed. So far they've been unsuccessful, but who knows what the future will bring.

TAWNY PIPIT

*

Not many birds have been featured in the title of a British film, but one that has is the tawny pipit. Despite only being a rare visitor to our shores, it starred in a now long-forgotten wartime movie, which celebrated the importance of the natural world to the British at a time when the nation faced potential annihilation.

In the eponymous film, *Tawny Pipit*, released in 1944, the bird is a metaphor for the very essence of English village life – at the time, of course,

threatened by the menace of Nazism. The story centres on a pair of very rare tawny pipits, which have chosen to breed in a field on the edge of a sleepy Cotswold village. The nest is discovered by a recovering fighter pilot and his nurse, who immediately realize the birds are under threat from military exercises nearby, and from plans to plough the field to grow food for the war effort.

With typical English wartime spirit, the villagers rise to the occasion, and fight off the threats, which also include a dastardly egg-collector. All ends happily, with the clear message that nothing can challenge traditional English village life, in a typically heartwarming piece of wartime propaganda.

Ironically, in the years that followed victory in 1945, much of our lowland landscape was destroyed by chemical farming, which did more to wipe out Britain's farmland birdlife than anyone could possibly have imagined before the war.

In reality, tawny pipits are only occasional visitors to Britain from continental Europe, where they breed on sandy and rocky areas from dunes to mountainsides. They are a large and rangy bird, looking more like a wagtail than a pipit.

As their name suggests they are pale sandy-brown in colour, with a few subtle streaks, very different from our familiar meadow pipit. Much to his chagrin, the doyen of British bird photographers, Eric Hosking, had to use meadow pipits for the film, as of course he couldn't venture across the Channel into occupied Europe to film the real thing.

SERIN

*

Wherever you venture in continental Europe, from the leafy boulevards of Paris to the olive groves of Mallorca, and the Colosseum in Rome to the ruined temples of ancient Greece, the chances are you will hear a singing serin.

It's the urban birdsong that tells you you've crossed the English Channel and yet this tiny, canary-like finch remains resolutely Anglophobic as it continues to tantalize British birders and ornithologists. Hopping back and forth across the English Channel, it always teases at becoming a permanent colonist here, but never quite manages to do so.

Hopes were high that this continental finch would settle here permanently, especially as our climate is gradually becoming warmer. However, for reasons that aren't clear, something about our islands doesn't suit them. Yet they do like large parks and gardens, and are common and widespread just a hop across the Channel, so keep an ear out for the jazzy, needling song – you may win ornithological fame and fortune.

At twelve centimetres long and weighing just thirteen grams, the serin rivals the siskin and lesser redpoll as Europe's smallest finch. It looks like a miniature canary, with a grey and yellow face, yellow breast, streaky back and a small stubby bill. In flight, it shows a bright yellow rump – a useful field-mark.

Its song is very distinctive, a tinkling rattle like a cross between a goldfinch and a goldcrest, or a higher-pitched version of the corn bunting. This is often delivered in a meandering song-flight over suburban gardens.

Serins are a scarce but regular visitor to Britain, with the vast majority of records coming, as you would expect, from southern England. Back in 1967, during the famous 'Summer of Love', a pair of serins nested in a garden in Dorset. In the decade or two that followed, they also bred, or attempted to breed, in nearby Devon, Hampshire and Sussex.

Redwing
Red-legged Partridge
Common Eider
Ortolan Bunting
Pink-footed Goose
Bearded Tit
Common Pheasant
Brambling
Grey Plover
Jack Snipe
Rock Dove

✳ OCTOBER ✳

Short-eared Owl
Carrion Crow
Goldcrest
Crested Tit
Yellow-browed Warbler
Sooty Shearwater
Leach's Petrel
Cattle Egret
Shore Lark
Firecrest
Bobolink
Mourning Dove

✳ INTRODUCTION ✳

FOR ANY BIRDER, there's a day – or night – in October that marks the transition between summer and autumn. It's the point at which you hear a sharp inward sigh overhead and look up to see a flock of thrushes. These are redwings from Iceland or Scandinavia and over a million of them arrive here in an average autumn, as punctual as hollowed-out pumpkins. Step out at night and you'll hear their penetrating calls as invisible hordes keep contact with one another in the October blackness.

At the peak of these movements, usually around mid-month, groups sometimes totalling several thousand birds fly overhead, signalling the zenith of autumn migration. Along with the redwings you may see the larger, rangier and longer-tailed fieldfares, also lured in by our berries, worms and milder winter climate.

These winter thrushes stand out because they only breed here in very small numbers, but there are other, more familiar, migrants at this time of year. In the garden you may notice dusky blackbirds with dark bills, causing consternation among the residents. Some of these will be young continental birds, part of an autumn influx that also includes robins, chaffinches and song thrushes.

One of the most surprising arrivals is the goldcrest, which looks too frail to brave the open waters of the North Sea, but in October it can turn up almost anywhere. Tune in to its thin but penetrating calls and you'll detect these visitors in woods, coastal sand dunes or city parks, where they mingle with our home-grown birds. Follow up each high-pitched 'screep', and you might discover a firecrest, with its black and white eyestripe and golden neck-patch shining out like a jewel among the dark holly and ivy leaves it loves.

These are our smallest birds. At the other extreme are some of our heaviest flying birds, for the British Isles provides a vital winter refuge for wildfowl. Huge whooper swans fly in family parties from Iceland and Scandinavia to their traditional wintering sites in Scotland, Ireland and northern England, while their smaller cousin the Bewick's swan travels even further, from the Siberian tundra, to be here. Their loud bugling enlivens the fens and pastures where they nibble grain and root vegetables with sturdy black and yellow bills. Skeins of geese are pouring in too: brent geese from Russia, Svalbard and eastern Canada, and barnacle geese from Greenland and Svalbard.

Ducks arrive in force at this time of year, now in their smart winter plumage. Flocks of elegant wigeon, pintail and teal wing in from Scandinavia or Russia and dabble or graze for food in marshes and estuaries, alongside waders such as godwits, grey plovers and knots. Above them the last connection to summer slips away with the final parties of swallows and house martins trickling south.

But October has many other attractions. Here on the edge of the vast Eurasian landmass, bordered by the Atlantic Ocean, the British Isles are superbly placed to act as a magnet for lost or derailed migrant birds from all corners of the globe. North-easterly winds usher in exotic species from the north and east, while the dying remnants of American hurricanes whisk songbirds across the Atlantic.

No wonder that keen twitchers – obsessive hunters of rare birds – keep their appointment diaries free in October. At this time they travel to meet the migrants, congregating at extremes: Cape Clear Island on the south-western edge of Ireland, the Isles of Scilly, Outer Hebrides and Shetland where, like the White Queen in *Through the Looking Glass*, they can believe in as many as six impossible things before breakfast. The unexpected conjunctions of birds are impossible to predict. No one would have placed bets on a Siberian rubythroat in the same week and on the same archipelago as Britain's second ever Cape May warbler from North America. But in October 2013 this happened, on Shetland.

With new and unexpected migrants come questions to determine their legitimacy. There are all sorts of strange rules by which natural vagrancy is assessed. Did the bird take refuge on a passing ship and if so, was it fed by the crew or passengers? Worse still, could it have escaped from a consignment of caged birds? Each autumn the rumours rumble on and speculations mount, especially from those who missed seeing the bird, and so have an axe to grind.

Some extreme rarities in the UK may be common in their home range but receive a red-carpet reception over here. When a North American mourning dove turns up it acquires a mantle of glamour from being in the wrong place, even though on its home turf it is dismissed as a 'trash bird'. But however big the welcome for that rare vagrant, the extreme birders know that as they metaphorically raise their glasses to its presence, they're also commemorating the demise of countless others lost at sea.

Some rare October arrivals are a source of wonder because they may be charting new migration routes. Better still, these birds have a chance of making it back home. Yellow-browed warblers are frail-looking yellow and green migrants, yet every autumn hundreds of them manage to travel thousands of miles from their Siberian breeding grounds to make landfall in Britain, when they should by rights be in South-East Asia. Scientists now think that this is a breakaway population, which is spending the winter somewhere in southern Europe or West Africa, before returning to the Siberian forests to breed. But whatever the reason for their presence, no one can deny that finding one of these tiny sprites, when scanning through a flock of tits and warblers, brings a real sense of pride.

REDWING

*

The soft, thin 'seep' calls of redwings as they fly over us at night are as much a part of autumn as falling leaves, damp pavements and the smoke of bonfires. Sometimes you'll hear them through the sound of fireworks exploding all around when the tang of cordite fills the air, as they pour overhead in invisible flocks.

Redwings are streaming into Britain from the north and east – more than a million in total – having flown over the sea from Iceland and Scandinavia in search of a place to spend the winter. A diet of berries and invertebrates, especially worms, is much easier to find in our milder winter climate than in their dark, chilly birthplace.

Redwings are our smallest thrush, slightly smaller and lighter than the familiar song thrush, and get their name from the rusty-red patch on their flanks. You can also tell them apart from other thrushes by their darker brown upperparts and the prominent creamy stripe above their eyes. A handful of pairs breed in northern Scotland, but they are primarily autumn and winter migrants to the British Isles, and one of the most common and widespread of all the birds that visit us at this time of year.

Like most other songbirds, redwings migrate at night, and the sounds we hear above our heads are the calls they use to keep in contact with one another. When morning comes, these new arrivals gather in flocks in orchards or along hawthorn hedges, where they mingle

with fieldfares and blackbirds, many of which have also crossed the sea to be here.

If the weather turns colder, and especially when snow covers the fields where they forage for worms, redwings will venture into our parks and gardens to feed on berries and windfall apples. But should the hard weather persist, they soon move on, and head south and west in search of milder conditions. Redwings are nomads, and birds that spend one winter in Britain might well be found in eastern Europe the next.

RED-LEGGED PARTRIDGE

*

Puffing and wheezing like a steam train, with a plump body and short legs, the red-legged partridge is nevertheless a strikingly beautiful bird. It is found on many lowland farms, especially in southern and eastern England.

Sometimes called French partridges to distinguish them from our indigenous grey or 'English' variety, red-legged partridges are native to continental Europe, but were successfully introduced to Britain as a game bird from the seventeenth century onwards. They thrived in our countryside, and have been on the increase ever since, augmented by the 6 million or so birds released each year to be raised for shooting.

Most releases take place in autumn, which is why you're likely to see small coveys in the drier parts

of Britain at this time of year. Seen from a distance, crouching low in an arable field, they look rather like large clods of earth; but up close their beautifully marked plumage is revealed.

Their flanks are tiger-striped with crescents of pale grey, chestnut and black, while their face-pattern is predominantly white with a black mask. Their eye-rings, bill and of course legs are dark red. Admire them too closely, though, and they run rapidly away or take to the air, cackling loudly like demented chickens.

The song of the red-legged partridge, if it can be called that, is a rhythmic chuffing sound, rather like a distant steam engine. You'll hear this from the males in spring as they perch on a tree-stump or fence-post. The female will often lay two clutches of a dozen or more eggs, incubating one herself while her mate takes care of the other.

Soon after hatching the young chicks leave the nest, and follow their parents around like a gaggle of unruly schoolchildren. After just ten days they are able to fly, giving them a better chance of avoiding danger.

COMMON EIDER

*

As you sit on a harbour wall almost anywhere in the northern half of Britain, you may be surprised to hear what sounds like the shocked and scandalized cries of a pantomime dame, with particular echoes of the late comedian Frankie Howerd.

Look into the water below, and you'll see that this extraordinary sound is coming from a large, black and white duck: a male eider. Eiders are northern sea ducks, found all around the northern hemisphere, including the Atlantic, Arctic and Pacific Oceans.

They are most famous for the soft, downy breast feathers with which they line their nests – the original 'eider down'. Now that we mostly sleep under duvets, eiderdowns have become a thing of the past, so many people fail to make the connection between the bird and the household object. With the price of genuine eider down reaching as much as £500 a kilo, it's hardly surprising that this premium product is now the preserve of the super-rich.

Eiders are still 'farmed' in Iceland, where traditional farmers must collect from thirty nests to produce a single pound of down. They do so near the start of the breeding season, leaving enough down to avoid the eggs chilling, and allowing the female to pluck more from her breasts to keep the eggs warm until they hatch. After the chicks leave the nest they often gather with other broods in crèches, watched over by several females for greater safety against predators.

When on the nest, the female eider can be very approachable, relying on her barred brown plumage as camouflage. Drake eiders are far more brash: heavy, robust birds clothed in a patchwork of black and white set off with a smudge of pale green on their necks, and a soft suffusion of pink on their breast.

The drakes' calls may seem rather comical, and somewhat at odds with such a butch-looking bird, but they certainly impress the watching females. In Britain you're most likely to hear these strange sounds along the coasts of northern England and Scotland where eiders breed. One of their main strongholds is Holy Island (also known as Lindisfarne) off the coast of Northumberland, which in the seventh century was home to a monk named Cuthbert.

Later venerated as a saint, Cuthbert was one of the first people who protected birds, and he had an especially close relationship with this species. Today,

eiders are known locally as St Cuthbert's or Cuddy's duck, and can still be heard expressing their loud approval of their saintly protector along this scenic and windswept coast.

ORTOLAN BUNTING

*

The idea of eating a songbird is something that appals most of us, but some of our continental neighbours have no such qualms. And of all the small birds they consume, by far the most sought-after delicacy is a rather shy and obscure bunting: the ortolan.

Ortolan buntings are dapper-looking relatives of our yellowhammer, with rust-brown bodies and olive heads, a lemon throat and moustache, and yellow eye-ring. They don't breed in Britain, but a few do turn up here in spring or autumn on their way to and from their breeding grounds in northern Europe. The name comes via Provençal from the Latin word *hortulanus*, meaning 'belonging to a garden'.

Ortolans are tough little birds, with some even nesting beyond the Arctic Circle in northern Sweden and Finland; they also breed further south through the Low Countries, France and Spain. They spend the winter in Africa, along a strip running from Sierra Leone to Ethiopia.

As ortolan buntings pass through Europe on their way south, their arrival is welcomed by hunters with nets. Tradition demands that, once caught, the unfortunate birds are kept in the dark and fed on millet seeds. Having been fattened up, they are drowned in

Armagnac, roasted and then eaten whole, in a bizarre and complex ritual.

It is customary to drape a cloth over the head of the diner so they can savour the unique aroma. In the mid-1990s, about 50,000 ortolans were trapped each year to fulfil this misguided gourmet obsession, which was helping to accelerate the decline of this little songbird. Today the species is fully protected by the European Union Birds Directive, which forbids the capture, killing and sale of ortolans.

Nevertheless the custom continues, helped by some who really should know better. Just before he died in 1996, as part of his final deathbed feast, former French President François Mitterrand consumed several ortolans in the time-honoured manner – bones and all – beneath the traditional white cloth, a practice that has been suggested also serves to hide the diner's greed from a watching God.

PINK-FOOTED GOOSE

*

The sound of hundreds of squeaky bicycle wheels fills the air as crowds of pink-footed geese pour into Britain to spend the winter here, feasting on potatoes and sugar beet in their traditional wintering areas in Scotland and England.

To see and hear a flock of pinkfeet, as they lift off from their night-time roost on coastal mudflats and head away inland to feed, is a stirring experience. Strung out across the dawn sky, their long skeins and evocative sounds are a sure sign that autumn is well and truly here.

They have come across the seas in tens of thousands, travelling from Iceland or eastern Greenland, to spend the autumn and winter around the wide open estuaries of north-west England, southern and eastern Scotland, and East Anglia. Incredibly, over 80 per cent of the entire global population of pink-footed geese spend the winter here in Britain, with only the most northerly breeding birds, from Svalbard, wintering across the North Sea in Denmark, the Netherlands and Belgium.

Pink-footed geese can normally be seen feasting on cereal stubble, unharvested potatoes and the remains of sugar beet in open, muddy fields, where their dull greyish-brown plumage provides a useful camouflage. The species is rapidly increasing, especially in Norfolk, where sugar beet growing is on the up. The geese are able to take advantage of such changes in farming patterns because they migrate in family groups, so the parents can pass their knowledge of the best wintering areas down through the generations to their offspring.

Like most geese, pinkfeet are wary, and when feeding some will act as sentinels, keeping their heads up to look out for danger. On the ground, they can be told apart from other species of 'grey geese' by their darker head and neck, and small pinkish bill. But as they rise up in vast numbers into the sky, by far the easiest way to identify them is their chorus of high-pitched calls, one of the classic sounds of late autumn and winter.

BEARDED TIT

*

As you scan a reedbed on a blustery autumn day, a sound like the ringing of several tiny cash registers floats across on the wind. This metallic 'ker-ching, ker-ching' is made by one of the most specialized of all wetland birds: the bearded tit.

Bearded tit must surely win a prize for the most unhelpful British bird name, for this endearing little bird is neither bearded, nor a tit. Its evolutionary origins are a mystery: once thought to belong to the parrotbills, a tropical African and Asian family, DNA tests now suggest that this species is more closely related to the larks. Given its preferred habitat of reedbeds, more suitable alternative names are 'bearded reedling' and 'reed pheasant', but neither of these has ever really caught on. In any case, the male tits sport not a beard but a flamboyant moustache, the envy of any Chinese mandarin, either side of their short, stubby bill.

Male bearded tits are a gorgeous colour: a rich, warm, tawny-buff, set off beautifully by a greyish-mauve head, yellow bill and that smart black moustache. Females lack the moustache, and are slightly plainer and duller, but both sexes have a long tail, which helps them balance as they perch on a reed stem. This long tail can be easily seen in flight as they briefly dash across the top of a reedbed, before plunging back out of view.

Bearded tits love reeds. They spend virtually their whole lives there, feeding on insects in summer and reed-seeds in winter, and build their nest using reed-stems and flower heads. So the best places to see them are the vast coastal reedbeds of East Anglia, though they have recently colonized newly created wetland areas inland, including the Somerset Levels.

They often disperse some distance in autumn: two females spent one recent winter in a tiny reedbed on the Serpentine in London's Hyde Park, much to the delight of the capital's birders and curious passers-by.

Knowing where they are is one thing; catching sight of them among millions of swaying reeds is another. Sometimes you'll see a flock at the bottom of the reed-stems, where a channel of open water runs past. Usually though, their call is your best guide, allowing you to search for these slender, long-tailed birds as they dart in and out of the stems.

COMMON PHEASANT

*

The harsh, double-bark of pheasants is a sound inseparable from most of the British countryside, yet these exotic-looking birds really belong no nearer to this country than the Caucasus Mountains of south-west Asia.

But thanks to us, common pheasants are cosmopolitan creatures. As one of the world's most widespread and successful introductions, they have been released in about fifty different countries, and can now be found on every continent except Antarctica.

The pheasant is such a common sight that we take it for granted. Yet the cock's coppery plumage and red face-wattles, coupled with a tail that's as long again as his body, make him a strikingly beautiful bird. Captive breeding has also produced a number of colour variations and you may see birds with or without white neck-rings, with metallic greenish plumage and even, on rare occasions, pure white specimens.

Originally brought to Britain by the Normans, or possibly even earlier by the Romans, the pheasant has been part of our rural scene for so long it is effectively now a native bird. The reason, of course, is that they are very good to eat and also provide good 'sport' for those who enjoy shooting birds, due to their rapid flight. Yet its ubiquity is entirely artificial: at least 30 million pheasants are specially bred in captivity and released into our countryside each year to sustain the multimillion-pound game industry.

The annual release of so many birds inevitably has an effect on our landscape: not least because since organized pheasant shooting first became popular, following the Enclosure Acts of the early nineteenth century, many woods and copses have either been spared from the axe or specially planted to give the birds cover.

This, along with the supplementary seed put out to feed pheasants in winter, has provided both habitat and extra food for small seed-eating birds such as finches, buntings and sparrows. On the debit side, many natural predators such as crows, foxes and birds of prey have been 'controlled' (i.e. trapped, poisoned or shot) to protect the released pheasants. It is even said that in the early twentieth century one gamekeeper used to shoot nightingales as their singing disturbed his precious chicks.

Entomologists worry about the effects that such large numbers of birds have on insect larvae, especially the caterpillars of butterflies and moths. There's also evidence to show that pheasants have reduced the populations of slow-worms and adders.

The male's coarse rallying call, which usually comes with a loud flurry of wing shaking, is often heard from deep cover where the bird hides away from predators. Pheasants often call in response to loud noise or vibration, and there are stories of them calling before earthquakes strike, and even of birds in Kent reacting to the sound of gunfire across the English Channel during the Second World War.

BRAMBLING

*

On a chilly autumn day, as you kick through the fallen leaves, a beech wood can seem almost devoid of life. But then, from somewhere above the canopy, comes a series of loud, nasal calls, as if the birds are saying 'bubble-and-squeak'. Bramblings have arrived back for the winter.

Bramblings are the northern equivalent of the much more common and familiar chaffinch, and breed across huge areas of Scandinavia and Russia, where they nest in birch and pine forests.

Each autumn they head south in search of seeds: they are particularly fond of beech-mast, the small, pyramid-shaped nuts produced by the beech tree. If the crop is a good one, enormous flocks will gather to feed and roost. Indeed the largest recorded single gathering of any bird species in the world is of a flock of 70

million bramblings in Switzerland, during the winter of 1951–2, which equated to a very large proportion of the whole global population.

For a bird that can gather in such enormous numbers, bramblings aren't all that familiar, even though they do occasionally come to feed at garden bird-tables. Imagine a chaffinch dressed in the colours of autumn, with a dark head, soft peachy tones to the body and tortoiseshell mottling on the back and flanks. If you have any doubt at all about these birds' identity, just wait until they take off, when the giveaway is their brilliant white rumps that are evident as they fly away.

Bramblings often join chaffinch flocks and with practice you can pick them out as they fly over by their more nasal calls. We don't often hear them sing because bramblings are almost exclusively winter visitors to Britain, although they do breed here occasionally, always in Scotland. But on sunny spring days, if you're lucky, you may hear the wheezing song of the males before they leave for the northern forests.

GREY PLOVER

*

When you hear the call of the grey plover echoing across the shimmering mudflats of an estuary in autumn, this haunting three-note whistle seems to embody these wide open spaces around our coasts. But if you catch sight of the bird, you may be in for a disappointment. Grey plovers live up to their name, in autumn and

winter at least, being stocky, grey waders with short legs, a short bill and a large dark eye.

While grey plovers may have a rather drab plumage outside the breeding season, in spring and summer they undergo a complete makeover. In the breeding season they are far better suited to their North American name, black-bellied plover, with the black extending from their face all the way down to beneath their tail, contrasting beautifully with a spangled silver back and wings. We are rarely lucky enough to see grey plovers in their full breeding finery, though the last stragglers passing through in May are often well advanced in terms of their summer plumage.

Watch them feeding out on the open mudflats and you'll see little of the nervous energy we associate with smaller waders. Grey plovers are far more considered in their feeding methods, and are exponents of the 'run, stop, peck' technique. This is a strategy chosen by many of the plovers, which use their comparatively short bills to pluck worms and crustaceans from the surface, rather than probing deep into the mud like longer-billed waders such as the curlew and oystercatcher.

Grey plovers don't form flocks out on the estuary, but space themselves out and may even defend the same patch of ooze from one winter to the next. Although they look rather like their cousin the golden plover, when grey plovers fly they reveal their black armpits, properly known as the axillary feathers, and give their unique call.

They breed in Arctic Siberia and North America, where they lay their clutch of four speckled eggs among the mosses and lichens of the tundra. Occasionally a few non-breeding birds will spend the summer here, and returning birds arrive from July onwards, when their mournful whistles ring out across the expanses of glistening mud.

JACK SNIPE

*

The jack snipe is a bird with a split personality. In winter it's silent and secretive, so much so that few British birders ever get a good look at one. But in summer, it becomes far more extrovert: the male birds perform display flights over their soggy territories, with an extraordinary song, likened to the sound of a distant horse cantering along a road.

The bad news is that if you want to hear a jack snipe sing, you'll need to pay a midsummer visit to Scandinavian bogs and mires, where these small waders breed in damp tussocks.

When the ice seals their northern breeding areas, jack snipes head south and west, and many spend the winter in the British Isles. They like worm-rich, muddy areas, with short grass or rushes where they can hide. These little waders are superbly camouflaged: crisp yellow stripes down their dark backs break up their pattern when they are among the grass, so you're unlikely to see one until it suddenly rises almost from underneath your foot.

From a bird hide though, you stand a better chance of seeing one feeding. As they probe among low vegetation, they often have a strange bobbing motion, as if they were on hinges, and this odd habit will sometimes lead your eye to them.

Jack snipes are so confident that their camouflage works that some birds will even allow themselves to be picked up by hand.

'Jack' is an adjective meaning 'small' and these birds are indeed noticeably smaller than the common snipe, and have much shorter bills, a feature that you can pick out in flight. An old name for them is 'half-snipe'.

Unlike common snipe, which have a hoarse, rasping call, jack snipes are usually silent as they fly away and most will not fly far before they land and hide again. Common snipe, on the other hand, have a zigzag flight known as 'towering' and usually fly a long way before they settle.

ROCK DOVE

*

Dodging pedestrians on grimy city streets, or brooding their young in the echoing vaults of sea-caves in the far north of Scotland – these are the alternative lifestyles of the rock dove, a bird with a foot (or wing) in two very different worlds.

The birds that Woody Allen memorably described as 'rats with wings' are, for many city dwellers, the bane of urban life. Feral pigeons, as domesticated rock doves are known, live alongside us, despite attempts by various politicians, including the former London Mayor Ken Livingstone, to ban them from our city streets and squares. These quintessential urban birds are accused of bullying songbirds at bird-tables and spreading disease.

But whatever you might think of the street pigeon, as ornithologist Eric Simms named it, you have to admire its extraordinary adaptability. The same species in myriad forms has, over millennia, been cosseted by pigeon fanciers, used to deliver vital wartime messages and bred as fancy white birds to be housed in dovecotes, where their droppings were once used to manufacture an ingredient of gunpowder.

But there's another side to this fascinating species. Truly wild rock doves – shy, retiring creatures, which shun any contact with humans – still live in their original habitat among the caves and sea-cliffs of north-west Scotland. Here they fly through the spray from the crashing waves, showing off their immaculate ash-grey plumage, twin black wingbars and white rump-patch.

They're a paradox for some birders, who can get quite sniffy about the street pigeon, but enthuse over their wild ancestors. It can be genuinely hard to tell which ones are the natives and which are feral, as the latter have now spread into their ancestral home and are interbreeding with pure wild birds. How long the native rock dove can survive as a British bird is open to question; its days may well be numbered. But how will we know when it's finally gone?

SHORT-EARED OWL

*

The unexpectedness of seeing an owl flying around in broad daylight is only matched by the short-eared owl's grace and agility. This is one of our most spectacular birds of prey and the calls of the male alert you to his dramatic display flight.

A hunting owl looks surprisingly pale and long-winged as it quarters over meadows and moor-lands, and has some superficial resemblance to a female hen harrier, another species that hunts over this bleak, open landscape. But with a good view you'll see its yellow eyes glaring out of a round facial disc and the pale wing-patch at the base of its long primary feathers, which stands out even in poor light. What you won't see as it flies are the 'short ears', which aren't really ears at all, but tiny feather tufts.

Short-eared owls are nomads, roaming over vast areas of open countryside and breeding where they find their preferred habitat of moorland or long grass. Their favourite prey is small mammals, especially voles and mice, but because voles in particular are more common in some years than others, the owl population fluctuates in response to its food supply.

This reliance on voles forces them to travel in search of food, so each autumn many fly across the North Sea from Scandinavia to winter here in Britain. They often arrive at the same time as migrating woodcock and for this reason used to be known as the 'woodcock owl'.

Watching a short-eared owl fly in off the North Sea on an autumn day, sometimes harried by passing gulls, is a slightly surreal experience for us, but for the owl it's a natural response to the urge to find food. In some years far more arrive than others, with influxes reaching areas where they are not normally found in great numbers, such as the south-west of England.

Some short-eared owls stay to breed and boost our small resident population, most of which is in northern England and Scotland. The females nest on the ground, usually in dense heather or young conifer plantations. Males display to their mates in flight by clapping their long wings and calling to advertise their territories – but if you approach too closely they will soon bark their disapproval.

CARRION CROW

*

In his *Dictionary of the English Language*, Samuel Johnson defined the crow as 'A large black bird that feeds upon the carcasses of beasts'. The carrion crow's grisly reputation, along with its dark shape and harsh, menacing calls, can indeed send a shiver through the blood of even the most level-headed.

Crows have always suggested an element of foreboding. That businesslike bill, glittering eye and funereal plumage more than hint at death and destruction, so it's not surprising that the collective noun for a flock of crows is a 'murder'. And who can forget the gatherings of crows in Alfred Hitchcock's spine-chilling film, *The Birds*? (Though in the original book by Daphne du Maurier, the attackers were not in fact crows, but gulls.)

Here in Britain, carrion crows are highly successful birds, common in both town and country. Despised by gamekeepers as nest-robbers, they are also arch-scavengers – black mobs of them crowd our rubbish tips along with the ubiquitous gulls. But they're also birds we should admire for their intelligence and adaptability.

Aesop in his *Fables* told the story of a crow that dropped stones into a pitcher until the water level rose, so that the bird was able to drink. Carrion crows have also been seen dropping seashells on to rocks to break them open and have even, in mid-flight, plucked fish from the surface of a river. They're birds that never cease to surprise. One of the strangest sightings involved crows hanging upside down from telegraph wires; perhaps just for the pleasure it gave them. Inscrutable creatures, crows.

In northern Scotland, Ireland and the Isle of Man carrion crows are replaced by their close relative the hooded crow or 'hoodie', which is grey apart from its black head, wings and tail. But in lowland Scotland, England and Wales, telling carrion crows apart from the rest of their family – ravens, jackdaws and rooks in particular – can be confusing. The carrion crow is the one with the fewest obvious features: lacking the jackdaw's grey shawl, the rook's greyish-white base to the bill or the sheer bulk of the huge, buzzard-sized raven. Or you can always listen out for that harsh, ominous call.

GOLDCREST

*

Goldcrests can be tantalising birds, at times merely a whisper of sound from deep within blankets of conifer needles, but sometimes appearing so close that you don't even need binoculars. The high-pitched calls and pulsing ventriloquial song make the tiny goldcrest hard or sometimes downright impossible to detect, and their size doesn't help. Goldcrests are by a whisker our smallest bird, roughly nine centimetres long and weighing just five grams – the same as an A4 sheet of paper or a 20 pence coin.

These scraps of feathers are fidgety midgets, constantly on the move, as they inspect twigs and leaves for invertebrates. If two goldcrests meet you might see

them raise their fiery crown-feathers in display or threat – an unexpected flash of colour on a bird that is mainly olive green. Males have orange crowns, the females yellow ones.

They build their fragile nests out of spiders' webs, moss and feathers among the leaves of conifers – from huge plantations to single trees in suburban gardens – often weaving the structure on to the very end of a branch to keep the eggs and chicks as safe as possible.

Throughout the spring and summer, male goldcrests sing their rhythmic song at such a high pitch that many of us find it harder to hear as we get older. But in October and November their sharp needling calls can be heard almost anywhere, including gardens, woods and even coastal sand dunes. This is because at this time of year large numbers of goldcrests pour into eastern Britain from continental Europe, especially Scandinavia.

The journey that they make across the North Sea was once considered impossible for such tiny birds. Because they arrived around the same time as wintering woodcocks, some people believed that they travelled on the waders' backs, and so the tiny goldcrest became known as the 'woodcock pilot'.

CRESTED TIT

*

Travel to the ancient Caledonian pine forests of northern Scotland and you may well hear the soft, purring trill of the crested tit.

Although crested tits are quite common and widespread in continental Europe, in both broad-leaved and coniferous woodlands, in the UK they are confined to the central Highlands of Scotland, where they live almost exclusively in mature pine forests, with a dense understorey of heather and plenty of dead trees where the birds can make their nest.

Their best-known population is in Speyside, where the woods around Loch Garten, famous for their nesting ospreys in spring and summer, are also the year-round home of a thriving population of crested tits.

They're a delight to watch as they perform acrobatics among the lichen-covered pine twigs or probe the brushes of pine needles for insects. Their best field character is in their name, so as the only small British bird with a crest, you shouldn't find them difficult to identify. If you have any doubts look for a black line bordering a frost-grey face.

Crested tits usually breed in hollow tree-stumps, although a pair has been spotted nesting in an old red squirrel drey. By late April or early May the female has laid her clutch of five or six eggs and by early June young birds are roving through the pine woods with their parents.

But crested tits don't usually travel far, which may explain why they are absent from many apparently suitable areas of pine forest elsewhere in Scotland. Sightings south of the border are very rare indeed and the handful that have been seen in southern England may well be wandering birds from France or the Low Countries, which are marginally less sedentary than their northern counterparts.

YELLOW-BROWED WARBLER

*

A loud and urgent 'soo-ee', among the curled and wind-blasted leaves of a coastal sycamore or sallow in October, is guaranteed to set a birder's pulse racing. It may well prove to be a coal tit, or even an odd chiff-chaff, but there is something about that call that seems strangely unfamiliar.

Although it's hard to locate in the north-easterly gale that sets the leaves fluttering, eventually it appears in full view: a delicate and graceful sprite, hardly bigger than a goldcrest, moss green and yellow in colour, with a citrus stripe above its eyes and two pale yellow wingbars. It is a yellow-browed warbler, once a very rare vagrant to Britain, but now a regular autumn sight and sound.

What's remarkable is that these tiny waifs breed in Siberia and winter in South-East Asia, so why do we hear and see them in growing numbers in the UK every year? Each autumn several hundred birds, sometimes many more, turn up anywhere along the coast between the Isles of Scilly and Shetland, although they are much rarer inland. Autumn 2013 was a bumper year, with yellow-brows the most common migrant on some days along the east coast.

Just why we see so many yellow-browed warblers in Britain is something of a mystery. The standard theory is that these are 'lost' birds, which have migrated in completely the wrong direction from their Siberian breeding grounds, in a phenomenon known as 'reverse migration'. Instead of heading south-east, they have gone north-west, passing over Scandinavia and being blown across the North Sea to end up here in Britain, never able to return home.

But many scientists now believe that these birds are not storm-driven vagrants, but genuine migrants: a small, pioneering population that is dispersing over new routes, and discovering new wintering areas.

If enough birds survive the journey, and then manage to return to Siberia to breed, they may even establish a permanent wintering population in western Europe; indeed it is highly likely that they already have, possibly in the Iberian Peninsula. Ornithologists aren't all agreed on this but, while the debates go on, yellow-browed warblers continue to grace our coasts every autumn.

SOOTY SHEARWATER

*

A windswept, east coast headland on a blustery autumn day. Out at sea, gannets are passing by: dazzling shards of white against a metallic-grey sea. Then a brace of darker, smaller birds overtake them, skimming low over the waves. They appear entirely sooty grey in colour, until they turn to show their underwings, revealing a bright silvery flash, and confirming their identity as sooty shearwaters.

Sooty shearwaters are one of the great global travellers, found in almost all the world's oceans. Yet the closest they actually breed to Britain is way down in the South Atlantic, on islands such as the Falklands off the coast of South America. They travel further to be here than any other regularly occurring British bird.

They are also one of the world's commonest seabirds, with an estimated global population of 20 million, including vast breeding colonies off the coasts of Chile and New Zealand. But despite this, they are classified as 'Near Threatened' by the global bird conservation organization BirdLife International, because of declines as a result of overfishing, and the potential threats from climate change. The young, known as 'mutton birds', are still harvested for food, oil and feathers at some colonies, with up to a quarter of a million birds being taken every year.

Sooty shearwaters nest in burrows and after breeding head thousands of miles north to their feeding grounds in the North Pacific and North Atlantic. They undertake one of the longest journeys of any migratory animal: birds fitted with electronic tags in their burrows in New Zealand did a round trip of almost 64,000 kilometres to feed off Alaska, Japan or California before returning home. They often scavenge around feeding whales or fishing boats and have a wide diet, which includes fish, squid and krill.

Here in the UK sooty shearwaters can turn up almost anywhere around the coast in late summer and autumn. In flight they are dark, slim-winged birds, larger than the much commoner Manx shearwater but with the same graceful, shearing flight. As you watch them disappearing into wave troughs then soaring effortlessly over the crests, their wingtips almost skimming the water, it's hard not to marvel at the vast areas of ocean they've covered on their journey around the globe.

LEACH'S PETREL

*

Night falls on the remotest island group in the British Isles, the far-flung archipelago of St Kilda. As darkness envelops the vast cliff-faces and offshore stacks, a sound starts up: a call like no other, which can only be described as sounding like an amusement arcade in full swing. It is the call of our most mysterious and enigmatic seabird: Leach's petrel.

Only the remotest islands around our far north-western coasts provide sanctuary for Leach's petrels, one of the most difficult of all our breeding birds to see. This isn't because they are particularly rare – about 50,000 pairs breed in Britain – but because they breed on just four remote island groups in the whole of the British Isles (North Rona, the Flannan Islands and off Ireland's County Mayo, as well as St Kilda) and also lead a predominantly nocturnal lifestyle.

Like their close relative the storm petrel, Leach's petrels are small, starling-sized birds, superbly adapted to a life at sea. Along with fulmars and shearwaters, the

storm petrels are known as 'tubenoses', because their bills have a special tube along the top, which enables them to expel salt from the seawater they need to drink. In common with most seabirds, they are surprisingly long-lived, with an average lifespan of twenty years, although some can live for up to thirty.

After feeding trips for plankton and small fish, they return to their colonies, thronging the air like bats and calling to their mates underground with that bizarre, mechanical call.

Leach's petrels leave their breeding colonies in early autumn, and head out to the open ocean to spend the winter in the Bay of Biscay or off the coasts of West Africa. As they head south, there is a rare chance to catch sight of these elusive seabirds. For Leach's petrels have an Achilles heel: they are very vulnerable to oceanic storms, so autumn gales may force them inshore or even inland, where they occasionally turn up on reservoirs and lakes.

These events are known as 'wrecks', and for keen birdwatchers the privilege of seeing these tiny seabirds is tinged with fears for their wellbeing. Happily, though, not all birds founder and many are able to reorient themselves and return to the open ocean, where they can forage safely for food for the rest of the autumn and winter.

CATTLE EGRET

*

In any wildlife film set in Africa, one of the commonest sights is a flock of white, gull-sized birds perching on the backs of buffaloes or elephants, or flocking to a waterhole to drink.

So to see a family party of these small white herons wandering among a herd of cows on a marshland in the shadow of Glastonbury Tor came as something of a surprise to birdwatchers back in 2008, when cattle egrets bred for the very first time in Britain on the Somerset Levels.

Although the sight of these resourceful birds may have seemed out of place in the West Country, those 'in the know' weren't caught entirely unawares. Cattle egrets are one of the world's most successful and widespread birds, and one of only two species (the other being the Arctic tern) to have been recorded in all seven of the world's continents including Antarctica. In the autumn and winter of 2007, dozens of cattle egrets had turned up in the UK, mainly in the south and west of England. These sociable birds stayed together for the winter; and while most then returned south to continental Europe, two pairs stayed on and bred alongside the more familiar grey herons and little egrets in two Somerset heronries.

Unlike most herons, cattle egrets are not completely reliant on watery habitats. They are also pretty hardy and adaptable: one bird wintering on the Isles of Scilly used to roost in an open greenhouse to keep warm at night.

This toughness, together with the birds' strong urge to roam, has been the secret of their success. At the turn of the twentieth century, the species was only found in the Old World, across a wide swathe of Europe, Africa and Asia, with a small population in Australia. Then, following a major storm, a flock was swept across the Atlantic Ocean and made landfall in South America. Within a few decades they had begun to spread north, through the Caribbean and into

North America, where today they are common.

Their cousin, the little egret, is already widespread, especially in southern Britain, so how can you tell if it is the rarer bird you are seeing? Whereas little egrets have a clean, pure-white plumage, and a black bill, cattle egrets are more creamy-white in colour, with orange plumes on their head and back during the breeding season, and an orange-yellow bill. They are also slightly smaller, more compact and less elegant than little egrets.

The cattle egrets that bred in Somerset were almost certainly from southern Europe, and their arrival here is a logical consequence of their recent spread northwards through Spain and France. Despite that first breeding success, they haven't managed to consolidate and become a permanent colonist, even though small numbers continue to turn up here each year. Given the cattle egret's track record, though, it is surely only a matter of time before they become as familiar a sight as their cousin.

SHORE LARK

*

The marshes strewn along the north Norfolk coast are a magnet for birders, especially in October when migrants are still passing through and the first winter visitors are beginning to arrive from the far north.

Among the vast flocks of geese and wild swans, and the waders wheeling around as the tide comes in, are a group of smaller birds, roughly the size and shape of skylarks: shore larks.

To find a flock of shore larks feeding and calling along the strandline of a beach is a real highlight of an autumn day's birding. They are striking birds: paler and sandier than skylarks, their most noticeable features are the pale, lemon-yellow face, bordered by a black band across the upper chest, and black patches across their eyes.

Shore larks are a scarce but regular winter visitor here in Britain, mostly sighted where saltmarshes meet the beach along the east coasts of Scotland and England, where they sometimes join forces with two other birds from the far north, snow and Lapland buntings. Despite their striking black and yellow face-pattern, they can be extremely hard to spot, crouching down to avoid the blast of an easterly gale. They're also very mobile and can be a real challenge to find, especially as flocks tend to be small too, usually comprising fewer than twenty birds.

They are also known as 'horned larks', because in the breeding season the male birds sprout a pair of black crown feathers that can look rather like satanic horns. In Europe they breed on the Scandinavian tundra, where the males sing on high fells streaked with snow, and the females line their nests with white gull feathers.

Shore larks have a widespread global range, breeding across much of North America all the way south to Colombia, the sub-Arctic and on mountain ranges elsewhere, including the Atlas Mountains of Morocco. They have very occasionally been found breeding on the high tops of the Scottish Highlands, but have not yet managed to colonize Britain permanently as a breeding bird.

FIRECREST

*

The goldcrest is well known as Britain's smallest bird. But it has a relative that runs it very close in the size stakes, being only marginally bulkier: the firecrest.

An encounter with a firecrest in your local park, churchyard or even in your garden is a moment to savour, for this colourful cameo of a bird can turn up almost anywhere.

Like the much commoner goldcrest, firecrests are a mere nine centimetres long, and weigh just five or six grams. They can often be confused with their cousin: they share the olive-green plumage and brilliant orange or yellow crown-feathers, but the firecrest embellishes these with black eyestripes, dazzling white eyebrows and bronze patches on the sides of its neck, giving it a more striking and vivid appearance.

Each autumn, firecrests arrive from across the North Sea, many of them passing through Britain to winter further south on the Continent. But some do stick around, finding a suitable sheltered spot, often near the coast, where evergreens, especially holly, ivy and rhododendron bushes, give them cover and a place to look for insects.

Being so small and constantly on the move uses a lot of energy, so some firecrests may be taking advantage of the urban heat-island effect by wintering in city shrubberies, often in cemeteries or churchyards. It's therefore well worth looking and listening out for this beautiful visitor during autumn and winter. The firecrest's song is subtly different from the goldcrest's: a string of accelerating, high-pitched notes, lacking the pulsing rhythm or terminal flourish that goldcrests usually feature in their songs. The call, though, is trickier to pin down to one species or the other.

Firecrests are scarce but have been increasing in the UK since they were first found breeding here in the early 1960s. It is highly likely that they were overlooked before this date, as once ornithologists realized they were nesting other colonies were rapidly discovered.

Today there are thought to be about as many as 1,000 breeding pairs, mostly in old conifer forests in southern and eastern England, with strongholds in the New Forest and the East Anglian Brecks. But outside the breeding season they are more widespread and there is a quiet pleasure in discovering this flash of brilliance on a dull, cold autumn or winter day.

BOBOLINK

*

As the chill winds of autumn begin to blow, migrant birds right across the northern hemisphere are heading south to spend the winter in the tropics, where they can find enough food to survive before returning north the following spring to breed. Just as here in Europe there are many species that leave us at this time of year, so the same is true across the pond, in North America.

To migrate south from eastern Canada and the north-eastern states of the USA, the quickest and most direct route is not overland, but flying out into the western Atlantic Ocean, then heading down to the Caribbean or South America.

This route has the added advantage of avoiding the danger of predators such as hawks; but it also has one major disadvantage: should the tail-end of a hurricane or tropical storm be blowing, migrant birds

are likely to be driven off course, and carried far out into the middle of the Atlantic.

The vast majority of these unfortunate birds fly until they drop exhausted into a watery grave. But a tiny handful manage to keep aloft, and fly eastwards until they finally reach land, after a journey of more than 3,000 kilometres. These are the sought-after 'Yanks' – vagrant American species that delight birders at hotspots from the Isles of Scilly to Shetland. Whether they ever make it back to the USA we don't know, but given that the prevailing winds blow from west to east it is doubtful.

One such vagrant is the bobolink. You might never have heard of a bobolink, for it is very rare in Britain, and its true home is the grasslands of Canada and the northern states of the USA. They look like large finches, but belong to the family of New World blackbirds, which are most closely related to buntings. Because the breeding males have black and white plumage, they are sometimes called 'skunk blackbirds' and cherished for their exuberant, bubbling song, which has been described by one North American naturalist as 'an outbreak of pent-up, irrepressible glee'. The birds that reach Britain aren't quite so striking, as they are in their streaky juvenile or winter plumage and resemble bright, yellowish house sparrows.

The first bobolink was found on the most south-westerly point in Britain, the island of St Agnes in the Isles of Scilly, in autumn 1962. In the fifty years or so since, about thirty more have turned up, mostly in the south-west, and all in September or October. October is the key month for North American songbird vagrants and the bobolink is one of over fifty species that have made it across the Atlantic.

Many of these have got here under their own steam, some trickling down via Greenland or Iceland perhaps, some in direct flight across the ocean. Some birds are thought to have hitched a lift on passenger and cargo ships as they travel eastwards and these are generally accepted as *bona fide* vagrants. However if the bird is actually fed, then its ability to have arrived here unassisted is under question. This is just one of the many aspects to judging the acceptability, or otherwise, of rare visitors to our shores. Rare birds are a minefield.

Those who pass judgement, the members of the British Birds Rarities Committee, are known as the 'Ten Rare Men' (since it was established in 1958 not a single woman has yet served on the committee). They are kept especially busy by a flood of autumnal observations, which, who knows, might even include a bobolink.

MOURNING DOVE

✳

On a November evening towards the end of the last millennium, Maire MacPhail looked through the window of her home on the island of North Uist in the Outer Hebrides to see an odd-looking pigeon sitting on the garden fence. The bird looked tired; as well it might have done, for it turned out to be only the second mourning dove ever to have occurred naturally in the British Isles.

Mourning doves are slightly smaller than our familiar collared dove, with a grey-brown back and pinkish underparts, black spots on the wings and a long, pointed tail. The name comes from their plaintive cooing call. They are one of the most common and widespread birds in North America, with an estimated population of almost half a billion individuals. Their range extends from southern Canada, south throughout the United States to Panama and the West Indies.

Wherever it had come from, the individual found by the eagle-eyed Mrs MacPhail had made an epic voyage across the Atlantic to the edge of Europe, where it eagerly gobbled grain in a Hebridean chicken run. It attracted several local birders, but stayed for just one more day, to the intense frustration of an army of twitchers who were already planning how to get to one of the most remote and far-flung places in the British Isles, in order to see the bird and add it to their 'British List'.

Ten years earlier, on 31 October 1989, the first ever mourning dove to be discovered in Britain had appeared in a ringing trap on the Calf of Man at the southern tip of the Isle of Man, but had died of exhaustion the next day. A third bird turned up in 2007, also, amazingly, on North Uist. This time it had the good grace to stay alive, and to stick around for more than a week, allowing hard-core twitchers from mainland Britain to travel across to the Hebrides to see it.

In the past twitchers have broken speed limits, chartered boats, planes and helicopters, and run miles to catch up with a rare bird, especially one that has hardly ever occurred before in Britain. But when it comes to the mourning dove, why would they go to such extreme efforts to see a bird that, for the price of a transatlantic flight, they could easily see where it belongs, in its native North America?

After all, the sighting of a mourning dove on this side of the Atlantic is the equivalent of our familiar woodpigeon turning up in New York's Central Park. Yet the reaction of twitchers shows that even the most commonplace bird can acquire the cachet of rarity, if it appears where it is not expected. So while you're waiting for a mourning dove to arrive, why not revel in the sight of one of our most subtly beautiful birds, a woodpigeon, instead?

Jackdaw
Barnacle Goose
Bar-tailed Godwit
Siskin
Black-headed Gull
Golden Plover
Common Crane
Linnet
Pied Wagtail

 NOVEMBER

Dunlin
Marsh Tit
Willow Tit
Hawfinch
Black-tailed Godwit
Tree Sparrow
Twite
Goshawk
Little Auk

INTRODUCTION

AS FIREWORKS light up the night sky and winds tear the last tattered leaves from the trees, for many birds November is a time for hunkering down. In the garden, local blackbirds skirmish with their Scandinavian cousins, gorging on berries after their cold flight across the North Sea. Redwings and fieldfares fan out through the countryside on a quest for fermented fruit: orchards full of windfall apples are often full of chuckling thrushes, especially after an early frost, which softens the fruit and makes it easier to eat.

More birds are still arriving, though. Continental woodpigeons and starlings continue to pour in and swell our resident numbers. In woods, on heaths and sometimes even in town gardens, russet woodcocks that may have flown from as far as Siberia spring up from underfoot and twist off on barred, whirring wings. On eastern coasts, a real treat is the sight of short-eared owls fanning low over grassy fields or, if you're very lucky, coming in off the North Sea, mobbed by gulls as they head gratefully towards the sanctuary of the beach.

Not all of these birds are coming here from abroad. A scruffy corner of a field or a patch of rough ground is enough for a pair of stonechats, descending from the high moors to find easier pickings. On mild November days these small bundles of charisma are a delight to watch as they gnat-catch from sprays of dock or fence-posts. In the open fields beyond you may see golden plovers, golden only in the autumn sunlight, but spectacular when flocks take to the air, dazzling first white, then dark as they twist and turn in perfect formation against the lowering clouds. Resident and Scandinavian birds mingle in these flickering flocks.

The falling leaves make some birds a little easier to see. Hawfinches are notoriously elusive in summer, but our small resident populations are boosted by continental arrivals in late October and November. Look carefully around yew and hornbeam trees and you might see one fly up from the ground or 'tick' loudly from a treetop. In whirring flight they look stumpy and short-tailed and have white see-through panels in their wing-feathers. With no leaves around, you could try getting to grips with marsh and willow tits. Both are now scarce woodland birds, though their decline has been patchy and they may be overlooked in some places.

The local lake or gravel pit is well worth a scan at this time of year. In summer mallards, coots and the occasional tufted duck may have been the staple fare, but now there's always a chance of something more exotic to brighten the short days: a zebra-striped drake goldeneye or a harlequinade of shovelers, straining the surface for tiny water creatures on which they greedily feed.

On washlands along our rivers wigeon and pintail numbers are building up and among them may be Bewick's swans from Russia or whoopers from Iceland. In western Scotland, especially on the Solway Firth, thousands of barnacle geese from Svalbard graze the salty turf. Barnacle geese from Greenland winter in western Ireland and Islay in the Hebrides, yapping as they corkscrew down on to the pastures, a technique for quickly losing height known as 'whiffling'.

Not all birds heading south from Svalbard are as obvious. When November winds whip up the wave-crests of the North Sea, small dark shapes speed south through the spume – little auks escaping from the Arctic's icy winter grip. These diminutive seabirds have nested in millions on high Arctic cliffs and are now heading for the open oceans where they will spend the winter.

But if seawatching isn't for you – and it is an acquired taste, especially during wintry gales – then the relative calm of an estuary may be an acceptable substitute. Out on the expanses of food-packed mud are flocks of knots, dunlins and redshanks, together with larger curlews and godwits, all probing the ooze for worms and minute molluscs. On an autumn afternoon, you can watch them wheeling in clouds above the tide-race while their dining table is washed clean by the incoming water. As they gather in packs to roost at high tide, their combined orchestra of trills, whistles and piping calls makes a fitting end to a late November day.

JACKDAW

*

On a chilly evening in November, as dusk falls over our towns, villages and countryside, you'll hear a cheery, familiar sound: a conversation echoing across the landscape. Look up, and you'll see ragged flocks of jackdaws, returning to their woodland roosts along routes they and their ancestors have followed for centuries. As they pass overhead, only slightly darker than the sombre sky, each bird calls out the first, sharp 'jack' of its name, to keep in contact with its companions.

Jackdaws are the smallest of our eight species of crow, about the size of a feral pigeon. Apart from their size, you can tell them from the other mainly black corvids – ravens, rooks and carrion crows – by the distinctive grey patch on the back of their necks, their short, stubby bills and piercing pale bluish-grey eyes.

They're swaggering, streetwise scavengers, the Artful Dodgers of the bird world, renowned – along with other members of their family – for stealing shiny or glittering objects to adorn their nests. Young jackdaws have a reputation for getting into scrapes, and injured birds can often make excellent unofficial 'pets' before eventually returning to the wild.

Jackdaws are mainly birds of the lowland countryside, happiest high up on church towers and chimneys. In autumn and winter they're sociable birds, feeding in fields where they flip over cowpats and probe the turf beneath for grubs, often in the company of rooks and carrion crows. On rubbish tips, they scavenge alongside other birds, taking to the air like a sootstorm in a flock of grey and white gulls. Perhaps it's because of their sociability and cheery sound that many people find jackdaws more appealing than other members of the crow family.

But one aspect of these birds' behaviour makes them much less popular. Jackdaws have an annoying habit of dropping sticks down chimneys, in the hope they'll lodge there to create a platform on which their nest can eventually be built. Long after the breeding season, when householders try to light the first fire of autumn, they often get a nasty surprise as their sitting room fills with smoke from the blocked flue. Much hard work later, the chimney is clear, and there are several bin-bags full of twigs waiting to be collected – courtesy of an industrious pair of jackdaws.

BARNACLE GOOSE

*

Under a glowering dawn sky on the borders between Scotland and England, a vast flock of barnacle geese takes to the air. Yapping like manic terriers, skeins of these small, neat birds are leaving the safety of their night-time roost on the mudflats, and heading inland to graze in open fields.

Barnacle geese – a pleasing vision in black, white and pearl grey – are winter visitors from some of the most northerly places on the planet: Greenland, Svalbard and Arctic Russia. Each autumn, as darkness begins to envelop the lands within the Arctic Circle,

they leave their breeding grounds and head south. They exchange these remote, wild places for the rich grazing pastures of western Scotland and Ireland, especially the whisky-producing island of Islay and the estuary that divides Scotland from England, the Solway Firth. The geese – more than 30,000 of them – congregate there in such numbers that from a distance, entire fields seem to disappear under a soft, grey mantle.

The annual arrival of these geese in the UK each autumn and their unexplained disappearance the following spring gave birth to their strange association with barnacles. The cleric Gerald of Wales, writing in the twelfth century, said that he'd seen more than 1,000 barnacle geese hanging by their beaks from seagoing timber, after which they fell into the water or flew away.

This was long before the science of migration was understood, and all sorts of strange theories were suggested to explain the seasonal movements of birds. We now know that what the curious cleric had seen were not birds at all, but goose barnacles, a large crustacean whose beak-like shells are suspended from long neck-like stalks, which are often washed up with driftwood on beaches.

Even so the somewhat bizarre belief that goose barnacles developed or transformed into birds persisted for over 500 years, until finally superseded by the equally outlandish explanation that the birds migrate vast distances across the surface of the globe. Outlandish, yes; but also, of course, true.

BAR-TAILED GODWIT

*

Bar-tailed godwits are not the most colourful, musical or strikingly patterned of the waders that grace our shores in autumn. But they do have one claim to fame: of all the world's migrant birds, they make the longest non-stop journey across the globe, flying more than 11,000 kilometres – almost 7,000 miles.

The peculiar name, which this species shares with its larger relative the black-tailed godwit, probably originally came from its call, but is also considered to refer to the fact that these plump birds are good to eat: 'god-wit' means 'good creature'. The seventeenth-century dramatist Ben Jonson refers to the godwit's gastronomic value in *The Alchemist* when Sir Epicure Mammon notes that if he acquires further riches, then even his footboy 'shall eat pheasants, calvered salmons, knots, godwits, lampreys,' highlighting the luxury of these wild fish and fowl.

The two species of godwit are superficially similar: both are large, leggy waders, and both have a predominantly rusty-orange plumage in spring and summer, moulting to a duller brown in autumn and winter. They can indeed, as their names suggest, be told apart by the patterns on their tails, but a better way to identify them is that in flight the black-tailed reveals a prominent black and white stripe along its wings, while the bar-tailed has a more uniform wing pattern. Bar-tails are also stockier and shorter-legged, with a slightly upturned bill, and prefer saltwater to fresh-water habitats.

Bar-tailed godwits breed in the high Arctic and migrate south for the winter, gathering on beaches and estuaries all around Britain, where some stay put while others head down into coastal West Africa.

But on the other side of the globe, where the vastness of the Pacific Ocean makes stopovers on land less practical, bar-tailed godwits undergo one of the most extraordinary physical tests of any of the world's birds. After breeding in Alaska, they fatten up on worms and crustaceans to almost double their bodyweight before heading out to sea. Scientists knew that the godwits migrated all the way to New Zealand; but they assumed that they did so by hugging the Pacific Rim and stopping off to feed at tiny islands along the way.

Then, in 2007, they tracked one tagged bird as it flew right across the open ocean for nine whole days, 11,000 kilometres over the vast expanse of water. During this epic flight the bird lost half its body weight, and the only way it managed to survive was by shutting down one half of its brain at a time to sleep on the wing. Finally, it and its companions arrived in New Zealand where they spent the winter, only to embark on yet another epic journey back to Alaska the following spring.

SISKIN

*

With a flash of yellow wingbars and a chorus of twanging calls, siskins are coming into our gardens as never before. Once mostly confined to the remote pine forests of northern Britain, siskins have become one of our commonest garden visitors. More than any other species, the siskin's fortunes have been transformed by its ability to cash in on our love affair with birds.

Back in the 1960s, when garden bird feeding first began to take off, a popular way to attract birds was to hang up peanuts encased in red mesh bags, bought from local hardware stores and pet shops. These bore a vague resemblance to the alder cones on which siskins feed in the wild, and seemed to act as a super-stimulus to these small, streaky, green and yellow finches. Soon siskins were appearing in gardens all over southern Britain – a welcome new arrival on the suburban scene.

Siskins nest in conifers, so the maturing of vast commercial plantations of larches, firs, spruces and pines during the latter decades of the twentieth century enabled the bird to extend its breeding range southwards as well.

When you first see them, it's easy to think of siskins as small, compact greenfinches, although their plumage is much streakier. Males have a black cap and bib and a yellowish face, while females and young birds are plainer. But both sexes have a broad yellow wingbar, lemon rump and tail-patches, which are easy to pick out in flight. When they're not in gardens, you'll often see them along the banks of streams and rivers, where they feed in alders alongside flocks of another tiny finch, the lesser redpoll. They're also fond of larch and fir cones and will gather in flocks of a hundred or more where the seeds are plentiful.

As they clamber acrobatically among the branches, they can be hard to pick out especially against a leaden autumn sky, but they can be identified by their nasal calls. As winter gives way to spring, you'll sometimes hear a flock singing in chorus from the treetops, a farrago of twitters interwoven with peculiar bleating sounds. When the breeding season arrives and siskins are back in their favourite conifers, this song is part of an elaborate courtship display. This includes a 'butterfly flight', during which the male impresses his potential mate by flying slowly around his territory on widely spread wings.

BLACK-HEADED GULL

*

Produce a bag of stale bread at your local park pond or lake and you'll soon be engulfed by a screeching blizzard of black-headed gulls. It's easy to take them for granted as they float and bicker above the ducks, geese and swans, but these really are one of the most graceful and aerobatic of our familiar birds. An entertaining way to test their agility is to throw a piece of bread upwards, and watch as they snatch it out of the air, much to the frustration of the assembled waterfowl below.

'Black-headed' is a bit of a misleading description of these gulls at any time of year. In spring and summer they have chocolate-brown hoods, and when they're not breeding they lose the hood altogether – all that remains are one or two small, dark smudges, as if the bird has forgotten to wash its face.

This is by far our commonest small gull and throughout the year you can identify them by their delicate flight action, red legs and the white flash on the front edge of their angular wings. Their call is also very distinctive and was the inspiration for Richard Adams naming the gull 'Kehaar' in *Watership Down*.

Although today we are used to black-headed gulls in our towns and cities, they were not always found there; Victorian nature writer W.H. Hudson, writing at the turn of the twentieth century, considered them something of a rarity in London. Even today, they are primarily an autumn and winter visitor to urban areas, breeding on marshes, moorlands and coastal dunes, mostly in the northern half of Britain.

If you walk among these colonies, a cloud of mobbing birds will rise to alert their neighbours to your presence. But this tactic didn't work against egg-collectors who, in the past, took large numbers of eggs and young birds to sell. One colony in Norfolk provided over 40,000 eggs in a single year at the beginning of Queen Victoria's reign.

Some of the black-headed gulls you see around the park lake, or pulling worms out of your local football pitch, may have travelled a long way to spend the winter here. Ringing records show that birds from Finland and Poland regularly winter in the UK, before adopting their dark hood early in the New Year and heading back east to breed.

GOLDEN PLOVER

*

A flock of lapwings circles over a ploughed field on a bleak November day, before settling to feed. As they drop down to land, among them you see a flock of smaller birds, with wings like knife-blades and bell-like calls ringing out above the incessant 'pee-wit, pee-wit'. These are the lapwings' classic companions during autumn and winter: golden plovers.

At this time of year, golden plovers are easy to overlook, as they are so similar in colour to the ground on which they are feeding. But on a sunny day, they transform into slim-winged beauties in the air, flickering rapidly white and gold as both sides of their wings are exposed to the sunlight.

Although many of our wintering golden plovers come from Iceland and Scandinavia, they also breed on moorland and high ground in the north of England, northern and central Wales and Scotland. In their spring finery they might as well be a different species: both sexes have a black breast and face bordered in white, with rich gold spangling on their backs. The sound of a golden plover in song-flight, echoing over a swathe of heather moorland at dawn, is one of the first indicators that spring may be about to arrive in these bleak, windswept places.

The golden plover also has a small but significant claim to fame as the unwitting originator of one of the world's bestselling books. Back in November 1951 the managing director of the Guinness Brewery, Sir Hugh Beaver, was among a shooting party in County Wexford in south-east Ireland. He and another member of the party had an argument about whether the golden plover or the red grouse was the fastest-flying British game bird.

Having discovered that no reference book appeared to hold the answer to this conundrum, Sir Hugh had an idea: to produce a book containing the answer to this and many other questions relating to superlatives and extremes. Four years later, in 1955, the *Guinness Book of Records* was born.

More than half a century after this incident, there is still debate as to which is our fastest-flying game bird. Both golden plover and red grouse have been estimated to reach speeds of more than 100 kilometres per hour, but until a truly scientific experiment is carried out, we still can't be sure which is the quicker.

COMMON CRANE

*

In the skies over Somerset, a sound not heard since Tudor times resounds once more across this wide, wet landscape: the bugling of cranes. Soon after you hear them they lumber into view on broad, fingered wings, like a skein of giant, elongated geese: all necks and legs. Circling low over the marsh, mirrored in pools of floodwater, the cranes finally pitch in among the withering sedges. After a gap of almost half a millennium, Britain's tallest bird is back.

Their presence here is a triumph of science, willpower and hope. This is not a natural return; nor even is this wetland itself 'natural': it was created, and the cranes were brought here, by us. The Great Crane Project is modern conservation incarnate, with all the debate and controversy that entails.

With their stately posture, grey bustle of tail plumes like a Victorian lady's dress, and red, black and white faces, cranes are not an easy bird to ignore. They were once widespread across lowland Britain, but a combination of land drained for farming and settlement and persecution – cranes are reputedly very good to eat – meant that by the end of the sixteenth century they were already extinct as a British breeding bird. Their ghostly presence lingered on in place-names such as Cranfield, Cranbrook and no doubt inspired the fictional Cranford, but their only appearance here was as an occasional wanderer from mainland Europe.

Then, in the last year of the 1970s, a small flock of cranes drifted off course as they migrated north from Spain or France to their breeding grounds in Scandinavia. They landed on the far eastern corner of

Britain: the Norfolk Broads. Fortunately they found the habitat to their liking, and established a small but growing colony of breeding cranes – the first to nest here for more than 400 years.

Gradually, this tiny nucleus grew larger, and the birds extended their range elsewhere in eastern Britain. But their biggest boost came with the Great Crane Project, a partnership of several conservation bodies dedicated to restoring breeding cranes to wetlands throughout the UK. The project aims to release 100 birds into the wild over five years, establishing a core population on the wetlands of the Somerset Levels.

Reintroducing any bird – especially one as shy as the crane – is never easy. First, crane eggs are taken from the booming population in Germany and incubated at the Wildfowl and Wetlands Trust HQ at Slimbridge in Gloucestershire. Once the chicks hatch, they are raised by staff wearing special 'crane suits' to imitate the birds' parents. This is to ensure that the youngsters do not form an attachment to humans, which could prove dangerous when they are finally released into the wild.

The project is not without its detractors. Some people believe that to raise and release the cranes in this manner is interfering with nature, and should not be done. But given the dire state of much of Britain's wetland wildlife, and the damage we have already caused to our natural heritage, most are in favour of the scheme.

A number of cranes pass through the British Isles each year in spring and pairs have now established themselves in the East Anglian fens, in Yorkshire and most recently in north-east Scotland. Wild birds are now consorting with the released ones in Somerset and Gloucestershire and, as boundaries blur, the sight of a flock of these majestic birds taking to the air with a chorus of trumpeting calls is something to celebrate.

LINNET

*

Few sights and sounds are quite so redolent of the farmed countryside as the sharp, metallic calls of a flock of linnets flitting and bouncing along a hedgerow in tight formation. Sadly this is becoming increasingly rare, for as with so many of our farmland birds, the linnet's fortunes are on a steep downward curve.

Nevertheless, on late autumn and winter evenings you can still hear the musical chorus of a flock of these slender finches as they gather to roost for the night in dense, scrubby thickets.

Linnets – or 'linties', as they're known north of the border – are neat, attractive little finches that breed in farmland hedgerows and in scrub, especially gorse and hawthorn, on heaths and commons. Both sexes are slim, with a brownish plumage and pale flashes in their tails and wings, which are especially noticeable in flight. But during the spring and summer the male is transformed into a thing of beauty, as he blushes rose pink on his chest and forehead.

As if he knows he has suddenly become good-looking, he perches high on the top of a gorse bush or hedgerow shrub and delivers a sweet and musical babble to impress his mate. Sadly, the linnet's looks and song also impressed our ancestors. The Victorians prized them as cagebirds, commemorating this in the music-hall song 'My Old Man, Said Follow the Van':

Off went the van with me home packed in it;
I followed on with me old cock linnet . . .

There is a more sinister side to the upbeat tune and comic lyrics: like many songbirds in Victorian times, linnets were often blinded in the mistaken belief that they sang more sweetly when they couldn't see.

Outside the breeding season, linnets gather in large flocks, often numbering several hundred birds, to feed on weed-seeds and the seeds of oilseed rape and flax left behind after harvesting. In fact linnets get their English name from the French *linette*, which comes from *Linum*, the scientific name for flax.

PIED WAGTAIL

*

With only a few weeks left before Christmas, eager shoppers are crowding along city centre streets in search of stocking fillers and other gifts. But above the beeping of cash registers and the noise of children's tantrums comes an altogether sweeter sound: the high-pitched, two-note call of the pied wagtail.

The pied wagtail is a bird we see so often that sometimes we take it for granted. It certainly lives up to its name, being both black and white and constantly wagging its tail up and down as it searches for food. Its meandering but oddly purposeful motion was noticed by the poet John Clare, for whom the bird was 'little trotty wagtail'.

As they bounce overhead like puppets on a piece of string, pied wagtails emit a characteristic call – 'chis ick', with the emphasis on the second syllable. This has led London birders to dub the species 'the Chiswick Flyover', though it is a sound that can be heard far beyond the bounds of the capital, throughout most of Britain.

During the spring and summer, pied wagtails are largely solitary, pairing up to breed but rarely seen in groups. But as soon as autumn comes, the nights start

to draw in and the temperature drops, they turn into highly social birds, gathering each evening in large flocks to roost for the night.

Safe in their urban heat island, these communal roosts also offer collective vigilance, heightened when the birds congregate in well-lit areas such as shopping centres or motorway service stations, whose bright neon lights act as a deterrent to predators. Not that this always works in their favour: birds roosting above the furnaces of a Midlands glass-making factory during the 1980s were regularly visited by a hunting tawny owl, which found easy pickings among this mass gathering.

By day, you can often see pied wagtails in fields where they feed on insects, but they're equally at home on our streets, gleaning prey from pavements and road surfaces. They seem to like car parks and in the breeding season it's not uncommon to see a male bird attacking his own reflection in a car wing-mirror, in the mistaken belief that another bird has muscled into his territory.

But it is at their winter gatherings that they are at their most charismatic and magical, squeezing into their nocturnal roosts while chattering merrily away to one another like noisy Christmas decorations – a sharp reminder of nature's ability to adapt to our own artificial world.

DUNLIN

*

In the middle of the night, as the waters on a coastal estuary begin to recede, a call like a football referee's whistle signals that not all birds are going to sleep. Like many waders, dunlins must feed when the tides allow, and so under cover of darkness these tiny birds head out on to the vast expanses of mud to find food.

At dawn, as the tide comes in, they mass into huge flocks, twisting and turning around the skies in tight formation as they look for a place to roost. From a distance the flock looks like an animated swirl of smoke.

Dunlins are workaday winter waders, a birder's staple on the open estuaries where they feed. They belong to a group of small shorebirds that American birders have christened 'peeps', because of their trilling calls.

They're no bigger than a starling, with long, curved bills, and run around on the mud, probing so fast that it looks as if they're stitching the ooze together. What they're searching for are teeming masses of tiny snails and worms, a rich food resource and the reason why our islands are so important as a winter refuge for waders and wildfowl. As they scuttle around the feet of the larger and statelier curlews and godwits, they look rather like mice. In autumn and winter dunlin are grey and white, but when spring comes and they moult into breeding plumage, with chestnut backs and black bellies, they can't be mistaken for any other waders.

Dunlins are found right across the temperate regions of the northern hemisphere, with about 350,000 wintering in Britain, having travelled from their breeding grounds in Scandinavia and Russia.

They do breed in the British Isles too, though in much smaller numbers, and can often be found nesting on the same boggy moorland as the golden plover. Because they share the habitat and arrive at around the same time in spring, they are known as the 'plover's page'. To see them in full glory, though, visit the flower-rich coastal machair grasslands of the Outer Hebrides where in late spring displaying dunlins rise and fall above meadows of clover, buttercups and orchids while lapwings and oystercatchers wail and shriek all around.

MARSH TIT

*

Like the Dartford warbler, Sandwich tern and garden warbler, the marsh tit is not very well named. It doesn't live in marshes, but is usually found in broad-leaved woodlands, so 'oak tit' would be a more accurate moniker.

Because marsh tits don't have the bright colours and striking patterns of blue or great tits, it's easy to overlook them. The secret is to listen for their call, rather like a discreet sneeze, allowing you to pick them out as they flit through the branches.

Late autumn and winter make a good time to get acquainted with these quietly attractive birds, because while they temporarily join roving bands of other woodland species in search of insects and spiders, they often remain in their territories when those other birds move on. In some apparently deserted oak woods in winter, the only sound may be the 'pit-choo' of a pair of marsh tits.

If they stay still you can appreciate their subtle fawn-grey plumage, white cheeks and black cap and bib. But be warned. That's also a good description of the very similar willow tit, so it's safer to rely on the marsh tit's distinctive call as your guide.

You can find marsh tits in older woods throughout England and Wales, but they're absent as breeding birds from Ireland and only just manage to reach the very far south of Scotland. Even in their southern strongholds they are declining in many places, for reasons that aren't entirely clear, but may be a result of the loss of the woodland understorey because of overgrazing by deer.

Like most members of the tit family, marsh tits don't travel far. Indeed they are one of the most stay-at-home birds in Britain, defending their wood-land territories throughout the winter. When spring comes the male sings and investigates nest-holes in old trees, where in time his mate will incubate a clutch of whitish, rust-speckled eggs.

WILLOW TIT

*

It's hard to believe, but one regular British breeding bird was not detected here at all until the very end of Queen Victoria's reign; and even then, much to the chagrin of British ornithologists, it was found by two Germans.

The discovery occurred when Otto Kleinschmidt and his colleague Ernst Hartert were examining a tray of skins at the British Museum in Tring. Although the birds were clearly labelled 'marsh tit', the men soon realized that two of the specimens were a species with which they were familiar from back home: the willow tit. The other details on the labels stated that these birds had been 'collected' (i.e. shot) in the suburbs of north London.

Until then, it had been assumed that of this closely related pair of very similar species, only the marsh tit occurred in Britain. Three years later the willow tit was finally confirmed to be breeding, and earned its rightful place as a British bird – the last regularly occurring species to be recognized.

To be fair, the two species are remarkably similar: greyish brown, with paler cheeks and a black cap and bib. Given really close views, the willow tit appears bulkier and more 'bull-necked', has a pale patch on its wing and, supposedly, a sooty rather than glossy black cap. But these features can be very hard to spot, so by far the best way of telling the two apart is by sound. While the marsh tit gives a sneezing 'pit-choo' call, the willow tit has a buzzing, nasal 'chay, chay', and the song is a series of loud 'see-u' phrases; but even so, placing a firm identity on any individual bird requires a detailed knowledge of both species. The latest visual aid to telling them apart is that the marsh tit has a pale grey spot at the base of the upper mandible of its bill, which can apparently show up in the field. No, really.

Coming across a willow tit is a very special experience nowadays, as the species is in rapid decline, especially in the south of Britain where it has inexplic-ably vanished from many of its former haunts. Because they excavate their own nest-holes, willow tits like damper habitats than marsh tits and are fond of wet coniferous or deciduous woodland with willows, alders and elder bushes. Hearing that nasal call can be the highlight of a damp November day out for any birder.

HAWFINCH

*

A sharp 'tik' call from a treetop, or a flurry of white tail-tips disappearing into the canopy means that hawfinches are about.

Despite their large size – hawfinches are half as long again and more than three times the weight of a goldfinch – these birds can be very hard to see, unless you're in a known location. The best way of spotting them is to listen for those loud, robin-like calls coming from the very top of a hornbeam or cherry tree. Wait patiently and they may well appear, on whirring wings. In winter hawfinches are easier to come across, because not only do they gather in small flocks at traditional sites such as Lynford Arboretum in Norfolk and Bedgebury Pinetum in Kent, but our small breeding population is boosted by continental birds.

If you do spot a hawfinch, they are handsome birds, softly coloured in rusts, beiges and fawns, and sporting that gigantic, parrot-like beak. In flight, they look very dumpy and short-tailed, and show a broad white wingbar and white tips to the tail-feathers.

Hawfinches are very fond of the kernels of seeds such as hornbeam, yew and cherry trees. Few birds have the strength to crack open cherry stones to get at the soft kernels inside, but it's a steal for our largest finch. It can exert immense pressure with its beak – more than 12 kilograms per square centimetre, or 180 pounds per square inch – crushing the hard seeds with ease. No wonder bird-ringers are always wary when handling hawfinches, as that vice-like bill would make short work of a finger or thumb.

The hawfinch is currently in sharp decline, with as few as 500 pairs now breeding in Britain. Its strongholds include the New Forest and Forest of Dean, where you still have a chance of hearing that sharp, clicking call and glimpsing the bird itself, as it perches momentarily on the very top of a tree before flying away.

BLACK-TAILED GODWIT

*

Head and shoulders above most spring waders – in size as well as appearance – there are few more splendid sights than a black-tailed godwit in all its summer finery. The deep russet-orange plumage is complemented by a long, orange and black bill and, in flight, a distinctive black and white wing pattern.

You will see birds in breeding plumage as they pass through the British Isles on their journey north in spring. But fewer than a hundred black-tailed godwits breed here, mainly on the damp grazing marshes of the Nene Washes near Peterborough. This is one of the last remaining patches of the Great Fen, a huge, boggy wetland that would once have covered vast swathes of eastern Britain.

Back in medieval times, when the fens supported millions of breeding waterbirds, black-tailed godwits were common enough to be regularly served at royal feasts, where this plump wader was considered a great delicacy. (See Bar-tailed godwit for more on this.)

Black-tailed godwits are still common here in autumn, when almost 50,000 birds arrive from Iceland. They stop to feed on saltmarshes, freshwater marshes and wetlands throughout lowland Britain, but as the winter progresses most move further south, to France and the Mediterranean.

Oddly, male and female godwits split up soon after the end of the breeding season, and may spend the winter several hundred miles apart. In spring, both males and females stop over here on the way north to Iceland to breed, arriving at almost exactly the same time as one another. But tardy males must be careful: if they fail to return early enough, their mate will 'divorce' them and take a new and available partner.

TREE SPARROW

*

We take sparrows for granted, rarely giving them a second glance. But in some rural locations it pays to take a closer look at any sparrow flock, for it may include the house sparrow's rarer cousin, the tree sparrow. Keep your ears open too for its dry 'tek, tek' calls coming from within a hedge.

With its chestnut cap, bright white cheeks and generally more dapper appearance, the tree sparrow looks like a house sparrow that has scrubbed itself up

for a special occasion. Unlike house sparrows, whose sexes appear very different, male and female tree sparrows are identical. They also prefer a place in the country to an urban lifestyle, a preference that in recent years has led to their downfall.

The way we manage our countryside – tidying up hedgerows and woodland, spraying our farmland with insecticides and planting arable crops all year round – has considerably reduced the numbers of tree sparrows, by depriving them of food and nest sites. Where colonies do survive, it is usually with a helping hand from us, with nestbox schemes where the sparrows can breed, plus supplementary food in the form of seeds to help them through the winter.

But although tree sparrow numbers are falling in Britain, they are still widespread across Europe and Asia, where in the eastern parts of their range they replace the house sparrow as the classic urban bird. Because they feed on seeds and grains, they are often considered a serious pest, which led to one of the most extraordinary episodes in the long relationship between people and birds.

In China, during Chairman Mao's 'Great Leap Forward' of the late 1950s, tree sparrows were accused of competing with people for precious grain and were proclaimed an enemy of the state. Citizens were mobilized to march around banging drums, blowing whistles and setting off firecrackers to prevent the sparrows landing. Millions of obedient citizens took part and it's thought that tens of millions of birds perished of exhaustion.

It was then that the problems really started. By killing so many sparrows the Chinese had removed a key species from their rural and urban ecosystems; for sparrows do not only eat seeds, but invertebrates too. As a result, numbers of insects – especially locusts – boomed, causing massive damage to crops. This in turn led to the Great Chinese Famine of 1958–61, during which an estimated 30 million people died of starvation. A salutary lesson of what can go wrong when we tamper with the natural world.

TWITE

*

Known as the 'mountain linnet', and in Scotland as the 'heather lintie', the twite is indeed the upland equivalent of its commoner cousin the linnet. Like that species, it is a small, plainish brown finch, and can be identified by its sandy-coloured plumage streaked heavily with dark brown, short yellow bill and, in flight, a pink tinge to the rump.

In winter twites head south to feed around salt-marshes and beaches, especially in the north and east of the UK, where they can be picked out from mixed finch flocks by the loud 'twa-it' calls that give them their name.

To see twites in summer in the British Isles, you'll need to visit some of our most scenic spots: the Western Isles of Scotland, the moorlands of northern England, or the west coast of Ireland. Twites are birds of heather moorland and traditional farmland, nesting in the shelter of wiry clumps of heather and feeding on weed seeds around crofts. But not just any moorland will do: it's the intimate mix of small-scale farming and rough upland scrub that seems to suit them best, which explains why the twite is in sharp decline as these long-established habitats disappear.

Losing the twite would also mean losing the only representative of the Tibetan bird fauna to be found in Britain. For this species evolved in the mountain ranges of central Asia, and the small numbers breeding in northern Britain and Scandinavia are more than 2,500 kilometres from the nearest populations in the south-west of that vast continent.

GOSHAWK

*

Loud yelping sounds from deep in a conifer wood betray the presence of a goshawk, one of our rarest and most elusive birds of prey. Wait near a forest viewpoint and if you're lucky you'll see the hawk itself, powering over the tree canopy like a shark crossing a reef.

Goshawks have long maintained a shadowy presence in our landscape. When Leslie Brown published his authoritative *British Birds of Prey* in 1976, he said that there was little point in writing at length about a bird that was only rumoured to breed here sporadically. Now goshawks are established in many woodlands, including well-known locations such as the Forest of Dean in Gloucestershire and Kielder Forest in Northumberland. But even though we know more about them, these shadowy birds of prey retain a sense of mystique.

The goshawk is a larger and more powerful relative of the far more widespread sparrowhawk. Its name derives from 'goose-hawk', probably from medieval falconers' practice of flying this species against geese, though in the wild goshawks far prefer woodpigeons, rabbits and squirrels.

Weighing 1.5 kilograms, a female 'gos' is hefty, as big as a buzzard and much heavier and bulkier than her smaller mate. As with the sparrowhawk, this size difference between the sexes allows a pair to exploit a wide range of prey. Superficially similar to sparrowhawks, goshawks are grey above and pale below, with fine dark barring across their underparts. They also have a broad, white stripe above their piercing yellow eyes. In flight they can be identified by their larger size and barrel-chested appearance, as well as their more pointed wingtips.

By far the best time to see goshawks is in early spring, when they soar high over their woodland territories. With luck and patience you'll witness their dramatic switchback displays, during which the birds plummet down through the air with closed wings, then open them to swing sharply upwards.

Goshawks breed in many types of woodland, but prefer conifers, where they build their bulky nests of sticks. They're very secretive during the breeding season, but they need to be, for illegal persecution is still rife from those few gamekeepers who fear their impact on game birds, as well as from a small but determined band of egg-collectors.

It was similar persecution that had eliminated goshawks from Britain by the late Victorian period, and the birds that breed here today are mainly descendants of captive goshawks, released at various times during the twentieth century. Whatever its origin, to watch one glide across a forest clearing is a breathtaking experience.

LITTLE AUK

*

As late autumn gales sweep on to our shores, it takes a hardy soul to go 'seawatching' in the hope of sighting ocean-going seabirds as they pass by our coasts.

Among the gulls and gannets, small flocks of guillemots, razorbills and puffins fly low over the waves on their whirring wings. They look small enough in comparison to the larger seabirds, but then they are joined by a flock of even tinier, black and white birds, which look far too minute to be able to survive in such a harsh environment. They are little auks, which at just

eighteen centimetres long (not even as big as a starling) are easily the smallest member of their family to occur regularly in Britain.

As they head south from their breeding grounds in the high Arctic, little auks generally stay far offshore. But when stormy weather does bring them close by, they can sometimes be seen in vast numbers. On occasion flocks numbering thousands have been counted as they pass east coast watchpoints such as Filey Brigg and Flamborough Head in Yorkshire. In gales or fog hapless birds can sometimes be swept inland and end up floundering in fields. Some may even be led astray as they merge with flocks of starlings.

Little auks are one of the most numerous seabirds in the world, with around 12 million pairs breeding on high Arctic cliffs and mountainsides from Canada through Greenland and eastwards to Svalbard and Russia. A colony thronged with birds is a dazzling sight as swarms of auks fly in from fishing trips bringing food for their chicks, which are hidden in clefts between rocks or under boulders.

In Greenland, the birds are caught in long-handled nets and harvested for a traditional dish known as 'kiviaq'. To create this delicacy, several hundred auks are crammed into a sealskin, which is rendered airtight with seal fat. The birds are then left to ferment for several months, before being eaten by those with a taste for the unusual – and very strong stomachs.

Whooper Swan
Fieldfare
Teal
Long-tailed Duck
Gadwall
Water Rail
Mute Swan
Brent Goose
Shelduck
Ptarmigan

DECEMBER

Sanderling
Snow Bunting
Purple Sandpiper
Lesser Redpoll
Dipper
Robin
Red Kite
Knot
Starling
Song Thrush

INTRODUCTION

SHORT, DARK DECEMBER DAYS aren't always conducive to bird-watching. If the weather remains stable, and there's enough food around, most birds are happy to stay put this month, feeding busily in the few short hours of daylight that remain.

For smaller species, which lose more heat in proportion to their surface area, this is a testing time, so the food we provide can often make the difference between life and death. Family groups of long-tailed tits stream through our gardens, cashing in on balls of fat and suet. Coal tits dart to and from the bird-table to grab seeds and peanuts, which they stash away to eat later. Goldfinches illuminate the grey winter days with flashes of brilliance. And in the late afternoon, as the street-lights begin to come on, blackbirds bicker in shrubberies before settling down to roost for the night.

In orchards, where fieldfares chatter over windfall apples, balls of mustard-coloured mistletoe are caged in the branches like lumps of stranded seaweed. Near them, you may see a mistle thrush on guard, rattling out a warning to anyone intent on stealing his precious berries. This defence works on most birds, but crafty blackcaps often sneak in under the thrush's radar to plunder the nutritious fruit. Wintering blackcaps are now common in many places, having arrived in autumn from central Europe. They're very partial to mistletoe and are probably more efficient than the thrushes at spreading the plant's sticky seeds by wiping their beaks on twigs.

The settled feel to December's birdlife is disrupted when bad weather arrives and many birds are forced to move on to find food. Then you'll see flocks of winter thrushes struggling overhead, often accompanied by parties of golden plovers, lapwings and skylarks, all bound for warmer, ice-free feeding grounds to the south and west. If harsh conditions persist on the near Continent, ducks and geese also head west for the relative warmth of our reservoirs, estuaries and marshes.

Not all birds are so easily budged. A white Christmas can never be guaranteed across most of the British Isles, but on the high tops of the Cairngorms it's a virtual certainty. Nearly all the breeding birds here have headed down to lower altitudes by December, as winds howl around the summit boulders and scour the snow into deep drifts. But our toughest bird, the ptarmigan, remains, now almost pure white instead of brown or lichen grey, scratching a living from this bleak winter habitat. Some snow buntings, which have bred here on the high tops, survive on scraps picked up around the ski-lifts, but most have headed away to the coast where they join others from Scandinavia and Iceland, scavenging for seeds at the top of the beach.

Although winter's grip is tightening, there are signs of spring even before Christmas. Along fast-flowing streams in the north and west, a rich, sweet song cuts through the roar of the torrent. In midwinter, dippers are proclaiming their linear territories and if you look on mid-stream boulders you'll see each bird flashing its white bib, while bobbing up and down like a jack-in-the-box.

They're not alone: if conditions stay relatively mild then the first great tits will be tuning up from mid-month, their 'tea-cher, tea-cher' song bringing hope of longer days. Song thrushes will also sing in midwinter and if the temperatures stay up, by the end of a mild December they'll join the ubiquitous robins, all carolling away as the first waxy snowdrop flowers appear. But it's a false start to spring and, almost inevitably, more testing times lie ahead.

As December fades, some spectacles accrue extra layers of meaning as we reflect on the year that's passed. On slowly freezing floodwaters, wild swans whoop among packs of whistling wigeon and piping teal. In a few well-known sites, vast numbers of starlings twist and mingle over reedbeds or pierheads as dusk falls, forming outlandish, plasma-like shapes. On dark afternoons, red kites assemble from all points of the compass, circling over hills draped with woods in which they will roost together.

Best of all, when birdsong is extinguished and as the year breathes its last, a pale, moth-like shape fans over a distant meadow, first jinking this way and that, then hugging the line of a hedge. All thoughts of cold and damp are forgotten as you watch a hunting barn owl beating its ancestral bounds, until it too is swallowed by the darkness and you trudge home, crunching through leaves stiffening with frost, to celebrate another New Year.

WHOOPER SWAN

*

The British are used to swans adorning our park ponds and rivers. These are the resident mute swans, but their nobility is somewhat undermined by an almost improper tameness, not helped by their ungrudging acceptance of the grubbiest ponds or canals as places to breed. That certainly isn't the case for the visiting 'wild swans', which grace us with their presence during the winter months: Bewick's and whooper swans. The whooper is the larger – indeed it rivals the mute swan as Britain's biggest bird.

A skein of ghostly whooper swans bugling as they pitch down on a pasture blue with dawn frost is a sight to cherish, and one that enlivens lakes and flooded fields in northern Britain during the winter. These stately birds have flown here from their breeding grounds in Iceland and Scandinavia, where their usual diet of waterweeds, grasses and herbs is now buried under snow or locked beneath a thick layer of ice.

So they head south, to take advantage of our lush countryside, kept ice-free during most years by the warming Gulf Stream, which provides them with the grazing they need. A handful of birds stay on to breed in Britain: mostly in northern Scotland, but with a few pairs in Northern Ireland too.

Whoopers travel in family parties, the greyish cygnets learning the migration routes and the best feeding and roosting spots from their pure white parents. They can fly at great heights: in December 1967 a radar operator in Northern Ireland spotted a flock of swans – almost certainly whoopers – at an altitude of 8,200 metres, not far off the height of Mount Everest.

The largest wintering flocks are in Scotland, Northern Ireland and northern England, though the several thousand birds that gather each evening in the Ouse Washes of East Anglia are now floodlit to allow visitors to watch as they feed. Here you can easily compare the whoopers with their smaller relative: they are not only noticeably larger, but also have longer necks than Bewick's swans.

The bill pattern is another clue: the easiest way to remember the difference is that whoopers have a mainly yellow bill with a wedge of black at the tip, while Bewick's have a mainly black bill with a patch of yellow at the base. Mute swans have black and orange bills.

The elegance and pristine beauty of wild swans have inspired writers and musicians for centuries. Indeed because it is the largest and commonest swan in Russia, it is likely the whooper swan was the inspiration for Tchaikovsky's famous ballet *Swan Lake*.

FIELDFARE

*

Suddenly our roadside hedges are alive with birds: the fieldfares have arrived. These chuckling flocks of multicoloured winter thrushes plunder orchards and throng hedgerows across the whole of the British Isles.

Fieldfares are one of our largest thrushes, and very handsome too. They have slate-grey heads, dark chestnut backs and a black tail, while their pale yellowish underparts are patterned with dark arrows. It's their rattling calls and high-pitched squeals, though, that often alert you to a ragged flock overhead, frequently accompanied by their smaller cousin the redwing.

Fieldfares are one of our commonest winter visitors. The birds we see are most likely to have been born in Scandinavia, where they nest in loose colonies. They're aggressive birds and will work together to attack predators such as hooded crows, dive-bombing them with a messy fusillade of faeces. This aggression spills over into winter, too. Fieldfares regularly chase off other birds at garden bird-tables, especially in hard weather, and there are several accounts of them attacking and even killing each other in battles over food.

An orchard full of frost-bitten apples will attract fieldfares and other thrushes from miles around, which descend in clacking hordes to gobble up the fruit, sometimes reaching several thousand birds in a single flock. Berries are one of their favourite foods in winter, but you can also see large flocks in short grassy fields, looking for worms.

Although they will stick around if there's plenty of food, fieldfares are great wanderers, so when the weather becomes too cold they move on, usually heading south and west. They're not faithful to their wintering grounds either, so those spending this winter with us could be hundreds of kilometres away next year.

TEAL

*

As you walk across a marshy field, trying not to get your feet too wet, you could be in for a surprise. Hidden in the ditch or channel running alongside you, a flock of birds is getting increasingly agitated, until the moment they can contain themselves no longer. They leap vertically up into the air, calling out as they fly fast into the distance, then land again on an undisturbed area of the marsh.

These are teal and given this typical behaviour, it's not surprising that a group of these diminutive ducks is known as a 'spring'. At just 330 grams (less than one-third of the weight of a mallard), the teal is our smallest duck, and also one of the most striking-looking. The drake is a perfect example of beauty in miniature, with a chestnut head and dark, bottle-green mask over his eyes, edged with a thin border of yellow. The body is greyish, with wavy markings known as 'vermiculations' (from the Latin for 'worm'), a white stripe just below the wing, and a flash of custard-yellow bordered with black beneath his tail.

The female, as with most ducks, is far plainer, enabling her to incubate her eggs safely out of sight of predators. In flight, both sexes show a flashy emerald-green wing panel known as a 'speculum', from the Latin for 'mirror', because it catches the light. This is a useful way to identify teal when the males lose their bright plumage during the summer months.

In winter, you can find teal on almost any body of water, from wide-open estuaries to freshwater marshes, dabbling in the shallows. As spring approaches, the males begin to display, raising their tails to show that eye-catching yellow patch. All the while they whistle softly in a piping chorus that, from a distance, sounds like tiny bells being struck. The sound of the male's call is probably the origin of word 'teal', and unusually among our common British birds, this species has never been known by any other name.

LONG-TAILED DUCK

*

In a sheltered bay on Scotland's east coast, flocks of ducks are bobbing amid the breakers. Among the black and white eiders and coal-black scoters there are a handful of smaller, paler birds, with whippy tails and musical calls. These are long-tailed ducks, whose cries gave rise to their Scottish name 'calloo', and the even more evocative 'coal-and-candlelight'.

In winter plumage, male long-tailed ducks are a pleasing blend of black, brown and white, set off with a slender tail – no wonder the species is sometimes called a 'sea-pheasant'. In the breeding season they exchange their white head feathers for darker ones, and grow chestnut plumes on their dark backs. Throughout the year the drake's bill is black with a pink splash, as if he's been eating strawberry ice cream. The females have a quiet charm, but eschew the male's adornments for a more practical plumage, vital camouflage when they're incubating their eggs.

Long-tailed ducks breed along coastlines in the Arctic, from the southern part of Hudson Bay in Canada, through Greenland and Iceland, to Scandinavia. In autumn they head out to sea, wintering across a huge area of the globe from the Pacific coast of the USA in the west to Lake Baikal in the east. In Britain they spend the winter in large flocks off the coasts of Scotland and northern England, where they dive to depths of up to sixty metres to catch shellfish. In spring, before they head north, males often perform their courtship display to accompanying females, but so far they have never been tempted to stay and breed here.

The long-tailed duck is perhaps the only bird that has had its name changed because of political correctness. Until recently, it was known in North America as the 'Old Squaw', a name that reflected the males' calls, a rather garrulous sound supposedly reminiscent of elderly women gossiping. But when a group of biologists from the United States Fish and Wildlife Service became concerned that Native Americans might be offended by the term 'squaw', they petitioned the American Ornithologists' Union to change the bird's name to that used elsewhere in the English-speaking world: 'long-tailed duck'.

GADWALL

*

It's not all about looks. Time was when the subtle, understated plumage of the gadwall would have thrilled any British birdwatcher. Not all that long ago, the sight and sound of this comparatively drab duck among the gaudy mallards and shovelers was an unexpected bonus during a winter day's birding. The male gadwall's deep, rasping call may not be particularly attractive, but it was good to hear, given that until a few decades ago the gadwall was rather a scarce species in Britain.

Most of our breeding population of this dabbling duck originates from birds released in Norfolk during Queen Victoria's reign, while in Scotland the gadwall first bred on Loch Leven in the early twentieth century. These could have descended from released birds or might have colonized naturally from continental Europe, where they are common and widespread.

In winter, our 1,600 or so breeding pairs are swamped by about 25,000 birds from further north and east, which like many other ducks head to Britain to take advantage of our mild winter climate and plentiful food.

Whatever their provenance, gadwall are quietly attractive. The drake's plumage is a rich palette of greys and browns, each feather finely vermiculated. The duck looks very like a female mallard, but is slightly smaller, and like her mate has a white wing-patch – the speculum – that on a mallard is glossy purple.

Despite their rather innocent-looking appearance, gadwall can be sneaky thieves, exhibiting what scientists call kleptoparasitic behaviour. They enjoy eating aquatic plants, but don't bother diving down into lakes themselves to collect them. Instead, they wait for birds such as coots to bring up the foliage beyond their reach, and then seize them right out of the mouths of their unsuspecting victims.

WATER RAIL

*

The origins of many familiar expressions are lost in the mists of time, but we do know how the phrase 'thin as a rail' came about: it refers to one of our most mysterious and elusive birds, the water rail. Like its cousin the corncrake (also known as the 'land rail'), water rails have an exceptionally slim body, compressed laterally to enable them to pass easily through the dense stands of reeds where they spend the majority of their lives.

In winter our populations of water rails are boosted by wandering birds from continental Europe, which can and do turn up anywhere: one lost bird found its way into the dining hall of a Worcestershire school, where it was photographed creeping along a pelmet – and was inevitably dubbed the 'curtain rail'.

Usually the only clue to a water rail's presence is a strange, penetrating sound, often likened to that of a piglet squealing in distress. This rather tortured call is sometimes referred to as 'sharming', and often signals a stand-off between two rival rails.

Water rails are very secretive, living in dense vegetation in marshes and fens in locations scattered throughout lowland Britain and Ireland. As they mince along the edge of reedbeds, you can see that they are noticeably smaller and slimmer than moorhens, chestnut and black on top and bluish-grey below, with a distinctive zebra-striped patch on their flanks.

If you disturb a water rail from the side of a ditch, all you'll see as it darts off is a pale triangle of under-tail feathers or a pair of dangling legs as it flies weakly away. But the bird's most striking feature is its long, blood-red bill, which it uses to probe for insects, frogs and fish.

It can be striking in more ways than one. In winter the shy water rail sometimes puts its bill to more sinister use. When their marshy homes freeze over, many water rails wander widely in search of alternative sources of food. Some end up in gardens where they skulk near bird-tables. Hiding in the foliage, they wait for an unsuspecting songbird to land on the ground to feed, then dash forward to impale their unfortunate victim with that pickaxe bill.

MUTE SWAN

*

Stately and serene, often bringing a touch of glamour to rather unpromising surroundings, the mute swan is our largest and heaviest breeding bird, and one that absolutely anyone can recognize. Few species have given rise to so many myths – most of them nonsense. The mistaken assertion that 'a swan can break a man's arm' is a favourite among pub bores, as is the belief that the Queen owns every swan in Britain, thus relegating this majestic bird to the status of a royal pet.

In fact a swan is more likely to break its own wing than your arm, even if they can be quite aggressive if you approach them too closely. And although the Crown does in theory retain the right of ownership of all unmarked mute swans on open water, in practice swans are a truly wild British bird.

Another myth about mute swans is that they are silent. In fact they have an extensive if somewhat tuneless repertoire of snorts and hisses, while travel writer Paul Theroux compared their creaking wingbeats as they fly overhead to the sound of two people making love in a hammock.

To see mute swans at their finest, a visit to a swannery such as the one at Abbotsbury in Dorset is a must. There, mute swans were first fostered by monks over 700 years ago, many destined for the table. Now they are valued not for their edibility but their splendour; as they fly overhead on those creaking wings they really make a spectacular sight.

Like most large waterfowl, mute swans are plump and good to eat, so in the late fifteenth century the Swan Laws were introduced to govern their management and to prevent the common people from taking advantage of this abundant and accessible food source.

To ensure that the population was carefully monitored, the Royal Swan Master organized annual round-ups to count the birds, a custom that continues today in the 'swan-upping' ceremonies held every summer on the River Thames.

BRENT GOOSE

*

Few species of bird can claim to have stopped an airport being built, but the brent goose is one of them. During the 1970s the windswept marshes of Foulness on the Essex coast were earmarked as the site of London's third airport. But despite its unpromising name, Foulness was a paradise for wintering birds, including the then quite scarce brent goose, which fed on a plant known as eelgrass.

The conservationists won the day, and the marshes were left to the birds. Since then, numbers of brent geese have steadily risen, and more than 100,000 now spend the winter in Britain, though over the past decade or so the population has begun to fall once again.

Neat and compact, the brent is our smallest goose, about the same size as a mallard. They're tough birds, which breed on the Arctic tundra and then head south to spend the autumn and winter on saltmarshes round the British and Irish coasts, the biggest flocks being found in southern England and East Anglia.

Their rather funereal colours make them easy to identify: blackish heads and necks and grey backs with a wisp of white across the neck. Three different races can be seen in Britain, though one of them, the North American 'black brant', is only a rare visitor. The commonest is the dark-bellied race, which breeds in Arctic Russia and winters on the mudflats and estuaries of southern and eastern England and South Wales. The pale-bellied race, which breeds in Greenland and Arctic Canada, spends the winter mainly in Ireland, especially around the shores of Strangford Lough.

Both races prefer to feed on the succulent leaves of eelgrass, one of the very few flowering plants to grow in the sea. But when supplies run out, brent geese head on to farmland, seaside golf courses or playing fields, where they crop the turf with their short, stubby bills. Although they breed in the remote Arctic, they are tolerant of people and will often graze close to built-up areas. Then as dusk falls, they leave their feeding grounds and fly off with a chorus of rolling honks, to roost on mudflats and sandbanks beyond the reach of predators.

SHELDUCK

*

Neither a goose, nor a duck, but somewhere in between, the shelduck is one of the most striking and easily identifiable of all our waterfowl. From a distance, as they mix with flocks of waders spread out across the mudflats of an estuary, they can appear largely black and white, and indeed the word 'sheld' itself derives from an old word for pied. But as the incoming tide

drives them closer inshore, you can pick out their dark, bottle-green head, broad chestnut band circling the midriff, and bright red bill, which in the drake has a prominent knob at the base. The loud cackling call of the female carries well across the muddy expanses in which the birds feed.

Shelducks spend most of their lives on large areas of mud or sand, which they sift through to find water snails and other tiny marine creatures. They are mainly birds of the coast, but will breed inland, wherever they can find shallow water to feed and suitable nest sites.

Although they are comparatively large birds, shelducks nest in holes. Disused rabbit burrows are among their favourite places, but they'll also breed in tree cavities, sheds, outbuildings and even haystacks. Soon after hatching, the fluffy youngsters are led to a nursery area by their parents, where they mingle with other broods to form crèches of up to a hundred or more, under the watchful gaze of several adults.

Social as youngsters, shelducks are also gregarious when they moult in late summer. They do this at traditional moulting grounds in the Wadden Sea, a vast area of mudflats on the edge of the North Sea off the coast of Germany, where up to 200,000 birds gather in safety to grow their new winter plumage. However in recent years some British shelducks have chosen to stay at home to moult, at sites such as the Wash, the Humber Estuary and Bridgwater Bay in Somerset.

PTARMIGAN

*

As you slog across the high tops of the Cairngorm plateau in the middle of winter, where temperatures plummet well below freezing and winds can gust at almost 300 kilometres per hour, there are very few signs of life. There may be a few hardy hill-walkers and skiers, but there's also one bird that doesn't just survive up here in midwinter, but thrives: the ptarmigan.

In a contest for Britain's toughest bird, the ptarmigan would win hands down. No other species spends its entire life in one of our harshest environments, and is indeed brilliantly and uniquely equipped to do so.

These tough little grouse are true cold-climate specialists, found all around the Arctic from Canada to Russia, where in places such as Svalbard they have to cope with three months of almost complete darkness, and temperatures down to minus 45°C.

In the UK ptarmigan are confined to the Highlands of Scotland. They're the only British bird to turn white in winter, and one of only three creatures to do so (the others being the mountain hare and stoat).

Unlike most other mountain birds, which head down to lower altitudes for the autumn and winter, ptarmigan stay put in all but the harshest conditions, surviving on plants such as heather and bilberry. To help them withstand the extreme cold, they have feathers covering their nostrils, toes and the soles of

their feet to minimize heat loss. They also use their strong feet to dig for leaves and twigs under the snow, and excavate snow bunkers where they can take shelter from strong winds. Being more or less pure white, apart from a black tail, they're also well camouflaged from predators such as patrolling eagles.

In summer, ptarmigan moult most of their white feathers and turn brownish, to blend in with the vegetation; then in autumn they moult again, becoming as grey as the boulders among which they feed. You can still locate them, though, from the croaking calls the males use to charm their hidden mates.

SANDERLING

*

Twinkling along the tideline, so fast that their legs become a blur, sanderlings can be the highlight of a winter walk along a windy beach. These shoreline sprinters are tiny waders – even smaller than a starling – and are pure white below and silvery grey above, with a dark shoulder patch and beady black eyes.

But it's the sanderling's sheer turn of speed that captures our attention, dodging the incoming waves before chasing after the waters as they retreat, frantically probing the sand for morsels of food.

In winter, when conserving energy is important, this dashing about looks like wasted effort, but sanderlings do have a strategy. By searching the freshly disturbed sand and shingle, they increase their chances of catching small invertebrates, which come up to the surface to cash in on food delivered by each breaking wave.

Sanderlings may look rather cute (they are often compared to a child's clockwork toy) but they are tough little birds. The ones we see in winter have often bred in Siberia, though the species breeds virtually around the globe, on tundra mostly within the boundaries of the Arctic Circle.

On their breeding grounds, sanderlings lose their whitish winter plumage and turn rich chestnut mottled with black on their back, wings, head and upper breast, remaining white on their lower belly. They rear their young on stony areas near water where there's a rich supply of insects, especially flies and their larvae.

You can occasionally see this fly-catching behaviour from sanderlings that have flown south to our beaches in late summer, when some of them may retain a vestige of their brighter summer plumage before moulting into their ghostly winter garb.

SNOW BUNTING

*

Trudge along a deserted beach in the teeth of a howling winter gale, and you might – if you're lucky – send up a flurry of 'snowflakes', or as they are properly known, snow buntings. On the ground these tiny seed-eaters look like just another flock of little brown birds. But as they take to the air they explode into a blizzard of white, calling softly as they swirl around the winter strandline.

Snow buntings are mainly winter visitors to Britain, often joining up with other buntings and finches in mixed flocks on saltmarshes and beaches on our northern and eastern coasts. But far to the north, in the Scottish Highlands, they can also be found during the spring and summer. Fewer than a hundred pairs of this tough little bird breed here, among the corries and boulders of the Cairngorm plateau, well over 1,000

metres above sea level. The ornithologist and author Desmond Nethersole-Thompson, who studied them in this harsh environment, described the snow bunting as 'possibly the most romantic and elusive bird in the British Isles and certainly the hardiest small bird in the world'.

Here, the snow bunting's sweet, melodic song may have a backing track of belching ptarmigan or a grunting reindeer. Yet these Scottish mountaintops are about as far south as this species ever nests. For these are truly Arctic birds, breeding well above the Arctic Circle in Alaska, Siberia and Svalbard. Across much of their range, snow buntings nest not in high mountains but down at sea level: step off the plane at Iceland's Reykjavik Airport and you'll even hear them singing in the car park.

During the breeding season the males are white with contrasting black wing-tips. But in autumn and winter they lose this pied livery and become browner, more like the females. Some snow buntings do stay put on the Cairngorms over the winter, hanging around the restaurant at the top of the ski-lifts in the hope of grabbing a few crumbs from passing skiers, hikers and climbers to supplement their usual diet of seeds.

PURPLE SANDPIPER

*

Some birds are extroverts, either using their brightly coloured plumage or loud calls to draw our attention. Others are more modest, keeping themselves to themselves. Despite its colourful name, the purple sandpiper firmly belongs in the latter camp.

Purple sandpipers make their home on the very edges of land and sea, where waves break constantly over seaweed-covered rocks. Their name makes them sound more exotic than they really are: it refers to a purplish sheen on their back and breast feathers, which you can generally only make out in very good light or when the birds are moulting into breeding plumage. But purple sandpipers are almost exclusively autumn and winter visitors to Britain, so the usual impression we get is of a rather dumpy, greyish-brown wader with short legs.

The purple sandpiper's drab plumage makes complete sense when you see them in their winter home, as it enables them to camouflage themselves perfectly against the dark, slippery rocks. They are easy to overlook, mainly because being quiet and confiding they will often let you approach quite close before shuffling off. The best way to find them is to scan through a flock of the more colourful and active turnstones, with which they often associate.

When you do finally get a close look at a purple sandpiper, it's the subtle features, such as the yellow base to the bill and white smudge near the eye, that stand out. They also have a pale belly and yellowish legs.

As you'd expect for a bird that feeds on rocks, purple sandpipers are less common in the south-east of Britain, though they will also forage around harbour walls and breakwaters. Very rarely they turn up inland on migration, but don't stay around for long.

Our wintering purple sandpipers come from much further north in Scandinavia or even Canada, but this subtle and unassuming wader is also one of our rarest regular breeding birds. Since 1978 a tiny population, usually ranging between one and five pairs a year, has nested on the high tops of Scottish mountains, in remote, almost inaccessible sites more than 1,000 metres above sea level.

LESSER REDPOLL

*

On a winter's afternoon, a gently flowing stream is lined with leafless alder trees, crowded with a bumper crop of brittle cones. In the topmost branches, a small flock of birds is feeding industriously, hanging like tiny acrobatic parrots among the slender twigs. When something panics them, they dash away in a tight flock making a chorus of jingling calls, like the rattling of loose change. This is our smallest finch: the lesser redpoll.

Once known as the 'red-headed linnet', redpolls are superficially like their larger and more widespread cousin. In size and shape, they also resemble siskins, which they often accompany on foraging journeys through riverside alders.

Getting a closer look at these canopy-dwelling birds can give you an aching neck, but it's well worth it. They are mainly streaky brown, but sport a neat black bib and the crimson patch on the forehead from which they get their name. Males often have a rosy pink flush across their chests, adding to their charm. They are lively, active little birds, which will sometimes allow you to get fairly close, then explode into flight en masse for no apparent reason, heading off elsewhere to feed.

Various varieties of redpolls can be found across the northern latitudes of the globe, but deciding how many different species they comprise is a tricky task for ornithologists. Those found in the UK, and also along a narrow strip from the Channel coast of France to Norway, are the smallest and brownest of all. They are now known as 'lesser redpoll' to distinguish them from the confusingly named common (or mealy) redpoll, which is a scarce winter visitor to Britain, paler in appearance and a mite larger.

Further north, on the tundra at the edge of the tree line, larger, frosty-white birds called Arctic redpolls brave the snow and ice. These tough little birds also occasionally turn up here in winter, usually in mixed flocks of lesser and common redpolls.

Our own lesser redpolls breed in small numbers throughout Britain, with their strongholds in Wales, the Scottish Borders, East Anglia and Kent. They prefer birch woods or young conifer plantations, especially on the edges of moorlands and heaths.

Back in the 1960s they enjoyed a population boom, especially in southern England, where birds regularly performed their display flights over suburban gardens. Since then, however, numbers have fallen, possibly as a result of the decline of birch trees in our woodlands, and the gradual replacement of conifers with broad-leaved varieties – beneficial to most species, but not, it seems, to the redpoll.

DIPPER

*

On a cold December day, when few birds are singing, the bright, rambling song of a dipper is always a pleasure. The sound is louder than you might expect from such a diminutive bird; it has to be, for dippers spend their lives alongside rushing water, and must compete to be heard.

Dippers sing in winter because they are early breeders, so the males begin marking out their particular stretch of water even before the start of the New Year. The male perches on a water-splashed stone or tree-root to deliver his song, which has all the volume and energy of a wren on steroids – strangely appropriate, as that is exactly what a dipper looks like.

Seen from behind as it bobs up and down on a rock, the dipper's blackish-brown plumage and cocked, stubby tail does indeed remind you of a giant wren. When it turns round, though, the flash of white from the bib, and chestnut belly beneath, leave no doubt as to its identity.

No other perching bird in our islands is as well adapted to an aquatic lifestyle as the dipper. They breed along fast-flowing, well-oxygenated streams and rivers, mainly in the north and west of the UK. Here you'll see them perched on stones in mid-current, their portly shapes bobbing nervously up and down as if on hinges. And you're bound to hear their sharp, metallic call: a high-pitched sound that, like the dipper's song, can easily be heard above the sound of the babbling water.

Dippers feed on aquatic invertebrates and to find these they need to tackle the torrents head-on and dive in; no mean feat for a buoyant creature not much bigger than a sparrow. The dipper uses its wings to propel itself down to the stream bed, and then walks along the bottom by gripping stones with its claws, while searching for insect larvae and freshwater shrimps. To rise to the surface again, it simply lets go and floats upwards. In spring, the catch is carried off to its hungry brood of youngsters, huddled together in a football-sized nest either tucked under a bridge, or hidden among tree-roots.

ROBIN

*

'Robin on a leafless bough, Lord in Heaven, how he sings!' The poet W.H. Davies is one of many writers to celebrate the robin's winter song. But at this time of year, real live robins are considerably outnumbered by their image on millions of Christmas cards.

The robin redbreast, as this dapper little bird is often known, is probably our most recognizable small bird and has always featured strongly in British folk-lore. It was the cock robin that was reputedly slain by a sparrow's arrow, and robins are said to have covered the babes in the wood with leaves. But it's during the festive season that our national bird really takes centre stage.

Christmas cards became popular around 1860 and robins featured from the beginning, carrying letters in their beaks or lifting doorknockers. They were often referred to as the little postmen, because until that time postmen wore red coats and were nicknamed redbreasts or robins, so the association between the familiar winter bird and the person who brought Christmas greetings was irresistible.

Even when postmen's uniforms changed to navy blue with red trimmings, we continued to associate robins with Christmas. This may also be because robins are famously tame, and in harsh winter weather often come to our doorsteps in search of food. For this reason, and its endearing appearance, we consistently choose the robin as the nation's favourite bird, disregarding its frankly violent behaviour.

Robins may look cute, but they are notably feisty and defend their territories vigorously, attacking any intruders in a flurry of wings and claws. At times, they will even fight to the death – yet we stubbornly ignore this, preferring a more positive, homely image.

Another reason we love robins is because of their song; and in particular, their unusual habit of singing all year round. Like all songbirds, robins sing in spring when the males need to attract a mate and repel their rivals. But robins sing in autumn and winter too: a welcome soundtrack to the shortening days, gathering mists and ripening fruit.

The robin's autumnal song has an ethereal, wistful quality: starting loudly with a series of rippling notes, but then fading into wisps of sound, which seem to evaporate on the misty air. Again, we cannot help but ascribe our own feelings to this purely biological process. So while the robin's song may sound melan-choly to us, in keeping with the season, for the bird itself it has one simple purpose: to defend the territories that male and female robins establish once they've moulted. This is unusual behaviour for a British bird, because few of our perching birds hold territories outside the breeding season, and only in the case of the robin does the female regularly sing.

In his classic study *The Life of the Robin*, first published in 1943, ornithologist David Lack described the 'woodlands, parks and hedgerows of England parcelled out into a series of smallholdings' – each representing the territory of a robin. Maybe that is another reason we like them so much: they remind us of ourselves.

RED KITE

*

On a cold, winter's evening, as dusk approaches, dark wraiths circle over the woods, squealing in the gathering gloom: the red kites are coming to roost. These rangy, elegant birds float effortlessly in the sky, tilting their wings towards the fading sunset to reveal flashes of russet and gold, before dropping rapidly out of view.

Once – and not all that long ago – to witness this sight you would have had to trek to the remote, wooded valleys of central Wales, where the last few pairs of this graceful raptor were just clinging on. Centuries of persecution as 'vermin', encouraged by the offer of a bounty on the birds' heads, followed by an onslaught by gamekeepers and egg-collectors, had virtually wiped out red kites as a British breeding bird. In the first few decades of the twentieth century, numbers may have dipped to as low as four birds – with only one breeding female. The future of the red kite on these islands looked bleak.

But somehow, thanks to a dedicated coalition of local people and conservationists, who guarded the few remaining nests, the red kite avoided the fate of the sea eagle and osprey, two other raptors that were driven away from our islands by persecution. Gradually, during the second half of the twentieth century, the kite population began to grow; but it remained confined to a small area of Welsh woodlands, a fraction of its former range.

To speed the recovery of the species, in the late 1980s a bold and far-sighted decision was taken to restore the kites to suitable habitat in parts of England and Scotland, beginning with the Chiltern Hills to the north-west of London. This scheme was not without its opponents: some conservationists objected to the plan on the grounds that it was somehow 'interfering with nature'.

But when the reintroduction went ahead, using young kites from Sweden and Spain, the birds soon proved the doubters wrong, their numbers increasing quickly and rapidly extending their range. Today, just a quarter of a century since those first birds were released, and following further reintroductions in the East Midlands, north-east England, Scotland and Northern Ireland, red kites are now well established in many places in Britain. The best-known site remains the Chilterns: notably over the M40 motorway between London and Oxford, where large flocks of up to a hundred kites soaring in the air are a regular spectacle.

Ironically, now that red kites are reasonably widespread, for some people they have lost their former allure. It's as if we only value rarity; once a bird becomes common again we somehow no longer consider it special.

Yet once kites were an all too familiar sight: in Tudor times they were the street-cleaners of our towns and cities, snatching anything remotely edible from the gutters and streets. And not just edible: kites also gained a reputation for stealing garments and underclothes to decorate their nests, hence the line from Shakespeare's *The Winter's Tale*, warning 'When the kite builds, look to lesser linen . . .' More recently, kites appear to have broadened their kleptomaniacal tastes: teddy bears, odd shoes and even a toy giraffe have been found in nests alongside growing chicks.

The red kite has always been a shapeshifter – from urban street-cleaner to Public Enemy Number One, simply because it had talons and a hooked beak. Once its numbers had declined it was transformed into a target for egg-collectors, then became a tourist icon,

and was finally hailed as the epitome of conservation success. In the future, as numbers boom and the kite becomes more and more taken for granted, that success may begin to tread the tightrope of public opinion once again.

But when we stand and watch tens – sometimes hundreds – of kites floating over their woodland roosts on a winter's evening, we should all remember what we might have lost for ever, and give thanks to those whose vision and hard work brought the red kite back.

KNOT

*

Looking out over an estuary in the middle of winter, it's hard to imagine quite how much life is out there, just out of view. But what may seem a bleak expanse of mud offers a vital lifeline to tens of thousands of wading birds. During the brief 'golden hour' or so either side of low tide, they will spread out across the mudflats to feed, pecking frantically to grab as many molluscs, worms and crustaceans as they can, before the waters start to advance once more.

As they do so, you become aware of little gatherings of birds in the far distance. First a few dozen, then a few hundred, then thousands of knots are massing together, as every minute the tide forces more and more birds off the disappearing mud and into the air.

Gradually, as the waters return, the number of birds in these flocks becomes simply uncountable as they sweep across the sky in perfect unison, each desperate

not to fall victim to a passing merlin or peregrine. From a distance these vast flocks look like smoke as they alternately flash dark and light grey, making us wonder how they avoid colliding with one another in these breathtaking aerial manoeuvres.

Finally, just as the waters wash over the last fragment of mud, the knots head for the shoreline, settling in dense flocks on shingle banks or beaches, packing themselves in so tightly that not an inch of ground is visible.

As they come in to land they call: a flurry of low-pitched, grunting monosyllables, rather like 'knut' – the sound that gave the species its English name. The knot's scientific name, *Calidris canutus*, is said to be in tribute to the eleventh-century King Canute, who famously demonstrated, despite his best attempts, that even his royal power was not enough to hold back the tides. Other sources claim that the name has gastronomic origins: because Canute regarded knots – fattened up on bread and milk – as a delicacy.

A knot is about the length of a blackbird, though plumper and heavier. In winter it's nothing to write home about: a humdrum wader with shortish legs and bill, grey on top and white beneath. But in spring and summer there comes a marvellous transformation into a rich, chestnut plumage: hence the official name of the species, red knot. But this striking plumage is only seen here on late spring lingerers or passage birds, as they head north to their breeding grounds in the high Arctic.

The world population of knots is estimated to be more than a million birds, and the species is one of the great global wanderers, found on the coasts of six of the world's seven continents. But their apparent abundance may be misleading: almost all knots breed inside the Arctic Circle – the region most likely to be affected by climate change. Already the fragile polar ecosystems are undergoing rapid shifts: and if the tundra proves unsuitable, the world population of knots could plummet, making it one of the first casualties of global warming.

STARLING

*

Once, not all that long ago, a very special phenomenon would take place on winter evenings in our cities, towns and countryside. Gatherings of starlings, known as 'murmurations', would assemble at regular sites: from Victorian railway stations to city squares, and rural woodlands to seaside piers.

As they came together in the growing gloom, jostling one another to find the best place to roost for the night, they chattered like gossiping grannies, before finally falling asleep. These vast flocks swirled so densely over some urban roosts that their calls drowned out the rumble of traffic from the streets below.

But gradually, during the final decades of the twentieth century, these gatherings began to dwindle, and then disappear altogether. Many urban roosts were actively discouraged because of the mess the birds made and this, coupled with a sharp decline in starling populations right across Europe, means that today only a handful of winter roosts remain. Yet those that do continue to provide one of the most keenly sought of all nature's spectacles.

This is odd, really, because starlings are not generally one of our favourite birds. We should perhaps find them more attractive, with their glossy plumage gleaming with green and purple highlights in summer and dotted with white in winter. But they are often seen as 'bird-table bullies', who mass in unruly groups to push off the smaller birds, like sixth-formers asserting their authority in the school playground. But just as we regard the humble house sparrow with more respect now that it is in sharp decline, so the increasing scarcity of starling roosts has lent them the special aura they once lacked.

Many of these starlings are not really British at all, but have travelled from as far away as Russia to be here for the winter. These immigrants from the east swell our dwindling resident populations, which have declined by 70 per cent in the last few decades, for reasons not fully understood, but which include the loss of the pastures where they feed. So the midwinter murmurations are a sight to cheer us all at this, the darkest time of the year.

The reasons why starlings roost in such vast numbers are complex. On the surface, it looks like a good way to avoid predators, and there is no doubt that while a lone starling can easily be pinpointed by a passing peregrine or sparrowhawk, a twisting and turning flock of several thousand make it very hard for the predator to single out just one bird to attack. Roosting together – especially in a vast reedbed – also safeguards starlings from terrestrial predators such as foxes, and may also help keep the birds warm on cold winter nights.

But this does not fully explain why so many should gather in one place – some travelling from as far as thirty kilometres away – when they could surely roost in smaller groups closer to where they feed. One theory is that by congregating together in this way the weaker birds can associate with the stronger ones, and when they leave the roost the next morning can follow them to better areas to find food.

Whatever the reasons for these incredible gatherings, they certainly provide a draw for the increasing crowds of people who travel from far and wide to sites such as the Somerset Levels, where Britain's largest roost of at least 1 million birds assembles from November through to March. Brighton seafront and the pier at Aberystwyth in west Wales also attract birders and curious passers-by alike.

These 'starling tourists' are a modern-day phenomenon, gathering as punctually as the birds to witness the starlings' aerial displays during the hour or so before the birds finally go to roost. If they are lucky, these crowds enjoy the spectacle of huge flocks morphing into ever changing shapes, ranging from balloons to giant amoebas.

The displays can continue almost until the very last glimmer of light fades, at which point the birds respond to some unseen signal, suddenly spilling downwards like sand running through an egg-timer, and disappearing from view. Only then, when the starlings have landed, does the twittering begin: a low murmur, which gradually fades away as darkness falls.

SONG THRUSH

*

I leant upon a coppice gate
When frost was spectre-grey.
And winter's dregs made desolate,
The weakening eye of day . . .
At once a voice arose among
The bleak twigs overhead
In a full-hearted evensong
Of joy illimited.

Thomas Hardy's poem, 'The Darkling Thrush', in which he reflects on the closing hours of the tumultuous nineteenth century, and the uncertainties of the next, embodies the hope that birdsong can bring even at the bleakest time of the year.

But which thrush was it that Hardy was listening to? Conventional wisdom suggests that his 'darkling thrush' is the mistle thrush – the largest member of its family in Britain – that often sings from treetops in winter gales, earning its folk-name of 'stormcock'. Yet Hardy describes this particular bird as 'An aged thrush, frail, gaunt, and small', adjectives not normally applied to the large and robust mistle thrush.

Song thrushes are certainly smaller, but how regularly do they sing in winter? Between 1991 and 2001, the ornithologist David Snow kept records of singing song thrushes in his home village in Buckinghamshire. This species can be hard to census, and he wanted to find out how many birds held territories throughout the winter and how this might relate to breeding locations in spring.

What he discovered was that some song thrushes do sing all the way from late October through to the following spring, but that the number of singing birds varied from year to year and depended to some extent on the temperature; during severe cold spells, the thrushes fell silent. This picture is likely to be mirrored in other areas of the UK, but wherever you live, it's always a pleasure to hear a thrush in the depths of winter.

Another poet, Robert Browning, also wrote about the song thrush in 'Home Thoughts, From Abroad', composed more than half a century before Hardy's verse, in April 1845:

That's the wise thrush; he sings each song twice over,
Lest you should think he never could recapture
That first fine careless rapture!

Browning perfectly captured the distinctive nature of this bird's song, especially the habit of repeating each phrase two or three times before moving on to the next. Despite the repetition, this is far from tedious, for the male song thrush boasts a repertoire of more than one hundred different phrases, enabling him to vary his song continually. This is just as well, for during the course of a single breeding season he may sing more than a million phrases in all.

Tawny Owl

Raven

Magpie

Crossbill

Mistle Thrush

Great Tit

Rose-ringed Parakeet

Collared Dove

Bewick's Swan

Great White Egret

Greylag Goose

Black-necked Grebe

JANUARY

Glossy Ibis

Mandarin Duck

Lesser White-fronted Goose

Coot

Moorhen

Merlin

Shoveler

Blue Tit

Grey Wagtail

Hen Harrier

Great Northern Diver

INTRODUCTION

THE YEAR HAS TURNED and even though gloves, scarves and waterproofs are the rule, there's a hint of spring lurking among the lengthening days: you only have to listen to the growing chorus of birdsong and look for the leaves of wild arum beginning to unroll in hedgerows and waysides. If the weather's mild, great tits, song thrushes, robins, wrens and dunnocks are tuning up and there may be a chance of an early blackbird song. It doesn't even have to be mild to encourage mistle thrushes and you'll often hear their wild treetop songs, borne aloft by the gusts of a January gale.

For these birds, the real business of breeding remains many weeks away. But for some, it is imminent. Even in the north of Scotland, where snow is bending the resinous twigs of Scots pines, crossbills are beginning to nest; in fact some may lay eggs in January. Their natural cycle is dependent on the pine-cone crop and if the food is available they will nest at any time of year, in any part of the British Isles where there are conifers.

Ravens too are beginning to gather on sea-cliffs, crags and at the tops of trees; you'll see them twisting and rolling in pairs while the bleak, wintry landscape echoes with their gruff croaks. In our gardens, male collared doves intone amorously: and their mates could already be sitting on eggs in the shelter of a nearby fir tree. The night is also alive with sound: duetting tawny owls establish territories throughout late autumn and winter and the quavering hoots of the male, countered by the 'kee-wick' of the female, are best listened out for on still nights.

For many birders, January is the time to make plans for the coming year. Some birders start as they mean to go on, by trying to see as many species as they can on New Year's Day. Others are more altruistic, taking part in a regular survey for the British Trust for Ornithology (BTO). Whether the subject is wild-fowl or winter thrushes, this is an excellent time to learn the ropes before those confusing migrants arrive.

When snow and ice cover the Continent, our wetlands are a refuge for flocks of fleeing wildfowl, including Bewick's swans, pink-footed and white-fronted geese and a host of ducks, among them packs of wigeon, shovelers and elegant pintail, and diving ducks such as goosander and goldeneye. Even unpromising waters such as large, concrete-sided reservoirs are worth scanning for the stately battleship shape of a great northern diver. It's not concerned by the aesthetics, or lack of them: all it needs is open water and fish.

If you're near a saltmarsh or coastal reedbed, then it's worth braving the cold to see roosting birds of prey, harriers in particular. To watch marsh and hen harriers arrive at their evening gatherings is one of the great spectacles of winter. With slow flaps of their long, fingered wings, the harriers quarter the grasses, tilting and wheeling as the light fades. As they drop, other blunt-winged shapes row through the approaching gloom – short-eared owls swapping shifts with the harriers to start their night's hunting.

Dusking – staying out in the field until the very last dregs of daylight seep away – has other rewards. In the south-east, squadrons of slim, long-tailed parakeets fly over suburban housing estates to their treetop roosts. By day, these improbable aliens still manage to shock us with their emerald brilliance and raucous screeches among the bare branches of London parks.

Other birds also surprise us in midwinter, often in unexpected places. When the weather is coldest, visit your local sewage farm and scan the filtration pans. Warmer than the surrounding countryside, they are hotbeds of insect activity and a good place to see pied and grey wagtails, meadow pipits and goldcrests. In the milder south and west, you might find delicate chiffchaffs, some of which take their chances in our unpredictable winters and choose not to migrate. It's a risk for these frail insectivorous warblers, but often seems to pay off.

A scarce January jewel, which haunts sewage works, leafy cemeteries and a few gardens, is the firecrest. This scrap of feathers with a flame stripe on its crown, moss-green mantle and black and white striped face is one of the most beautiful of all our birds and often seems to disregard watchers as it searches the leaves of holly and ivy for food. On the darkest winter days, it's always a delight to find.

TAWNY OWL

*

The long winter nights are usually quiet, but as the New Year begins some nocturnal species have already begun to stake out their territories. Male and female tawny owls do so by performing a duet; together they create one of the best known of all British wildlife sounds.

Shakespeare, who knew his birds pretty well, apparently did not realize that not one, but two birds are involved in these utterances. In one of his earliest plays, *Love's Labour's Lost*, he wrote:

> *Then nightly sings the staring owl,*
> *Tu-whit, tu-whoo, a merry note . . .*

But what we are hearing is not a single call, but the male's long, quavering hoot followed by the female's sharp response. This tells any listening owls – both male and female – that this territory is well and truly occupied by a breeding pair.

The reason this is important – and the reason why tawny owls start defending their territories so long before they actually breed – is that they are one of Britain's most sedentary birds, rarely moving more than a kilometre or so from their birthplace. By late autumn, the grown youngsters from the previous year's brood are now fully mature, and begin to muscle in on their parents' territory. By calling incessantly through the long winter nights the incumbent pair are establishing their right to remain there.

Tawny owls are the commonest member of their family in Britain, with about 50,000 breeding pairs, in woodlands from Caithness in the north to Cornwall in the south. However, like several other sedentary species, they don't breed in Ireland, being unwilling to fly across large stretches of open sea.

They're also our most urban owl, often living close to the centre of towns and cities, so long as there are hollow trees or old buildings in which they can nest. Tawny owls are strictly nocturnal and often the only sign they're about is when you hear their night-time calls.

There are other clues, though: small birds often betray the presence of tawnies by mobbing them, so if you hear song thrushes, blackbirds and other species calling persistently near dense stands of evergreens, or among the foliage of a mature broadleaved tree, there's a good chance that a tawny owl is roosting there. Sometimes the persistence of the mobbing birds pays off and you'll see a large, round-winged, rufous bird coast silently through the canopy in search of peace and quiet. Although tawny owls will sometimes eat birds, they feed mainly on small mammals, as well as frogs, earthworms and large insects: even fish remains have turned up in some owl-pellets.

Tawny owls are early breeders, so later on in April or May it's worth looking out for a bunch of what look like off-white feather dusters perched on a branch. These are baby owls, still wearing their first downy plumage, indulging in a spot of 'branching' – emerging from the safety and darkness of their nesting-hole for the very first time. At dusk they call loudly for food, sounding like adult tawnies with a severe case of laryngitis.

RAVEN

*

A sound like a grunting pig – so deep in tone that you cannot imagine it being made by any species of bird – resonates in the skies above. You look up, and a huge, black bird with long, fingered wings and a wedge-shaped tail is flying overhead. It looks superficially like a crow, but something about its menacing cruciform shape, combined with that extraordinary call, tells you it is indeed something different: a raven.

Not so long ago, to hear the raven's sonorous croaks you would have needed to visit the remote uplands of Scotland, Wales or northern England, or the desolate landscapes of Dartmoor or Exmoor in the south-west. But now this haunting sound echoes throughout lowland Britain: as far south and east as the White Cliffs of Dover, where ravens are now nesting again after a long absence.

We may think of ravens as upland birds – hence the prevalence of the bird's name in places such as Ravenscraig or Ravenscar, meaning 'raven's rock' – but their original range extended right across Britain, including the medieval cities where they joined kites as street scavengers. However, from the Middle Ages onwards, ravens were ruthlessly persecuted, and in common with other large scavenging or predatory birds were driven back north and west to the wildest and least populated parts of our islands.

As persecution has lessened, the raven is reclaiming its long-lost realm and is now probably more widespread than at any time in the past couple of centuries. It's now even turning up on the outskirts of the capital, where since Victorian times, when the last wild birds were seen there, the only ravens have been the captive birds at the Tower of London.

Ravens are the largest perching birds in the world, even larger and heavier than a buzzard and much longer-winged and bigger-billed than any of our other crows. Globally they're one of the most widely distributed birds, equally at home in Arctic tundra or scorching desert. They also have an extraordinary vocabulary, which includes pig-like grunts, quacking calls and musical, bell-like notes.

Like other members of the crow family, ravens are highly intelligent, and have been observed indulging in what can only be termed 'play'. Birds have been watched rolling down snowy slopes on their backs with their feet in the air, over and over again, apparently for no other reason than to have fun. In flight they are fond of acrobatics, which include a version of the canoeist's half-roll, in which they fold in their wings and tilt their bodies upwards, before returning to their usual flight-pattern.

The size and impressive appearance of ravens has cemented them firmly in legend. The Norse god Odin kept a pair of ravens called Hugin (thought) and Munin (memory), which patrolled his realm, reporting daily on what they'd seen. Celtic lore associates ravens with battlefields: these carrion-feeders with their dark satanic bills would often be the first birds to arrive at the scene of carnage following a pitched battle. That's worth remembering as you struggle up a mountain path or stroll along a sea-cliff: be aware that the ravens soaring overhead have more than a passing interest in where you place your next footstep.

MAGPIE

*

Some birds, such as the robin and blue tit, are always welcome visitors. Others are not. Top of the list of 'garden villains' is, without doubt, the magpie, because of its habit of feeding on the eggs and chicks of other garden birds. Yet this dashing member of the crow family is not as black as it has been painted. Take a closer look and you'll begin to see why: that apparently pied plumage isn't just black and white, but gleams with iridescent greens, blues and purples, changing from moment to moment depending on the direction of the light.

Magpies have always had a rascally, streetwise image. They featured as opportunistic sneak thieves in anti-theft public information campaigns on television in the 1980s, though long before this the nineteenth-century Italian composer Rossini celebrated their kleptomaniac tendencies in his opera *The Thieving Magpie*. More recently, in Philip Pullman's *His Dark Materials* trilogy, the author named his metropolis of soul-stealing spectres Cittagazze: 'city of the magpies'.

Yet despite these sinister connections, our relationship with magpies has also been one of joy and celebration. Even now, at the start of the twenty-first century, many of us still salute a lone magpie, or recite the verse 'One for sorrow, two for joy, three for a girl, four for a boy' as we pass the bird. For those of a certain generation, those lines also evoke the opening titles of the 1970s children's TV series *Magpie*, ITV's hip alternative to the BBC's *Blue Peter*.

Saluting magpies is often hard work nowadays, for this species is undoubtedly becoming much more numerous than in the past. This is partly down to reduced persecution, but also because magpies are scavenging on the increasing amount of roadkill and cashing in on the waste food casually discarded on our streets. As a result, roosts of over a hundred birds – chattering away like rapid-fire machine guns – are becoming far more common.

As well as their habit of robbing the nests of other birds, and their ability to scavenge, magpies also feed on invertebrates, especially beetles. An early name for the species was 'maggot-pie', which some assume was a reference to their delight in probing carrion for maggots, but others say derives from the French *margot-pie*, an affectionate nickname for this fascinating bird, along the same lines as 'Jenny wren', 'Tom tit' and 'Robin redbreast'.

CROSSBILL

*

In the year 1251 a monk named Matthew Paris looked out of the window of his monastery at St Albans in Hertfordshire, and was astonished. Flocks of birds were plundering the fruit of the monks' apple orchard; but as Paris noted, these were nothing like any species he had ever observed before: 'In the course of this year . . . there appeared . . . some remarkable birds which had never before been seen in England, somewhat larger than larks . . . The beaks of these birds were crossed . . .'

These marauding invaders were of course crossbills: one of the most extraordinary and distinctive of all British birds, thanks to their uniquely shaped bills, in which the top mandible crosses over the bottom one.

Later, when the species became better known, the myth arose that the bird's mandibles had become twisted when they tried to remove the nails from Jesus's limbs at his crucifixion. In the process, the male crossbill was supposedly stained by Christ's blood; hence his brilliant, brick-red plumage.

The truth is more prosaic, though no less fascinating. Crossbills feed on the seeds of conifers such as Scots pine and larch. To break into the cones, they have evolved this specialized bill, whose crossed tips enable them to prise the cones apart to get at the paper-thin seeds within.

Because conifer seeds are available all year round, but are not always predictable as the crop sometimes fails, crossbills have evolved a complex, nomadic lifestyle. They nest earlier than any other British songbird, often starting in January, when incubating females may even have snow on their backs.

Once the chicks have safely fledged, they stay with their parents for several weeks afterwards. By midsummer these flocks may find that the food available in the area where they bred is running short, at which point they turn into nomads, wandering far and wide in order to find new places to feed. These seasonal movements, known as 'irruptions', sometimes involve many thousands of birds, and are what our thirteenth-century monk observed in his apple orchard.

Crossbills can be shy birds and feed high in the conifer canopy, where they can be very hard to detect, especially if they're not calling. Sometimes you can locate them by looking for a gentle rain of twirling pine seeds as these drop to the forest floor. But it's their call that usually gives them away: a loud, percussive 'clip, clip', which you'll often hear as a flock flies from one part of the forest to another.

If you do get a close look, they are strikingly beautiful: the males are brick red, the females olive green, and the young birds streaky and much greyer. Newly fledged youngsters can also be picked out by the shape of their bills, in which the distinctive crosses are only just beginning to develop.

Crossbills are very acrobatic, clambering along branches and hanging among the pine twigs like tiny parakeets, as they prise the seeds from their woody cones. This dry diet also gives us a better chance of seeing them, as crossbills often come to puddles and pools in the middle of woods to quench their thirst, dipping their bills into the water and then lifting their heads up so that the liquid flows down their throat.

MISTLE THRUSH

*

As a howling winter's gale sweeps across the open countryside, it's hard to imagine that any bird would choose to sing when it could be hunkered down, taking shelter from the wind. But one species is still belting out its wild, skirling song, to defy the worst of the weather. It is the mistle thrush, also known, appropriately, as the 'stormcock'.

Mistle thrushes are one of the earliest birds to begin singing in the New Year, long before spring has even hinted at its arrival. They perch on top of the tallest tree they can find, from where they deliver a performance that includes the rich, fruity tones of the blackbird, mixed with repeated phrases more reminiscent of the smaller song thrush.

There's a lot of confusion regarding our two resident thrushes, but the mistle thrush is easy to pick out by its much larger size and paler, more greyish plumage than the warm brown tones of the song thrush. Their flight appears rather laboured, as they progress with a series of short flaps followed by a slight dip on closed wings, giving the bird a bouncing motion. You'll often hear them call as they fly, with a loud rattle – rather like a comb being scraped across a piece of wood, or an old-fashioned football rattle. If you can see the white tips to their outer tail-feathers, that should clinch the identification.

For most of the year mistle thrushes are solitary or in pairs, but from midsummer into early autumn bands of them roam the countryside, feeding on open pastures, moors and playing fields. These are family groups, which have joined up with one another after breeding, but will separate before winter arrives.

In autumn, mistle thrushes live up to their name by jealously standing guard over clumps of mistletoe, a parasitic plant that lives in the tops of trees. A single thrush defends each ball of mistletoe and its sticky white berries against all comers, including other thrushes, using its beak, claws and bursts of those harsh, rattling calls. Occasionally, though, when a large flock of redwings or waxwings lands on a tree, the mistle thrush appears flummoxed by their mass arrival and has to admit defeat.

The males we hear singing in January hold large territories, with tall trees where they nest and areas of open grassland or parkland where they can search for worms and other invertebrates. They usually build their beautifully woven nest in the fork of a tree, but they will sometimes choose stranger places: one mistle thrush made its home in a set of traffic lights, right by a busy roundabout in the centre of Salford.

GREAT TIT

*

Cutting through the rumble of city traffic and the constant hum of the urban jungle comes one of our most familiar bird sounds: the 'tea-cher, tea-cher' song of the great tit. This metallic, rhythmic sound is instantly recognizable, and you can hear it in our towns, cities and countryside on mild winter days from mid-December onwards. It's the origin of the old country names 'saw sharpener' and 'carpenter bird', and has also been compared with a squeaky bicycle pump.

But great tits have more than one string to their bow, and that well-known song is only one of at least forty different vocalizations they make; each bird has a repertoire of up to eight different songs. No wonder that when even experienced birders hear a bird call or song they can't quite place, it often turns out to be just another great tit.

The explanation for this huge variety of songs is known as the 'Beau Geste Hypothesis', after P.C. Wren's 1924 novel about the French Foreign Legion. In the novel, the eponymous hero props up the bodies of dead soldiers around the walls of a besieged fort to suggest to the enemy that it is better defended than it really is. In a similar way, a great tit with a large repertoire may be able to persuade rival males that his territory is defended by more birds than just him, prompting them to seek their fortunes elsewhere.

The great tit's appearance matches its crisp, clear song: its black cap, yellow belly and white cheeks make it unmistakable. It is also very common, having been one of the most successful species in adapting to life alongside us, in our gardens. As birds that normally nest in holes in trees, they have readily taken to breeding in nestboxes and arrive at feeders almost as soon as we hang them up.

Now that they have become our neighbours, we can gain insights into their complex courtship behaviour: for example, male great tits will try to attract a passing female by peering out of the entrance of their nest-hole and moving their heads back and forth, flashing their white cheek-patches like a semaphore signal. If that doesn't work, they can always try singing . . .

ROSE-RINGED PARAKEET

*

Close your eyes, and nowadays London's Hyde Park can sound more like Mumbai or New Delhi than our capital city, thanks to the exotic screeches of rose-ringed parakeets. These long-tailed visions in emerald green, with a distinctive pink ring around the male's neck, came originally from Asia, where they are one of the commonest and most recognizable of all that continent's birds.

Rose-ringed (often called ring-necked) parakeets first began to establish themselves in the wild here in 1969, though there are reliable reports of odd birds from before this date, and at least one breeding record dates right back to Victorian times.

More than any other introduced British bird, their origins have been subject to extraordinary speculation. Some of the first flocks were seen around the suburb of Shepperton on the western outskirts of London, leading to rumours that they escaped from the set of *The African Queen*, which despite its apparently glamorous location was mainly filmed at Shepperton Studios. The main problem with this theory is that the Bogart and Bacall movie was made in 1951, making it hard to explain how these bright green birds somehow stayed hidden for almost two decades.

Another classic urban myth is that the doyen of 1960s rock guitarists, Jimi Hendrix, kept a pair of parakeets called Adam and Eve in his central London apartment, and (presumably in a drug-fuelled haze) released them into the wild to add 'psychedelic colour' to the capital. The date fits – 1969 – but once again there is no evidence that this event ever actually took place.

The more mundane, but undoubtedly more likely, explanation is that the parakeets – a common cagebird then as now – simply escaped or were released by the pet trade. Having arrived here, they did not starve or die of the cold, as many people expected of such a tropical-looking creature. These birds hail from the Himalayan foothills, where temperatures drop far lower than they do in the London suburbs; and in any case their arrival coincided with a huge rise in garden bird feeding. Being agile and acrobatic, the parakeets readily learned to cling on to peanut feeders, often driving away smaller birds with their colour and noise.

Since their arrival here, rose-ringed parakeets have divided opinion. In the 1970s one eminent ornithologist, Derrick England, put a strong case for eradicating them, in his words 'to stop the nonsense' of a parrot gaining acceptance to the official British List. But even if there ever were a window of opportunity to remove these birds, it has long gone: almost half a century after their arrival here they have spread to many parts of south-east England, with small pockets elsewhere, and the UK population is now close to 10,000 breeding pairs. They may not be universally popular, but many Londoners have now embraced them as part of our multicultural capital city, even though the flash of emerald among the bare branches of winter trees still feels slightly surreal.

COLLARED DOVE

*

It is hard to imagine Britain's suburban gardens without the monotonous call of the collared dove, which has been likened to a bored football fan trying rather unenthusiastically to encourage his team: 'U-NI-TED, UN-I-TED . . .' Yet at the end of the Second World War – well within living memory – this sandy-coloured dove with its distinctive black-on-white neck band was unknown in Britain, even as a rare vagrant.

As they crowd around the bird-table or drone from the rooftops, collared doves may seem rather unexciting, but their story is one of the most extraordinary of any British bird. The very first sighting here was of a single bird in Lincolnshire in 1952, the year that Queen Elizabeth succeeded to the throne; but the species was kept in captivity at the time, so this individual was widely considered to be an escapee. Then, in the spring of 1955, a pair of collared doves not only turned up in a garden on the north Norfolk coast, but actually bred.

The location was kept secret; which seems bizarre now that the bird's triple-noted cooing is so widely heard in Britain. Even so, news leaked out, and many birders made the pilgrimage to Norfolk to see them. They included a teenage Bill Oddie, who recalls peering avidly over the garden wall to catch sight of the breeding pair.

The following year, more birds arrived, and soon the trickle had turned into a flood. Within a decade collared doves had reached Wales and Ireland, and by the time of the first BTO *Atlas of Breeding Birds*, a national survey carried out between 1968 and 1972, they had spread throughout the country from Scilly to Shetland, even turning up on the remotest offshore islands.

Originally found mainly in villages, towns and suburbs – in Germany the species is known as the 'television dove' because of its habit of perching on rooftop aerials – during the 1970s the collared dove also spread to farmland, increasing tenfold during the decade. Today almost 1 million pairs breed in Britain.

The collared dove's arrival here wasn't entirely unexpected, because this bird, once restricted in Europe to the Balkans, had begun moving rapidly northwards and westwards during the 1930s. Its explosive colonization covered an estimated 2.5 million square kilometres in only forty years. Just what triggered the sudden change isn't known, but it may have been a genetic mutation, helped by the doves' ability to breed quickly and during every month of the year. Some will be sitting on nests somewhere in Britain, even in December and January.

The sound of collared doves often appears on TV soundtracks, as their cooing evokes a calm, rural scene. The only problem is when they are used on period dramas set in the eighteenth or nineteenth centuries, where their calls are as anachronistic as car horns or the ringing of telephones.

BEWICK'S SWAN

*

The musical honks of a skein of Bewick's swans as they emerge from a midwinter fog-bank and pitch in to graze on frosty pastures immediately summon up the spirit of wild places. These elegant birds, whose name commemorates the early nineteenth-century engraver Thomas Bewick, are also known as 'tundra swans'. They breed around pools in the mosquito-ridden flat-lands of Arctic Russia and fly south in autumn to avoid the ice that seals their Siberian home. Bewick's swans find a refuge from November to March on our com-paratively warm lakes and marshes, grazing on pastures and arable fields near open water.

Bewick's are the smallest of our three species of swan and superficially similar to their larger cousin the whooper swan. If on their own, so you can't compare size, the best way to tell which species you are looking at is by examining the bill pattern. Both whoopers and Bewick's swans have black and yellow bills, but on the Bewick's swan, the yellow area is noticeably smaller and doesn't extend below the nostrils.

The bill patterns of Bewick's swans are the key to a remarkable project. They vary a great deal between individual swans, leading to one of the most in-depth scientific studies ever undertaken of single birds within a species. Back in 1964, the ornithologist and conser-vationist Peter (later Sir Peter) Scott was watching the flock of Bewick's swans that visit the Wildfowl and Wetlands Trust HQ at Slimbridge in Gloucestershire with his daughter, Dafila. They noticed that each swan's bill pattern was unique, giving them the chance to monitor the life of each bird in a way that had never been done before, with any species.

Fifty years later, the continuing study has taught us a huge amount about the behaviour and ecology of this attractive waterbird. The swans travel in family parties that include the greyish cygnets. By identifying individuals, ornithologists can tell how long pairs stay together and measure their breeding success. Wild Bewick's swans that bred the previous summer in the remotest parts of the Siberian tundra are now gobbling grain under the Slimbridge floodlights just a few metres away – and it's an unforgettable encounter even for the experienced birder.

GREAT WHITE EGRET

*

A January evening on the Avalon Marshes in Somerset, where a large crowd of observers gathers to watch starlings perform their aerial dances before going to roost. As eager faces scan the sky, awaiting the star-lings' mass arrival, a large, white bird springs up from a hiding-place in the reedbed, and flies past on slowly flapping wings.

A birder spots it, and shouts out 'Great white!', causing momentary panic among the waiting crowd; until they realize, to their relief, that this is not a shark, but a great white egret, the most recent addition to the list of Britain's breeding birds.

The great white egret is Europe's tallest and most elegant heron, standing up to one metre high. Fifty years ago the nearest great whites to Britain were at Lake Neusiedl in Austria, and right up to the end of the last millennium this was only a rare visitor to our shores, with perhaps one or two records a year. But during the last decades of the twentieth century, great white egrets slowly began to move northwards and westwards, expanding their range into France and the Netherlands.

A few years ago, they began to turn up on the Somerset Levels, a newly created wetland habitat in south-west England. They liked what they saw and stayed, with up to half a dozen birds being seen at any one time. Eventually, in 2012, they bred at Shapwick Heath National Nature Reserve in Somerset, where two nests hidden deep in the reedbeds produced a total of five chicks, four of which fledged successfully. They bred again in 2013, and now this graceful waterbird seems set to become a permanent colonist.

Given good views, it is easy to tell great white egrets apart from their much smaller relative the little egret. They're pure white, with improbably long, serpentine necks and a slender bill, the colour of egg-yolk in winter and jet-black during the breeding season. In flight, especially from a distance, they can be mistaken for little egrets, but their longer legs trail well behind their tail, and their wingbeats are slower and much more ponderous.

The arrival of great white egrets in Britain is partly due to increased protection of wetlands and their birds, which enabled the species to make a comeback

following huge losses in the late nineteenth and early twentieth centuries as a result of the plumage trade, which used their feathers to adorn the hats of wealthy and fashionable women.

The creation of this vast reedbed habitat from a former industrial site – the land was dug for peat until a couple of decades ago – meant that when the birds did turn up in Britain there was already a suitable place for them to nest. This is a timely lesson for conservationists everywhere: if we create the right habitat, the birds will eventually find it. Now the future of the great white egret – and many other wetland species – depends entirely on how much space we will allow them in our crowded countryside.

GREYLAG GOOSE

*

On an East Anglian broad, a flotilla of geese dabbles among the pleasure boats, now moored for the winter. Hundreds of miles to the north, by a windswept Scottish loch, a gaggle of the same birds watch nervously as a white-tailed eagle looms overhead. These are the two very different worlds of the greylag goose.

Broadly speaking, most greylags breeding in northern and western Scotland are descendants of original wild birds, whereas the vast majority, if not all of those found in the rest of Britain, derive from deliberate reintroductions.

Many geese also arrive from Iceland to spend the winter here, so separating feral from native birds can be tricky. But identifying them as greylags is much easier. These are the biggest and bulkiest of our wild 'grey geese', and are easily recognized by their bright orange bills and pink legs. When they fly, you'll also see large pale grey panels on their wings and of course hear that familiar cackle.

The nasal calls of wild greylag geese might well remind you of domestic farmyard geese; and so they should, as they are one and the same bird. Greylag geese were first domesticated at least 3,000 years ago, originally in Egypt, making them one of the very first species of bird to be exploited in this way by human beings; only the chicken and duck have lived alongside us for longer.

Geese have been selectively bred for a range of products, including oil for lamps and feathers for arrows and bedding, as well as producing meat and eggs. Greylags domesticate easily, helped by the chicks' habit of 'imprinting' on the first living creature they see after they are born, including humans. This was first studied in depth by the Austrian biologist Konrad Lorenz, who became 'foster-mother' to many young geese. In his popular book *King Solomon's Ring* he describes the greylag goslings that followed him around his land and accepted him as their parent, 'with all the dignity characteristic of their kind'. Lorenz was one of the first scientists to study bird behaviour in the field, helping to create the science of ethology, and in 1973 – along with fellow pioneers Karl von Frisch and Niko Tinbergen – winning the Nobel Prize for his efforts.

BLACK-NECKED GREBE

*

A reservoir in the middle of winter may be thronged with birds, which thrive on these large areas of open water despite their apparently unwelcoming concrete surroundings. Among the flocks of noisy gulls, ducks and Canada geese, it's easy to miss a smaller bird, which frequently disappears under the surface as it dives for food. As it comes up again, its dusky plumage and bright red eye are unmistakable: a winter plumage black-necked grebe.

While little and great crested grebes are familiar, the sight of a black-necked grebe is always a pleasant surprise, because in winter they are very thinly distributed. To seek them out you'll need to visit one of their favourite wintering spots, which include harbours and shallow seas off the coast of Hampshire and Dorset. They also congregate at reservoirs on the western edge of London where watchers have to put up with the cacophony of jets passing overhead on their way to and from nearby Heathrow Airport.

At this time of year, black-necked grebes look like a slightly larger and darker version of the little grebe, with the same fluffy rear-end, but with a grey and white (rather than brown) plumage and eyes that shine like rubies. Black-necks are very similar to their close relative the Slavonian grebe, but have a duskier neck and a smaller, more upturned bill.

In the breeding season, though, black-necked grebes are transformed. The head and neck turn coal-black and they sprout golden ear-tufts – hence their North American name, 'eared grebe'. The combination of these features, together with their red eyes and chestnut flanks, makes them stunning birds, rendered all the more attractive by their capriciousness and elusiveness.

Although black-necked grebes turn up in winter and spring on a great variety of waters, they are very choosy about where they breed. Several pairs will nest on the same lake or pool, sometimes alongside colonies of screeching black-headed gulls, whose constant awareness and combative nature help protect the grebes from predators. Here, in relative safety, the black-necked grebes lay their eggs on floating nests of weed, and rear their tiny, stripy-headed chicks on a diet of aquatic invertebrates and small fish.

GLOSSY IBIS

*

Some waterbirds, such as egrets, have an air of elegance; others have a darker, more primitive appearance, reminding us that they descended from the dinosaurs. Its huge, downcurved bill puts the glossy ibis firmly in the latter camp.

Glossy ibises look superficially like curlews, though a closer look reveals a dark, green and bronze plumage, very different from the curlew's mottled brown. With their sleek feathers, which show highlights of chestnut and iridescent sheens of green, blue and purple, they look almost too exotic for Britain. They are rare in this country, but have increased dramatically in numbers in recent years.

The glossy ibis is by far the most widespread member of its family, and indeed one of the most cosmopolitan species in the world, breeding in the warmer regions of Asia, Africa, Australia, the Americas and southern and eastern Europe. If you visit the nearest breeding colonies, in the Camargue in southern France or the Danube Delta in Romania, you'll see these coppery-coloured birds on their stick-nests in trees by wide river channels.

Flocks of more than a dozen birds have arrived in the past few years, mainly in south-west England and Wales, often staying around for weeks or even months on end, and they can be quite approachable. Indeed one ibis remained in Kent and neighbouring counties for an incredible seventeen years from 1975 to 1992, occasionally disappearing for months on end before resurfacing again.

We have the habitat, and from time to time we have the birds, so it is surely only a matter of time before glossy ibises colonize Britain permanently, and become the latest in a long line of waterbirds, including little, cattle and great white egrets, to move northwards to breed here.

MANDARIN DUCK

*

An ornamental lake in Surrey's stockbroker belt, on an icy January day, is not the first place you'd expect to come across one of Britain's most colourful birds. But Virginia Water has long been known as a hotspot for the mandarin duck, whose dazzling beauty really must be seen to be believed.

Ginger whiskers, a blood-red bill, a broad creamy eyestripe and an iridescent purple chest are set off by a pair of extraordinary curved, orange wing-feathers, which stand up like a boat's sails. Females are various shades of greyish brown and beige, with delicate white spectacles. In their quiet way they are equally beautiful.

Despite their flamboyant appearance, mandarin ducks can weather the worst of our winters, surviving by grubbing for acorns, beechnuts and chestnuts in woodland. When disturbed, they rise almost vertically into the air and twist off through the filigree of overhead branches, making a series of oddly slurred whistles. They nest in hollow tree-trunks, and it's always surprising to watch the tiny ducklings tumbling out in late spring to join their parents on wooded pools and streams.

Mandarin ducks are a popular artistic motif in the Far East where, because they're often seen in pairs, they're a symbol of fidelity; in China, silk bed covers and pillows embroidered with mandarin ducks are traditionally given as wedding presents. Although they are protected right across their breeding range, which includes north-eastern Russia and northern Japan, their global numbers are still threatened by logging, industrialization and the drainage of their wetland homes.

Here in the UK, mandarin ducks are thriving, and although their secretive nature makes them hard to count properly, it is thought that there are more than 7,000 birds living in the wild. They were first brought here from China in the mid-eighteenth century, to a private collection in Richmond, Surrey. About a hundred years later, in 1866, a feral bird was shot on the River Thames in Berkshire, since when the number of birds living in the wild has been on the up, thanks partly to escapes from the Duke of Bedford's flock at Woburn Abbey in the early 1900s.

Although the mandarin duck's core range is in the Home Counties, there are also strong populations in, among other places, Devon, Gloucestershire, Worcestershire, Yorkshire, Derbyshire and parts of Scotland, with an isolated outpost in Northern Ireland's County Down. As the population expands, this is a duck that will soon add a splash of colour to your local pond or streams – that is, if it's not already there.

LESSER WHITE-FRONTED GOOSE

*

The lesser white-fronted goose has always been very rare in Britain, with fewer than 150 records since the first one was shot in Northumberland in September 1866 by a punt-gunner named Alfred Chapman. This wandering bird had travelled from its breeding grounds, somewhere from northern Russia west to Scandinavia, having gone astray on its autumn migration to south-eastern Europe. Yet despite its scarcity, this relative of the familiar white-fronted goose has played an unwitting part in the establishment of two of Britain's most cherished institutions.

As their name suggests, lesser white-fronted geese are smaller and daintier versions of white-fronted geese, which winter here in large flocks at traditional feeding grounds. One of these is Slimbridge on the Severn Estuary in Gloucestershire.

In 1945 the ornithologist and conservationist Peter Scott visited the grasslands along the estuary. While scanning through the vast flocks of white-fronts, he picked out a smaller, neater goose with a clear yellow eye-ring: a lesser white-fronted goose. At the time, there had only been a handful of records of this species in Britain, and its presence confirmed what Scott had already begun to realize: that this was an extremely special site for both common and rare wildfowl. He decided at that very moment that he would settle there and set up a research establishment to study ducks, geese and swans; thus the Wildfowl and Wetlands Trust was born.

Later, in the mid-1950s, Peter Scott began making television programmes for the BBC: his influential series *Look* helped to establish the BBC Natural History Unit in 1957. Bristol was picked as the location for the department largely because Slimbridge was now Scott's home, and it was easier to travel to Slimbridge from nearby Bristol than from London. Thus the scarce and relatively unknown lesser white-fronted goose played its small but significant part in the history of the BBC.

COOT
*

Feeding the ducks on the local park pond is one of those childhood memories we all treasure. But as we throw bits of bread to the mallards, and watch as the larger mute swans and Canada geese muscle in to grab a morsel of food, it's easy to ignore one of the most fascinating of the pond's inhabitants: the coot.

Coots are dumpy, charcoal-coloured birds of the rail family, related to moorhens. But unlike their cousins, they tend to spend more time on open water, especially in winter, when they gather on lakes and reservoirs in flocks of up to several hundred, sometimes even thousands. You can recognize coots easily by their white bill and white shield on their forehead, which gives rise to the expression 'as bald as a coot'.

They're famously feisty and will often fight each other over territory. They do so by leaning back on the water and lashing out at each other with their ridiculously huge, lobed feet. Sometimes these encounters can become so vicious that the loser sinks beneath the water and drowns, making the coot one of the few birds that will habitually fight to the death.

Coots have a limited but striking vocabulary, uttering a single, explosive high-pitched call like someone beating a metal rod against a stone. They use this to defend their little patch of water, at the heart of which is a floating nest made from aquatic vegetation, often built using a platform of overhanging branches, surrounded by water. In heavy rain, when pools and

lakes become swollen, you can watch coots hurriedly adding material to their nests to raise them and their precious eggs above the rising water levels.

Coot chicks wouldn't win a bird beauty contest. They look bald, too, with red and blue heads and a sparse covering of wiry black down. Coots are for the most part solicitous parents, tenderly feeding their offspring with morsels of pondweed. But there's a twist: if food supplies run short, they may be forced to choose which chicks to feed. And during extreme food shortages, coots have even been known to bite young begging for food, in some cases so repeatedly that the unfortunate chick is killed by its own parent.

MOORHEN

*

Most waterbirds need large expanses of water where they live and breed, but not so the most modest and overlooked of them all, the moorhen. Even the smallest pond, stream or ditch which has enough food and nesting places will provide you with the sight of a moorhen going quietly about its business. Often this species will remain hidden, only revealing its presence by uttering a short, explosive belch or quiet clucking sound.

A moorhen is easy to identify from its red and yellow bill, red shield on the forehead and greenish-yellow legs. From a distance the plumage can look very plain, but a closer view reveals a subtle blend of purple,

blue and dark brown hues, set off by a raggedy band of white along the flanks. As a moorhen swims jerkily across open water, it flicks its tail nervously, displaying two large white patches beneath.

The name 'moorhen' may seem puzzling, until you realize that it has nothing to do with moorland, but derives from the old word for marsh or mere. In the local park moorhens join jostling coots and mallards to snatch bread from around our feet, but they can also be very wary.

Moorhens are slimmer than their cousins the coots and much more agile. It can be a surprise to see one clambering after hawthorn berries high in a bush, or hear one calling at night as it flies over your house, patrolling the area for new places to feed.

Like coots and grebes, moorhens build a nest from bits of aquatic vegetation in or at the edge of the water, often making little attempt to hide their handiwork. Their nests are generally open to the elements, but one enterprising Yorkshire bird pulled a piece of dirty plastic over its back during heavy rain while brooding its clutch, discarding this makeshift cape each time the rain stopped.

MERLIN

*

A dull winter's day almost anywhere in the UK can be instantly enlivened by the unexpected sighting of a merlin. This magical bird is aptly named: appearing out of nowhere, hurtling over the ground on tight, compact wings as it flies in hot pursuit of a flock of skylarks or meadow pipits. Merlins are mercurial and you need to savour this fleeting encounter; it may be the only one you'll see all day.

At just twenty-five centimetres long – even smaller than a mistle thrush – the male merlin (or 'jack') is our smallest falcon. But he makes up for his small size with stamina and determination as he skims the heather or saltmarsh in quest of small birds. He is blue-grey above, tawny orange below and, when perched, looks rather like a male sparrowhawk. But when he takes off, the differences immediately become clear: merlins can put on dazzling displays of aeronautics, towering high in the air before plummeting down to race after small birds.

The brown and cream females are just as agile, but noticeably larger, which gives them the strength to catch bulkier prey. Both sexes have a characteristic tripping flight action, which can help you identify them even from a distance.

In the breeding season these diminutive falcons nest in deep heather on moorland in the north and west. In autumn they head down to lower altitudes where our own breeding birds mix with merlins from Scandinavia and Iceland and spend the winter hunting over open country, ranging though farmland, hillsides and coastal marshes.

Merlins have had a chequered past. Once valued as a lady's falcon, they were very popular with female monarchs including Mary, Queen of Scots; but more recently they have been persecuted for nesting on grouse moors. Afforestation of moorland habitats also reduced their numbers, as did the use of chemical pesticides during the 1950s and 1960s. From a low point of about 500 breeding pairs in the early 1980s, the population has now more than doubled, but the status of this tiny

falcon remains precarious. In winter they can turn up anywhere in open countryside, so it's worth giving any small bird of prey a closer glance.

SHOVELER

*

Swimming in tight circles, their huge, spatulate beaks sifting the surface of the water for food, shovelers are the avian equivalent of baleen whales. In the words of TV presenter Kate Humble, they look as if they have dropped a contact lens and are now searching intently for it. So even if you can't see the shoveler's bill, you can easily identify it by its bizarre swimming action.

When you do get a good view of that extraordinary bill, you'll notice that it has flanges on each side, which it uses to strain small creatures in the same way that large marine mammals such as the blue whale sift plankton.

Apart from their bill, female shovelers are similar in appearance and plumage to other female dabbling ducks such as the mallard and gadwall, being mottled brown in colour. When they fly, both male and female shovelers reveal a powder-blue patch on their wings. The drakes, though, are one of our most distinctive waterfowl, sporting a striking harlequin pattern including a glossy dark green head, chestnut flanks and a pure white breast. Their call is a strange mechanical 'g-dunk' sound, which you'll hear from birds as they take off or when they're flying overhead, looking as if they're being led by that long, broad bill.

Shovelers are rather scarce breeding birds, with fewer than 1,000 pairs scattered throughout the marshes and shallow lakes of lowland Britain. But in winter

our population is boosted by thousands of birds from continental Europe, which form small flocks on lakes and gravel pits, mostly in the south of the UK. Unlike mallards, though, they're rather shy, so you're not likely to see them taking bread on your local park pond.

BLUE TIT

*

Apart perhaps from the robin and the blackbird, no other garden bird inspires quite so much affection as the blue tit. Its cheek may be a clue to its popularity. For this tiny bird, only twelve centimetres long and weighing just eleven grams (less than half an ounce), punches well above its weight, jostling larger birds off the bird-feeders, and is often the first to take up residence in a newly erected nestbox.

Blue tits are one of the most widely distributed of all British birds and you can find them almost wherever there are trees. Although we think of them as garden birds, blue tits are most at home in deciduous wood-land, especially oak woods. They have the distinction of producing some of the largest clutches of any songbird, with up to sixteen eggs – that's a very crowded nestbox.

Their confiding nature and unique colour combination have also made blue tits popular. No other British bird has a blue cap and wings, olive-green back and yellow belly. The male and females may look identical to us, but blue tits can clearly tell each other apart, due to their special visual abilities. Birds can see colours in the ultraviolet spectrum that are invisible to us, and scientists have discovered that the male's blue crown feathers reflect this ultraviolet light, revealing his state of health. Because the more dominant and experienced males reflect more ultraviolet light, it is thought that the females use this characteristic to choose the fittest partner.

Blue tits also have a widespread reputation for mischief. In 1693 a French cleric, Father Jean Imberdis, wrote: 'Small is this naughty Fowl, yet it can wreak No small Destruction with its claws and beak'. He was complaining about blue tits' paper-tearing habits, which are not surprising considering that they habitually shred papery bark in search of insects on which to feed.

But in the middle of the twentieth century, blue tits took this talent to new levels when they began removing the foil caps from milk bottles left on door-steps, so they could reach the cream. Some blue tits were apparently so eager to get at the contents of the bottles they would even wait for the milk cart to arrive and chase it down the street. But with the decline of doorstep deliveries and our health-conscious switch from full cream to semi-skimmed milk, this behaviour has virtually died out.

GREY WAGTAIL

*

Few other British birds are as charming as the grey wagtail, a bird whose sharp, penetrating call – with a clear, metallic tone – can be heard by a mountain stream or over your local high street.

Despite their name, grey wagtails are often confused with their close relative the yellow wagtail, as they can have considerable amounts of yellow in their plumage. But yellow wagtails live in open water-meadows and on farmland and are purely spring and summer visitors, whereas grey wagtails are with us all year round.

During the breeding season the male grey wagtail is very handsome indeed, sporting a smart black bib and white moustache, set off with a steel-grey back and lemon-yellow belly. In winter, males lose the black bib and look more like the females and youngsters: grey above and peachy white below, with a splash of yellow beneath that long bobbing tail.

Grey wagtails boost their appeal by breeding in highly photogenic locations: shaded spots near fast-flowing streams and rivers, where they perch on water-splashed boulders in mid-torrent, dappled by the sunshine passing through the trees above. They nest under bridges, by lock gates or near a weir – anywhere that rapidly flowing water provides them with a continuous supply of insects to feed themselves and their young.

As you watch them teetering at the water's edge, plucking insects from the ground or hawking mayflies in the air, it's the tail that grabs your attention. It is as long again as its body, and always moving up and down, disrupting the bird's outline against the rushing water. Sometimes it's fanned briefly to show the white outer feathers, which catch the sunlight filtering through the streamside leaves. Pied wagtails, attractive birds themselves, look squat and stub-tailed in comparison.

In autumn, as the upland streams grow colder and lose their attraction for insects, grey wagtails often leave their waterside homes and come to town. The warmer temperatures in our urban areas provide enough heat to attract insects, so instead of perching on rocks in the middle of a raging river, they flit along tiled roofs or forage along grimy culverts, their sharp calls cutting through the thrum of traffic – a very different world, but clearly a profitable one for this graceful bird.

HEN HARRIER

*

On a cold winter's afternoon, it's tempting to head home as dusk begins to fall. But if you do so, you might just miss one of the most thrilling spectacles in the avian calendar: hen harriers floating into their roost.

Like other members of their family, hen harriers are long-winged, long-tailed, graceful birds of prey, which hunt by quartering low over rough ground such as marshes and moorland. As they search for rodents and small birds to flush out, they hug the contours of the ground, disappearing behind hummocks and following the lines of streams. When they disturb a bird such as a meadow pipit, they can be remarkably agile for such a large bird, twisting down and extending a sharp talon to seize their unfortunate victim in mid-air.

The male hen harrier is pearly grey with ink-black wingtips, and can look almost as pale as a herring gull against the sepia tones of a midwinter moor. In some lights, he is bluish: an old English name was 'blue hawk', while their Dutch name translates as 'blue chicken-thief'. Females and young birds are brown with a chequered wing pattern and a white band across the rump and dark rings across the upper tail, which is why they're often known as 'ringtails'. You're likely to see hen harriers in wide, open spaces, such as heaths, moors and coastal marshes, where the vegetation is long enough to conceal plenty of rodents and small birds.

In winter they can be seen throughout much of Britain, and in the late afternoon birds that rove widely during the day come together to roost in long grass or rushes. Saltmarshes are a favourite roost site and to see them arriving at sunset on a winter's evening over the Thames Estuary, their rangy shapes silhouetted against the distant lights of an oil refinery, is an unforgettable event.

In spring, hen harriers head north, to breed on moorland and in young forestry plantations. Male birds 'skydance' by plummeting towards the ground, before at the last possible moment pulling sharply upwards to repeat the manoeuvre. As they switchback over their territory above the heather moors in this dramatic manner, they stake their claim to potential nest sites. Once the male has found his partner and they have chosen a place to nest, you may be lucky enough to see the food-pass, in which he passes prey to the female in mid-air as a prelude to mating.

But the hen harrier's conspicuous plumage and showy courtship display has its drawbacks. Because they feed on grouse chicks, they have come into conflict with some landowners and gamekeepers across the UK. Even though they have full legal protection, hen harriers are still being unlawfully killed: 2013 was the first year since the 1960s in which they didn't breed successfully in England. Yet studies have shown that if this illegal killing were to end, there is enough upland habitat to support more than 300 pairs of these magnificent birds.

GREAT NORTHERN DIVER

*

Reservoirs may not look particularly appealing habitats, but in winter these vast areas of open water act as a magnet for waterbirds – and for birders eager to see them. Among the flocks of ducks and cormorants you may catch sight of another bird which, because it dives so frequently and stays under for such long periods, can be easy to miss: the great northern diver.

Great northern divers, as their name suggests, don't really belong on our concrete-girdled reservoirs in the south of England. They are birds of the true wilderness, breeding in remote parts of Canada, Alaska, the northern states of the USA, and eastwards through Greenland to their sole European outpost, Iceland.

Their wailing cries echo around the forested lakes where they nest, and no film set in the northern backwoods is complete without a soundtrack of their haunting calls – though Americans rather spoil the bird's romantic image by insisting on calling it the 'common loon'.

If the great northern diver sounds striking, then its appearance is just as dramatic: a hefty, dagger-shaped bill and sleek, submarine-like body, its plumage covered in graphic patterns of black and white stripes, dots and dashes.

On the water, divers sit low, ready to sink silently when danger approaches. Under the surface in pursuit of fish they become streamlined guided missiles, with that powerful bill at the business end and, at the rear, huge lobed feet for extra propulsion. On land it's a very different story. Here divers are ungainly, their legs set so far back on their body that they can hardly walk, and so need to make their nest right at the water's edge.

About 2,500 great northern divers winter around the UK coasts, mostly off Ireland and northern Scotland. Many of our wintering birds come from their closest breeding grounds in Iceland, but others travel from further afield, including Greenland or even Canada.

Rumours have long abounded that they breed on remote Scottish lochs: Arthur Ransome even wrote a novel based on that very premise, *Great Northern?*. But a careful review of past records found that none could be conclusively proven. Nevertheless it is always worth looking – and listening – out for these charismatic birds in remote parts of Scotland in summer; one day, who knows, a pair might just decide to stay on and breed. In the meantime, check your nearest reservoir this winter.

White-fronted Goose

Mallard

Wigeon

Great Spotted Woodpecker

Chaffinch

Wren

Dunnock

Long-eared Owl

Waxwing

Canada Goose

❄ FEBRUARY ❄

Skylark

Chough

Parrot Crossbill

Slavonian Grebe

Lesser Spotted Woodpecker

Golden Pheasant

Great Bustard

Black-throated Diver

Avocet

INTRODUCTION

IT MAY BE the shortest month, but February can sometimes seem very long indeed. Weary of winter and hungry for signs of spring, we greet each freeze-up, flood or snowfall with dismay – and we're not alone. February can be a taxing time for birds too, as their food supplies dwindle and winter's talons tighten on the land.

One of the hardiest and most welcome garden visitors is the waxwing. With its striking flashes of colour and exotic coiffure, it turns up regularly in towns and city gardens on a continuous quest for food. Flocks of waxwings can locate berries in the most unpromising places and swarm over the trees, perplexing the resident mistle thrushes who don't know which way to turn to protect their hoard. Waxwings deserve a medal for recruiting more non-birdwatchers to the 'cause' than perhaps any other bird.

Our gardens are important fuelling stations at this time of year. For farmland birds, such as the reed bunting or yellowhammer, bird-tables in village gardens offer a crucial lifeline. In town or country, almost anything can turn up. Look out for bramblings, redpolls and siskins among the greenfinches and goldfinches that crowd around the seed-dispensers. If you can spare an apple or two, you may attract redwings and fieldfares alongside the song thrushes and blackbirds, especially in hard weather. For blackbirds on low rations or with no food at all, the need to burn body-fat and keep warm can tip the balance between life and death in just a couple of days.

February can be fickle, however, and in milder spells those same blackbirds may try an experimental spring song or two from the rooftops. Chaffinches are also singing regularly by the second half of the month, when shiny green shuttlecocks of bluebell leaves pierce the leaf-litter on the woodland floor and constellations of yellow lesser celandines burst into bloom.

You know that spring must be imminent when you hear Shelley's 'blithe spirit', the skylark, burst into song over fields sprouting with winter cereals, usually towards the month's end, though the timing varies depending on whether you're in the north or south of the British Isles. One of the most obvious spring sounds this month isn't a song at all. In woods and parks – almost anywhere with large trees – great spotted woodpeckers are drumming. It's a territorial advertisement that the bird makes by tapping its bill rapidly on a branch or even a telegraph pole and because 'great spots' have hugely increased in the past few decades it's a sound we're hearing more than ever. If you're very lucky, you might even hear a lesser spotted woodpecker drumming. These tiny woodpeckers breed only in England and Wales and tend to drum high in the woodland canopy, though they will also use quite small trees in orchards or hedgerows.

Spring fever has already reached the rookeries where birds are stealing sticks and rebuilding nests in windswept, leafless treetops. Grey herons are up to the same tricks on a larger scale while ravens may be sitting on eggs now. Sparrowhawks begin their courtship display now, switchbacking over their territories in woods or parks with plenty of trees. In some western and northern woods you might see a displaying goshawk, its white undertail coverts fluffed into a pompom as it soars high over the conifers.

But in spite of these false springs winter can return at any time. 'February Fill-dyke' is an apt name for a month that tips copious rainfall on to already saturated ground. Where watercourses brim over on to fields, the drowned landscapes attract flocks of wild swans, wigeon and other ducks, grazing in tight packs at the fringes of floodwaters like minuscule multicoloured sheep.

Overhead, lapwings flop wearily and arrow-winged golden plovers flash white and amber against grey cumulus clouds. Among the tangles of short vegetation around the pools there will be jack snipe, cryptic as always and almost impossible to see until they fly up practically from underfoot. On rivers chocolate with their cargo of silt, peachy-white goosanders fish with saw-toothed bills, more by touch than by sight. Kingfishers look out of place in these drab, brown surroundings and stick to the margins where there's at least a chance of spotting prey in the clearer shallows.

While winter still has most of our islands in its grip, each year the last few days of the month are guaranteed to produce a precocious migrant or two: a sand martin maybe fresh from a trans-Saharan crossing, or a northern wheatear bouncing jauntily on top of a coastal headland. These are the advance guards, which mark the changing of the seasons and the unstoppable arrival of spring, now just around the corner.

WHITE-FRONTED GOOSE

*

Birds, like people, can be creatures of habit. Few are more so than white-fronted geese, which return each year to their ancestral wintering grounds on the bogs and saltmarshes of south-east Ireland, western Scotland and the Severn Estuary, with smaller flocks scattered elsewhere, such as the coastal marshes of Essex and north Kent. Across these wide-open, wild places the musical yapping of white-fronts – rather like a benevolent pack of dogs – is one of the classic sounds of winter.

White-fronted geese are so called because of the distinctive white patch around their bills, which extends up across their face ('front' is the French word for forehead), but they're often too far away to check. That's when their high-pitched calls help you distinguish them from other 'grey geese' such as pinkfeet and greylags, both of which share the same marshy winter home. You'll also hear the calls high above you when a long, V-shaped skein flies overhead on a chilly afternoon, heading towards their roost.

If you can contrive a closer view – for white-fronts are very wary of intruders – another distinguishing feature is the broad, black streaking across the white-front's belly, a feature they share with their much rarer cousin the lesser white-fronted goose.

White-fronted geese are handsome birds, but are now scarce, and in Greenland their numbers are rapidly declining. This is partly due to increased spring snowfall, which affects their ability to breed and feed, but possibly also because of competition with the larger and more aggressive Canada geese, which are spreading into the Arctic and pushing out their smaller and more delicate relative.

The majority of the 16,000 white-fronted geese we see here in autumn and winter have travelled from Russia, but Scotland and Ireland are also the winter home to virtually the whole global population of a distinctive subspecies. Greenland white-fronted geese breed on the tundra in the west of Greenland and look darker, with more black bars across their bellies and orange, rather than pink, bills.

But whichever white-fronted geese you see, they always evoke the essence of wild places, bringing a touch of the Arctic tundra to our own winter landscapes.

MALLARD

*

An hour or two spent feeding the ducks on your local park pond may yield little more than mallards, jostling aggressively with one another to get at the hunks of bread. But although these birds may seem reassuringly familiar, some have travelled much further than you might imagine.

Mallards are our most numerous and widespread ducks, found almost anywhere with fresh water. They are so ubiquitous that we perhaps take them too much for granted. For few birds are quite as eye-catchingly smart as a male mallard, with his glossy dark green head, white collar and curly black tail feathers – the origin of the name of a fashionable 1950s hairstyle known as the 'DA', meaning 'duck's arse'.

The name 'mallard' derives from the same root as the word 'male', and originally referred to the drake only, but now includes his mate too. Female mallards are more subtly plumaged, speckled in various shades of light and dark brown. The female's modest appearance is contradicted by her call, a loud and distinctive belly laugh. This is the famous quack we know so well, and is very different from the softer wheeze of the drake.

Mallards usually breed in marshy vegetation by the side of a river, pond or lake, but they also build nests in hollow trees. Some birds choose very public nesting places such as window boxes, roof gardens and high ledges, which require a breathtaking leap of faith for the newly hatched ducklings and a somewhat perilous journey to the nearest body of water.

But compared to the journeys some mallards make to get here in winter, this is (sometimes literally) a walk in the park. From late autumn onwards, mallards from continental Europe join our resident birds, more than tripling the UK population to over two-thirds of a million. Some of these birds may have flown from as far away as Russia and many infiltrate local flocks, even in town parks. So although they look familiar, the ducks that snatch your bread may have been born hundreds, if not thousands of kilometres away.

WIGEON

*

It's a foggy February day, when the mists swirling over the saltmarsh obscure all but the closest birds. Then, out of the murk and gloom, comes a chorus of wolf-whistles. Somewhere out there is a flock of wigeon.

Wigeon are dabbling ducks, closely related to mallards, shovelers and teal, but unlike their cousins they spend as much of their time out of the water as in it, cropping waterside pastures with their short, blue-grey bills. The drake is one of our most handsome ducks, with his chestnut head and a creamy-yellow forehead, which pleasingly contrasts with the soft grey body. The feathers of the females and young birds are the colour of autumn leaves: brown, orange and frosty white.

Fewer than 500 pairs of wigeon actually breed in the UK, mostly on remote Scottish lochs, where lone females shepherd their precious brood of ducklings across the clear, glassy surface. But in autumn this small breeding population is massively boosted by almost half a million migrants arriving from compass points to the north and east. They come from their breeding grounds in Iceland, Scandinavia and Arctic Russia, some travelling from as far away as the wilds of eastern Siberia.

The best place to see large flocks is on an estuary, where there's plenty of rough grass for the birds to graze. At low tide they also love to feed on the exposed eelgrass beds, and at high tide they either ride the waves or move inshore to mow these waterside lawns.

You often see them in tightly packed flocks, looking strangely like penned sheep. Just like sheep, wigeon are efficient grazers and fertilizers, especially when at places such as the Ribble Estuary on the coast of Lancashire and Merseyside there can be as many as 80,000 birds in winter. But wigeon are ducks to be heard as well as seen, and their surprising chorus can often be one of the abiding memories of a winter day's birding.

GREAT SPOTTED WOODPECKER

*

On a bright, cold February day, just as the early songsters are thinking about delivering a burst of song, one bird is defending its territory in a less conventional way: hammering its beak rapidly against the hollow branch of a tree.

Great spotted woodpeckers are the headbangers of our woods and forests. In late winter and early spring they really know how to grab our attention, advertising their territories by drumming loudly and persistently on tree-trunks and branches. And not just any old branch or trunk. Resonance is crucial as it allows the sound to travel further, so male woodpeckers will keep returning to the drumming posts that have the best acoustic qualities. Some birds even choose the metal plates attached to telegraph poles and create quite a din, which no doubt helps intimidate rival males.

We now take for granted the fact that woodpeckers make their drumming sounds by tapping rapidly with their bills, at an astonishing rate of up to forty beats per second. But it was only relatively recently that this idea was widely accepted, as many ornithologists were convinced that the sound was produced vocally. A birdwatcher named Norman Pullen settled the matter in 1943 by inserting a microphone into the branch of a dead tree. By watching the birds as they drummed, he soon proved that the sound he heard was in exact time with the movements of the bird's bill and its contact with the wood.

But that still didn't solve the other big question: why don't drumming birds get a headache? We now know that like all woodpeckers, the great spotted has a spongy mass of tissue between its bill and skull, which absorbs the impact.

For the majority of the year when they are not drumming, great spotted woodpeckers can be surprisingly elusive, as they flit unobtrusively around the woodland canopy. But they usually give away their presence by their sharp 'chik' calls, which carry well as the birds fly overhead or perch momentarily at the topmost point of a nearby tree. Once you become familiar with this distinctive sound you'll be surprised how common these birds are, even in our towns and cities, where they regularly visit bird-feeders to the dismay of smaller, less assertive species. They are handsome birds, with a striking black and white plumage that once earned them the name 'pied woodpecker'.

Unlike many of our woodland birds, which have mostly been in decline for the past few decades, great spotted woodpeckers have bucked the trend. Numbers have increased rapidly, and the population has increased more than fourfold since the late 1960s.

This may be because they are cashing in on food we provide on our bird-tables, but it may also be a result of the decline in starling numbers over the same period. Starlings compete with woodpeckers for nest-holes, and if there's a dispute, the starlings usually win.

Woodpeckers in general are reluctant to fly over large areas of water, which explains why there are ten species in continental Europe but only three (plus the scarce wryneck) in Britain. Until recently Ireland was the only European country with no resident woodpeckers at all, because the Irish Sea acted as a barrier to birds from Great Britain. But a few years ago they were discovered in woodlands along Ireland's east coast, and now the species is fully established there as a breeding bird. These new colonists probably flew across the Irish Sea from Britain, but woodpeckers do sometimes travel to the British Isles from Scandinavia, crossing the whole of the North Sea. But wherever they came from, the Irish great spotted woodpeckers, along with their counterparts growing in numbers in Britain, are a success story worth celebrating.

CHAFFINCH

*

On a mild day in February you may hear a rapid series of notes, speeding up towards the end, something that has been compared to a cricketer running up to deliver a ball. It is the sound of one of our commonest and most widespread birds: the chaffinch. The familiar song of the male chaffinch is a sure sign that spring is on its way.

But depending where you live, you may be hearing different versions of this song; for chaffinches, unlike most other birds, have distinct regional accents.

In parts of Scotland, for example, the chaffinch is known as 'the ginger-beer bird', because the last three notes of its terminal flourish sound like a request for the traditional soft drink.

Females can be mistaken for house sparrows, but they have clear white wingbars and show a greenish rump as they fly off. But with his blue-grey head, pink cheeks and underparts, a chestnut back and smart white epaulettes the male chaffinch really is unmistakable.

Here in the UK the chaffinch rivals the robin for second place in the league table of our commonest breeding birds (behind the wren in first position). It is also one of our most widespread species, found in urban and rural habitats from city parks and gardens to the pine forests of the Scottish Highlands, and most places in between.

The name 'chaffinch' refers to its habit of flocking in stubble fields, often in the company of other birds, to sort through the chaff for seeds. In less tidy times, when spilled grain was a regular feature in farmyards and stubble was retained for longer periods, these winter flocks were more widespread. Some observers – including the eighteenth-century author and naturalist Gilbert White – noticed a tendency for birds to segregate into flocks of males or females, which led to the chaffinch's colloquial name of 'bachelor finch', though this habit seems much less obvious today.

There are still bachelor chaffinches in some places, but sadly not of their own free will. The chaffinch's singing ability has given rise to a competition in the northern Belgian region of Flanders called 'vinkensport', or 'finch sport'. A row of cages is set out in the open air, each containing a male chaffinch. The birds are then encouraged to sing by the proximity of other males and a tally is kept of the number of different songs each bird sings. The winner is the chaffinch who's completed the most songs in an hour – the rules stating that each completed song must include that final flourish.

WREN

*

For one of our tiniest birds, the wren really does have a very loud song. It explodes out of the undergrowth in an ear-splitting rally of notes, delivered so rapidly they blur into one another to create a trill, before ending with a final flourish. When the singer shows himself, he perches momentarily on a fence-post or on top of a shrub, his tail cocked jauntily and bill open wide, trembling with the sheer effort of producing such a high-volume territorial advertisement.

For most of the year, wrens are hardly what we would call extrovert. Normally these plump, short-tailed little birds creep mouselike among banks of foliage or in crevices between rocks, where they probe with their short, sharp bill in search of tiny insects and invertebrates. In hard winters, wrens survive at night by roosting together, sometimes in old bird-boxes: as many as sixty-one birds have been counted entering a single nestbox.

The scientific name for the wren, *Troglodytes troglodytes*, derives from the Greek for 'cave-dweller'. This ability to find food and shelter means that, despite being small and vulnerable to heat-loss, wrens can live almost anywhere – from mountain crags and remote islands to suburban gardens and city parks. Its catholic choice of habitat, allied with the ability to raise two broods of five or six young during the breeding season, has put the wren way out in front as Britain's most common bird, with close to 8 million breeding pairs.

Not that male wrens have it easy. Their fussy partners demand that the male builds up to half a dozen 'cock's nests', using his extraordinary architectural skills to weave these loose balls out of moss, grass and feathers in different places around his territory, including shrubs, old buildings or even in the pocket of an old coat hung up in a shed. Only when he has completed this Herculean task does the female choose the one nest where she will lay her precious clutch of eggs, meaning that the majority of his efforts have gone to waste.

As she incubates the eggs, and then feeds the tiny young on a diet of insects and spiders, the male continues to sing away. Rather aptly, given that the North American name for this species is 'winter wren', he continues to do so well into the autumn and winter, so that barely a month goes by when you won't hear the wren's explosive song somewhere in the British Isles.

DUNNOCK

*

They say that you can't judge a book by its cover: some of the raciest novels have appeared in rather drab dust jackets. The same is true in the avian world: few British birds are as unassuming as the dunnock, yet few other birds can match its raunchy and unpredictable sex-life.

For most of the year, the typical view of a dunnock (or 'hedge sparrow', as it used to be known) is of a small, greyish-brown bird shuffling around beneath a bird-table or foraging for insects at the bottom of a garden hedge. But in early spring it turns into an extrovert, delivering its rather rambling song from the tops of hedges and garden shrubs.

Despite their traditional name, they are not sparrows, but belong instead to the accentor family, a group of half a dozen or so species mainly found in the mountainous regions of Europe and Asia. Only the dunnock has spread its wings and headed down into the lowlands, where it has adapted to living in hedgerows, woods and, latterly, our gardens.

Here in Britain the dunnock is an important host for baby cuckoos, a fact known to Shakespeare. To quote the Fool in *King Lear*:

> *The hedge sparrow fed the cuckoo so long*
> *That it had its head bit off by its young . . .*

This is one facet of the dunnock's private life that has been known for centuries, but it's only relatively recently that its complicated mating habits have been uncovered. We're used to the idea that most birds are monogamous, pairing up for life, or at least remaining faithful during the breeding season. But dunnocks are far more adventurous, practising both 'polyandry', where a female mates with more than one male, and 'polygyny' in which a male mates with several females.

Some territories are held by two birds – a dominant male and a subordinate male – both of which sing and both of which may mate with the same female. That's why you can often see groups of three or even four wing-flicking dunnocks in your garden in spring, each desperately trying to beat each other to win the crucial race to pass their genes on to the next generation.

LONG-EARED OWL

*

In a pine wood on a cold, crisp February night, only the sound of frost crackling underfoot breaks the eerie silence. Until, that is, a breathless hooting sound filters through the blackness: a long-eared owl is courting.

The moaning call of a long-eared owl sounds rather like someone blowing across the top of a bottle, and is much softer than the well-known hoot of the tawny owl. Like tawnies, long-eared owls are nocturnal, and one of our most elusive and overlooked breeding birds. They nest in conifer woods, copses and shelterbelts of trees near wide, open grasslands and heaths where they hunt for rodents.

Long-eared owls are rather scarce in the British Isles, with more in the north and east and in Ireland. They often go unnoticed though, because few people choose to venture into dark conifer woods on late winter nights. But if you listen carefully at this time of year, in the right places on a windless night, you might be lucky enough to hear that low hoot.

They often take over the disused nest of a crow or a squirrel drey, in which they lay a clutch of three or four pale, rounded eggs. These can be very hard to find, so in order to study the birds more effectively, ornithologists in East Anglia have encouraged the owls to nest in woven willow baskets.

When the young owlets first leave the nest they call continuously for food – a sound rather like a squeaky gate – and on summer evenings this can offer a valuable guide to whether long-eared owls have bred successfully.

Although they are scarce in spring and summer, when autumn comes our small breeding population is boosted by long-eared owls flying in from the Continent. This gives us a rare opportunity to observe them, gathering together at regular roost sites in thick bushes, where you can sometimes glimpse their distinctive silhouetted shapes by day, through a network of branches. If you do spot one, look out for the 'ears' – not actually ears at all but tufts of feathers – and the distinctive brown, black and buff plumage, as richly patterned as a Persian carpet.

WAXWING

*

Supermarket car parks don't feature high on most birders' lists of sites to see rare birds. But in winter it might be wise to make an exception, and listen out for the sound of trilling sleigh-bells overhead. Not the return of Father Christmas, but the signal that we are enjoying a waxwing winter.

Waxwings are plump, starling-sized birds, which breed in the vast conifer forests of northern Russia and Scandinavia, stocking up on flies during the long days of the brief, sub-Arctic summer. In winter they head south and west to gorge on berries, and if these are in short supply on the Continent the birds flood into the UK. The spectacle of these punk-crested plunderers swarming over the bushes in your local supermarket car park is guaranteed to attract everyone's attention.

And waxwings really are attention-grabbers, with silky plumage the colour of milky coffee, set off by black, Lone Ranger-style masks, long Mohican crests, yellow tips to their tails and strange red blobs resembling sealing wax on some of their wing-feathers: hence their name. In the air, waxwings look remarkably like a flock of starlings, but when they're perched you can see their long crests, even in silhouette.

The real joy of waxwings is their tameness, when their fondness for fruit brings them into town and can provide us with stunning close-up views. In autumn and winter, during a 'waxwing year', flocks of a hundred or more of these exotic-looking birds can turn up in gardens, even in the middle of cities, especially where ornamental fruit trees have been planted.

They are very fond of rowan and cotoneaster berries, but will also eat a range of other fruit from apples to mistletoe. During their smash-and-grab raids, after which they sit around at the top of tall trees or on television aerials digesting their haul, they can each guzzle as many as a hundred berries in an hour. A large flock soon strips all the berries from a single area, and then the birds rapidly move on to their next target, uttering those jingling bell-like calls as they depart.

CANADA GOOSE

*

In their native North America, skeins of migrating Canada geese have inspired a plethora of songs and poems, as well as a successful 1996 children's movie, *Fly Away Home*, starring Anna Paquin and Jeff Daniels.

Here in Britain, we have a less romantic attitude to this brash, pushy goose; there are regular calls for these noisy birds to be culled, to prevent them taking over our park ponds, destroying the surrounding grass and bullying the smaller ducks, coots and moorhens.

The reason why we have such different views from our cousins across the pond is simple. As their name suggests, Canada geese are native to North America, whereas here they are an introduced, alien species. They have, to be fair, been here for an awfully long time: the first reference is more than three centuries ago in 1665, when English diarist John Evelyn recorded them in the waterfowl collection of King Charles II at London's St James's Park.

Their impressive size and bold markings, especially their black necks and white flashes across the face, helped to make Canada geese very fashionable as an adornment to private estates during the eighteenth and nineteenth centuries. It was inevitable that some birds would eventually escape, and once they had, they soon found our countryside and parkland to their liking.

Canada geese are able to breed on surprisingly small pools and waterways, and because their size and aggressive behaviour keep predators and competitors at bay, they quickly established themselves. Today there are more than 100,000 birds at large, mainly in lowland England and Wales, but also in parts of Scotland and Northern Ireland.

Few other birds divide opinion quite as much. Many people hate them with a passion, but for others, the spectacle of a flock of these imposing birds winging their way overhead in a V-shaped skein, making those sonorous, honking cries, brings the call of the North American wild into our quiet suburban lives.

SKYLARK

*

On a fine day in February, a walk in the countryside may be enlivened by one of the most extraordinary displays of any British bird, the song of the skylark. Even as you hear it, you strain to see the bird itself, as it sings so high in the sky.

No other British bird is capable of sustaining such a loud and complex song while hovering so far above the ground, rapidly beating its wings to stay aloft, as the skylark. Some songs can last twenty minutes or more, as the bird displays to rival males while trying to impress a watching female with his physical fitness.

The song of the skylark is one of the classic sounds of summer, seeming to go on for ever as we scan the skies for a glimpse of the faraway bird, a tiny black dot in a sea of blue. But skylarks can be heard and seen in winter too, as they gather in flocks in harvested fields or – on those fine winter days that hint at the spring season to come – the males begin to sing once again.

Their plumage is as streaky as the stubble in which they feed, like lanky sparrows with a short crest and broad tail, rimmed with white. On newly ploughed fields larks look quite pale as they feed on grains, seeds and small insects among the furrows, but are well camouflaged when in pastures. Skylarks prefer a mixture of arable and pasture, and as mixed farming has declined, so have their populations. They're still widespread throughout rural areas but millions of birds have gone over the last forty years, as a consequence of agricultural change and the use of pesticides.

But the sound of the first skylark continues to mark a key turning point of the seasons for many country people as well as birders, and it has garnered its fair share of celebration over the centuries. Capturing birdsong in words isn't easy, but George Meredith's nineteenth-century poem 'The Lark Ascending', which in turn inspired the well-known musical piece by Ralph Vaughan Williams, comes closer than most:

> He rises and begins to round,
> He drops the silver chain of sound
> Of many links without a break,
> In chirrup, whistle, slur and shake,
> All intervolv'd and spreading wide,
> Like water-dimples down a tide
> Where ripple ripple overcurls
> And eddy into eddy whirls . . .

The skylark's very obvious song might seem extravagant and dangerous – a musical form of the peacock's tail that may impress potential partners, but at the same time could attract the attention of predators. Yet scientists have shown that when approached by a bird of prey such as a merlin, an older, experienced skylark will sing louder and more forcefully than a younger male. Instead of attracting the predator's attention, this bravado appears to put them off, as if the skylark is saying 'Okay, come and get me if you think you're hard enough!'

CHOUGH

*

As you walk along a coastal path in the west of Britain or Ireland, you may hear a sound less familiar than the usual cawing of jackdaws and the cries of gulls: a chorus of evocative 'chow-chow' sounds, whose echoes seem to hang in the air, just like the birds themselves. It comes from a flock of choughs, our rarest and most charismatic crows, which make their homes on top of the wind-blown sea-cliffs of the Celtic fringe.

Now confined to these Atlantic coasts, choughs were once far more widespread, but were forced back westwards by their specialized feeding habits, as lowland Britain became developed for arable farming, with rough pasture replaced by sterile fields of grass, wheat and barley.

Choughs are medium-sized crows, a little larger than jays or jackdaws, with a glossy blue-black plumage, large red feet and bright scarlet bills, which curve downwards like a scimitar. They use their bills to probe short turf for the grubs and pupae of beetles, moths and flies on which they depend. In hard weather,

when the ground freezes and insects are difficult to reach, choughs can switch to feed on the sandhoppers they find in seaweed along the strandline.

They are sociable birds, gathering in small flocks both on the ground, where they waddle and hop around, and in the air, where they hang and dive in the sea breezes with consummate ease, all the while uttering that curious call. Their aerobatic displays are phenomenal: you could accuse them of showing off, so expertly do they use the vortices of air around clifftops.

The name 'chough' may seem a puzzle, until you remember that the English language is a curious beast, and that the suffix 'ough' can be pronounced in at least ten different ways. So originally the name chough was pronounced 'chow' (as in the word 'plough'), to mimic the bird's sound; only later did it change to the modern-day 'chuff' (as in 'rough').

The main hotspots for choughs are in western Ireland, the Scottish island of Islay and parts of west and north Wales, especially Pembrokeshire. The last English stronghold for the species was Cornwall, where choughs still feature on the county's coat of arms. Choughs disappeared from Cornwall in the early 1970s, and plans were well under way to reintroduce them when, to everyone's surprise, wild birds from Ireland arrived back in the county in 2001. The following year they bred, and have now formed a small but growing population on and around the Lizard Peninsula.

Choughs usually nest in holes and crevices in cliffs, but will venture inland to breed in quarries and even old mineshafts. But wherever you see them, they are immensely charismatic birds and a treat to observe as they tumble and twist through the air, their cries echoing off the rocks all around.

PARROT CROSSBILL

✳

In a group of islands whose natural history is among the best known in the world, you'd think we'd know all there is to know about which birds breed in the British Isles. Not so: some birds are a curiosity and an enigma; and the parrot crossbill certainly fits the bill in both respects.

Like other crossbills, males are brick-red and females and youngsters olive-green. They also have that distinctive beak in which the upper mandible crosses over the lower one like a pair of pliers, which evolved to enable them to prise open pine cones to obtain the flaky seeds within.

Parrot crossbills are found from Scandinavia eastwards to north-west Russia, and are the northern equivalent of the more familiar common crossbill, which is found across much of Britain. Every now and then, flocks of parrot crossbills break out of their normal breeding range and head south and west across the North Sea in search of food, ending up in Britain.

However, they may be overlooked here, as telling them apart from common crossbills relies on good views, when it is possible to see that they live up to their name, with larger and thicker bills almost like a tiny parrot. The real experts who know them and their relatives well can distinguish them by their calls, which are marginally deeper in tone.

But in the forests of Strathspey in the Scottish Highlands, the situation is further confused by the presence of a third species, the Scottish crossbill, which has the distinction of being our only endemic bird – found in Britain and nowhere else in the world. In terms of bill size, the Scottish crossbills are intermediate in size and shape between parrot and common crossbills.

Confused? You're not alone. Even experienced ornithologists often have to admit defeat when confronted with birds that appear to be Scottish or parrot crossbills, but may actually be hybrids. To muddy the waters still further, scientists in Europe and North America now believe there may be a dozen or more different species of crossbills, each almost identical to one another, and only identifiable by their subtly dissimilar calls. At this point birdwatching gives way to bird listening and even then the calls have to be analysed using visual representations called sonograms.

What is not in doubt is that pure-bred parrot crossbills have nested in Britain on several occasions, notably after a major influx of these birds in the early 1980s, and that as many as a hundred pairs probably breed regularly in the pine forests of northern Scotland.

SLAVONIAN GREBE

*

A Scottish loch in spring and a south coast harbour in winter: both are home to one of our rarest birds, the Slavonian grebe. Named after a region of northern Russia (or, as some believe, a similarly named part of Croatia), this is the smaller cousin of the familiar great crested grebe. Like all members of its family, it lives an exclusively aquatic lifestyle, never venturing on to land, even to breed.

In spring and summer, the Slavonian grebe sports a rich chestnut neck and belly, a greyish black head

and back, and flamboyant golden ear-tufts – hence its alternative name of 'horned grebe'. They build a floating nest, into which the female lays up to five eggs, often covered with waterweed to hide them from predators.

When the chicks hatch, their stripy black and white heads give them the look of animated humbugs, paddling frantically along behind their parents or hitching a ride on their backs. Sadly the chicks often fall victim to otters or pike, and so numbers vary dramatically from year to year, with fewer than fifty breeding pairs managing to hang on in their remote Highland homes.

In winter, they change both lifestyle and appearance completely, forsaking freshwater habitats for marine ones. A boat trip around a south coast harbour such as the huge one at Poole in Dorset can provide views of birds that, with their contrasting black and white plumage, look more like auks than grebes. These may be British birds, but are more likely to come from Iceland or Scandinavia.

A few Slavonian grebes also turn up on inland waters such as reservoirs, where they can be remarkably trusting and allow you a closer view. Then you can make out their conspicuous vermilion eyes, as bright and shiny as redcurrants, which gave the species its various folk-names: 'devil-diver', 'pink-eyed diver' and 'water witch'.

LESSER SPOTTED
WOODPECKER

*

A far-carrying 'pee-pee-pee' call from the top of a tree in early spring is worth following up because it might well be made by a lesser spotted woodpecker. A century or so ago, almost every orchard in England would have echoed with this ringing call.

In those days, it was often called the 'barred woodpecker', to distinguish it from its larger relative the great spotted (or 'pied') woodpecker. Seen well, those names are a useful guide to separating the two: for while the lesser spotted has a series of narrow white bars across its dark back, the great spotted sports two prominent white patches, giving it a more contrasting appearance. 'Lesser spots' are much smaller though, about the size of a house sparrow, so can be very hard to detect as they climb along twigs too slender for their starling-sized relative.

Today few people get the chance to compare the two. While the great spotted has enjoyed a population explosion, and is now a regular sight on our garden bird-feeders and in our parks and woodlands, the lesser spotted has gone into steep decline, and perhaps as few as 1,000 pairs now breed here.

It is also very elusive, spending much of the time feeding on insects and other invertebrates, high in the tops of tall trees, where it's only betrayed by its call. In autumn and winter, lesser spotted woodpeckers often join roving parties of small birds such as tits, goldcrests and nuthatches in woodlands, along large hedgerows and by tree-lined rivers. But in late February males begin to stake out their territories in old orchards or woods by calling loudly and drumming softly, tapping their bill on a branch so rapidly that the sound has sometimes been described as a soft purring.

Unlike the loud, resonating sound of the great spotted woodpecker, the lesser spotted's drumming is far less easy to pinpoint and locate. By late April drumming is over and the woodpeckers attend to their young in a nest-hole hidden by the curtain of growing leaves. Unless you know their call, they effectively vanish until autumn.

So why has our lesser spotted woodpecker population gone into freefall? One possible theory is that they have been outcompeted for nest sites by the more successful great spotted woodpeckers. It's also possible that the loss of orchards and their connecting network of hedgerows have reduced nest sites and feeding areas.

Recent research has shown that breeding success is affected by cold, wet springs and that lack of food may be reducing the number of young that leave the nest. Female lesser spots often desert their young once they hatch and rove the woods in search of fresh mates, leaving the males to bring up the chicks. If the males are to raise them successfully, they need a plentiful supply of insects, which are harder to find in cold springs.

There's still a great deal to unravel about the decline of our woodland birds, but in late winter and early spring, it's well worth keeping your eyes peeled – and your ears open – for this charismatic and fascinating woodpecker.

GOLDEN PHEASANT

*

It's dusk, on a chilly winter's afternoon in the Norfolk Brecks, one of the coldest places in Britain at this time of year. The thickest tangles of young pines seem devoid of life, apart from the occasional bark of a muntjac deer. It's certainly not where you'd expect to come across one of our most dazzling and exotic birds – indeed a species widely considered to be among the most beautiful birds in the world.

Just as it becomes almost too dark to see, a flash of burnished gold illuminates the gloom, and a long shape emerges cautiously from beneath the dense curtains of pine needles, stepping gingerly on to the track in front of you. Gazing through binoculars, you strain your eyes, and catch a vision in glowing orange and scarlet: a cock golden pheasant.

Even with stiff competition from other members of its family, this is a pretty impressive bird. A bright sulphur-yellow crown is set off by a shawl of black and flame, vermilion underparts, green and blue back and long, tapering tail. Some have even attributed the origin of the phoenix legend to this firebrand of a bird.

Golden pheasants don't really look as if they belong in Britain; and they don't. Like other exotic-looking species such as the mandarin duck, they were brought here from their native home in the bamboo forests of central China in the late nineteenth century, following the misguided fashion for introducing attractive foreign species into the British countryside. They weren't just seen as adornments: some were put down as potential game birds, but they skulked in vegetation and refused to fly for the guns.

Unlike more prominent and more problematic introductions such as the Canada goose and grey squirrel, golden pheasants have not spread very far. They have been introduced in several places, from Sussex to south-west Scotland, but these populations have now mostly died out. The only truly self-sustaining populations nowadays are in the pine plantations of East Anglia, with the main stronghold on the sandy soils of Breckland, on the border between Norfolk and Suffolk.

As well as having a limited range, golden pheasants are also very shy, perhaps because that dazzling plumage makes them such an easy target for predators. The females are harder to see; like most female game birds they are far drabber than their gaudy mates. The best way to locate the birds is to listen at dusk in late winter and early spring for the raucous calls of territorial males deep in dense plantations.

Along with the golden pheasant another species, the equally striking Lady Amherst's pheasant, was also brought here from Asia in the nineteenth century, and released into the wild around Woburn Abbey in Bedfordshire. Their numbers peaked at around 200 pairs in the 1970s, but then went into a steep decline, and the species is now on the verge of extinction in Britain. Should the seemingly inevitable occur, this stunning bird will be the first alien species to have become accepted as an official British bird, but then to vanish from our island.

GREAT BUSTARD

*

When a bird disappears from its former range, and becomes extinct in Britain, it lives on in myth and folklore, but leaves a gaping hole in the places where it used to be found. So if it can be brought back, it can feel as if the landscape itself has been restored.

For almost two centuries, since the last pair of great bustards bred in Suffolk in 1832, the booming calls of these huge birds have not been heard in Britain. In those days the bird was highly prized: both to eat, and as a trophy, with stuffed great bustards being put on display in many a country mansion.

Weighing up to sixteen kilos, the great bustard is one of the heaviest flying birds on the planet. They are tall, too, able to look a roe deer in the eye. The plumage, especially of the male, is very striking: a combination of deep chestnut neck, mottled brown back, blue-grey head and neck and, in flight, black and white flashes on the wings, makes it impossible to ignore.

But for this majestic bird, size was to be its downfall. As well as making it an easy target for the newfangled shotgun, it also meant that great bustards needed vast, unspoiled areas to survive. In modern lowland Britain, hemmed in by hedgerows and criss-crossed with roads, such places no longer exist – except, perhaps, on the wide, open landscapes of Salisbury Plain in Wiltshire. Despite being surrounded by roads, factories and towns, this unique area has retained its ancient character, thanks to large parts being out of bounds to the public because they are used by the armed forces for military exercises.

So Salisbury Plain was the ideal place to reintroduce great bustards back into Britain, and during the past decade the Great Bustard Group has done just that. Their aim is to establish a self-sustaining population of these mighty birds by rearing and releasing bustards rescued from Russia, where their nests are often destroyed by farm machinery.

Whether this brave attempt to return great bustards to Britain will work is still open to debate, though in 2009 two nests were found, producing the first wild chicks to be reared in Britain for almost 180 years. If it does succeed, the sight of these incredible birds flying low against the big skies of Salisbury Plain will indeed be something to celebrate.

BLACK-THROATED DIVER

*

Few sounds are quite so evocative of the wilds of Scotland than the haunting calls of the black-throated diver. These soul-stirring cries, echoing across the waters of a steely grey loch at dawn and dusk, are often the only sound you'll hear in these austere places, where to experience them at all can require a long, hard trek from the nearest road.

In their breeding plumage, black throated divers could well be our most beautiful bird. Black and white they may be, but those contrasting shades combine to create a stunning pattern, their barcoded neck set off with an ebony bib and plush, grey head.

The black, dagger-like bill and broad, lobed feet are perfect for catching and pursuing fish, which the divers bring to their chicks in nests on the shoreline. Because their feet are set so far back on their streamlined bodies, divers can't waddle far and nest right by the water's edge. There's a snag though. Black-throated divers breed in some of the wettest and wildest places in Scotland, where rapid changes in water levels either flood the nests and eggs, or leave them high and dry, too far away from the loch for the birds to reach on foot.

So to help them, since the late 1980s conservationists have been providing tethered, floating rafts for the divers to use as nesting platforms, a scheme that seems to be working. Today the Scottish population is more than 200 pairs – up by more than 40 per cent since the rafts were first put in place.

In autumn and winter, black-throated divers change both their appearance and their lifestyle. They lose their striking breeding plumage and instead appear more uniform: dark above and pale below, with a prominent white patch on the flanks that helps to identify them at a distance. Like other divers, they prefer marine habitats at this time of year, and can be seen in small numbers off our coasts, though they remain rare inland in winter.

AVOCET

*

Few birds better show how we can help bring back lost species than the avocet. Its successful return from extinction here in Britain has become a proverbial example of how to intervene to restore both a bird itself and the places where it lives. And as if that weren't enough fame for this exotic-looking black and white wader, it has also been immortalized as the logo of the RSPB.

Avocets are fussy creatures, needing shallow, brackish water with small islands of mud or gravel where they breed, and a copious supply of aquatic invertebrates, which they sweep up using that remarkably slender, upturned bill. Until the early nineteenth century they nested on coastal lagoons created when sea walls were breached by high tides. But when these were repaired, the avocets had nowhere to go. This, combined with the depredations wrought by egg-collectors, soon drove the species to extinction in Britain.

A century later, during the Second World War, farmland on the coast of East Anglia was flooded once again, this time as a precaution against invasion by the Nazis. Avocets tried but failed to breed in Norfolk and Essex in the early 1940s, and it was not until 1947, two years after hostilities ended, that they finally managed to nest successfully at Havergate Island and at Minsmere on the Suffolk coast. Minsmere was purchased by the RSPB and became the charity's flagship nature reserve, with perhaps the greatest variety of habitats and breeding birds in any single place in Britain.

In the sixty years or so since their return, avocets have been a huge success. They soon colonized other parts of East Anglia, and have since spread north and west to breed at many wetland sites around the country, including inland at Droitwich in Worcestershire, where they nest on old salt workings below a massive radio mast. Despite their elegant appearance, they are cantankerous birds, often seeing off any intruders into their territory with a strident volley of calls.

In autumn, the 1,500 breeding pairs are swelled by an invasion of birds from further east, with about 7,500 avocets wintering here. These are mainly on south coast estuaries such as the Tamar and the Exe, where special boat trips run throughout the season to see these elegant and very special birds.

St Kilda Wren

Blackbird

Chiffchaff

Lapwing

Nuthatch

Treecreeper

Peregrine

Rook

Cetti's Warbler

Grey Partridge

Great Crested Grebe

MARCH

Sand Martin

Goldeneye

Snow Goose

Woodlark

Egyptian Goose

Alpine Swift

Ruff

Little Ringed Plover

Black Redstart

Ring Ouzel

INTRODUCTION

MARCH CAN BE an unpredictable month for birds, as well as for us. Some years, Britain bakes in an early spring heatwave; in others we freeze. Eventually though, the changeover between winter and spring begins, when departing winter visitors mingle with early spring arrivals from the south.

Over lakes and gravel pits, the flickering shapes of sand martins appear among flocks of wintering ducks, while chiffchaffs join parties of tits and goldcrests as they rove the woods in search of emerging insects. Perhaps the best harbinger of spring is a sprightly male northern wheatear, bouncing over the springy turf of a coastal headland or flashing his white rump among the furrows of a freshly ploughed field. This neat bird uses only a limited palette of colours, yet still manages to dazzle on even the dullest March day, seeming fresh and alert, unjaded by his recent flight across the Sahara Desert.

On grassy eminences on the coast and inland, look out for the first ring ouzels, which at this time of year are likely to be British birds on their way to breed in northern England or Scotland. Later, in April, Scandinavian ring ouzels also pass through, and are always a thrill to find.

There may even be exotic surprises in store, despite the earliness of the season. In most Marches, the first improbably exotic hoopoes flop like fan dancers over sand dunes and coastal grassland, probing with their long, curved bills for grubs hiding in the short turf. Look upwards, too, because in some years Alpine swifts arc over suburban skies on their impossibly long wings. Both of these are 'overshooters', which have travelled just a little too far on their return journey from Africa to southern Europe. When they fail to find a mate, they usually make good their error and head back south.

MARCH

March isn't only about spring migrants and rarities. Many resident birds are establishing their breeding territories in earnest and the dawn chorus is growing in intensity and volume. On mild, damp March evenings, as the last dregs of light begin to fade, the fluty song of a blackbird summons up spring in a few mellifluous phrases. If the weather is mild enough, his mate may already be sitting on her first clutch of eggs.

Mistle thrushes and song thrushes are also singing by now, swelling the suburban dawn chorus of great tits, blue tits, dunnocks, wrens and chaffinches. Long-tailed tits are early breeders, and are putting the finishing touches to their flask-shaped nests, which can contain well over a thousand feathers, as well as moss, animal hair and even fragments of tinfoil.

Far from suburbia, on sea-cliffs in the remote north and west of Britain, guillemots, razorbills and puffins are returning to their breeding colonies after spending the winter at sea; some may not have touched land since last July. At first their approach is tentative and they loiter in rafts on the sea beneath the cliffs. Not until spring is well under way will they begin nesting in earnest.

Waders, too, are starting to return. On traditional farmland, lapwings wail and tumble in their ecstatic spring displays, though these are now less common than they were even a few decades ago. In upland valleys and along Scottish rivers, the shrill peeping of oystercatchers seeking out breeding sites is a sure sign that spring is not far off. Curlews and redshanks begin to forsake the estuaries where they've spent the winter and return to upland pastures, where they probe the frost-free soil for worms and set about staking out their territories by performing their elaborate song-flights.

As we focus on the arrival of spring, it's easy to forget the characters that are slipping away with winter. All this activity can eclipse the muted departure of winter thrushes and finches. Not all winter visitors leave so quietly though. Sometimes, on mild March days, the woods are filled with a sound like the rush of a distant waterfall. This is the communal singing of a flock of redwings, sometimes hundreds at a time, tuning up before they leave for Iceland or Scandinavia. Their farewell chorus is a marker for the advent of April, and the entrance of spring, waiting impatiently in the wings.

ST KILDA WREN

*

On a blustery March day, on the remotest island group in the British Isles, a tiny bird is singing its heart out. Despite its small size – about twelve centimetres long and weighing just twelve grams – its pulsating song rises above the mighty waves that crash on to the shore below; indeed it can be heard up to a kilometre away. The name of this feisty songster? The St Kilda wren.

St Kilda is a group of islands, stacks and sea-pounded rocks on the north-western edge of Britain, more than sixty kilometres west of the Outer Hebrides. Exposed to all the elements the North Atlantic can throw at it, St Kilda is without doubt one of the most extreme and hostile environments anywhere in the UK – which, you might think, would make it the least likely place to see wrens.

But the wren isn't Britain's commonest breeding bird for nothing. It got to the top by its ability to make a home in almost every habitat, from city centres to coastal fringes, and virtually everywhere in between.

The wrens that live on St Kilda are the same species as the ones we see and hear throughout Britain; but after more than 5,000 years of isolation from their cousins on the mainland, they have evolved into a subtly different subspecies. St Kilda wrens are slightly larger, greyer and paler than those found elsewhere in Britain, and have a louder song, enabling the males to make themselves heard above the constant sounds of the wind and sea.

The St Kilda wren is one of Britain's rarest birds, with only about 250 pairs spread across this rocky archipelago. Like other wrens, they forage for tiny insects and spiders among the boulders and dry-stone walls that criss-cross the islands, and also search around the puffin colonies. The fertile guano produced by more than a million of these charismatic seabirds encourages plants, which are in turn home to small invertebrates. The wrens nest in sheltered crannies between the rocks, sometimes occupying vertical territories, stacked one above another on the steep and inaccessible cliffs.

The wrens can also be seen on the 'cleits': stone structures built by the extraordinary former inhabitants of this island to store the corpses of seabirds during the winter months. These hardy souls, known as 'the bird people of St Kilda', lived on the islands until 1930, when illness and hardship had reduced their numbers too low to sustain a permanent community. Today, all that remains of this lost civilization are the cleits and a row of tumbledown houses, on whose broken roofs and walls the wrens occasionally perch to deliver their loud and enthusiastic song.

BLACKBIRD

*

On a bright and chilly March evening, just as dusk begins to fall, an unmistakable sound echoes around the rooftops of our villages, towns and suburbs. Fluty and fruity in tone, with measured phrases divided by brief pauses, it tells us that however cold and icy the weather may be, winter will soon be over. It is the song of one of our best-known and best-loved birds: the blackbird.

Blackbirds are members of the thrush family, and the brown females and youngsters often have a few speckles on their throats and breasts, which reveal their connection with song and mistle thrushes. But at this time of year, it is the ebony male that takes centre stage. In Shakespeare's day, blackbirds were known as 'ouzels', and in *A Midsummer Night's Dream* Bottom perfectly describes the male: 'The ouzel cock so black of hue, with orange-tawny bill.' The only feature he missed out was the male's yellow eye-rings, which are as bright as early spring crocuses.

Throughout the winter, blackbirds have been roosting in thick undergrowth and announcing their presence with loud 'mik-mik' calls. These are part of our winter soundscape and, for the blackbirds themselves, are aggressive signals. When blackbirds roost they call as a ritualized warning to other blackbirds to keep their distance, although skirmishes don't often break out.

The reason why our resident blackbirds seem so edgy at this time of year is that their territories are under siege. Large numbers of continental blackbirds from Scandinavia, the Low Countries and Germany pour into Britain each winter to escape the freezing weather back home, and several thousand birds at a time can often be seen arriving on the east coast. But you don't need to live there to witness this phenomenon: you might notice small, restless groups of blackbirds in your own neighbourhood, often containing young males with black instead of yellow bills. They're usually pretty unpopular with the resident blackbirds, a sure sign that these are continental visitors.

In spring, the trigger for the male blackbird to begin to sing is a complex blend of day-length and temperature. So although they usually wait until the lighter evenings of March to start singing, in mild winters they may begin as early as January. Blackbirds often have two or three broods and exceptionally some pairs manage an astonishing five broods in a single

breeding season. So they are keen to get off to a flying start, laying their clutch of five or six greenish eggs speckled with reddish-brown spots in dense bushes or shrubs, often in gardens.

They proclaim their territories from the top of a roof or, especially in town, by perching on television aerials. But there aren't many places where you can't find blackbirds, and you'll hear them sing from trees, scrub, hedgerows and sea-cliffs virtually throughout the UK, apart from the high tops, where they are replaced by their much scarcer cousin the ring ouzel.

Because they're such common and widespread birds, they pack in their territories very tightly, so just as one song ends, another begins. This network was perfectly captured in Edward Thomas's evocative 1917 poem 'Adlestrop', where the writer's train makes an unscheduled stop at a small, rural railway station:

> *And for that minute, a blackbird sang*
> *Close by, and round him, mistier,*
> *Farther and farther, all the birds*
> *Of Oxfordshire and Gloucestershire.*

CHIFFCHAFF

*

With a beat like a metronome, the chiffchaff's unmistakable song is the overture to the long-awaited rush of spring migrants. These diminutive, olive-green warblers are among our first spring migrants to arrive, and are usually back on their breeding territory by the end of March, a good few weeks before most other warblers return from Africa.

In spring, singing chiffchaffs are easy to identify, as they persistently shout their name from perches in budding trees or blossoming bushes, pumping their tails up and down as if full of joy to be back. We say that they sing 'chiff-chaff' but our European cousins hear the same song rather differently: the Germans call this little bird 'zilp-zalp', the Dutch 'tjiftjaf' and the Welsh 'siff-saff'.

They breed in open woods, preferring taller trees than their close relative the willow warbler. The two are superficially similar, but chiffchaffs have dark legs and short wings, and a more open expression on their rather plain face. In spring and summer their repetitive song instantly sets them apart from the willow warbler's plaintive, tuneful cadence.

A typical view of a newly arrived chiffchaff is of a small, pale green bird searching among the flowers of a pussy-willow bush for pollinating insects. These hungry birds may have wintered in the Mediterranean area or even south of the Sahara. But they may also have come a much shorter distance. One reason why chiffchaffs are on the rise in Britain is that some have changed their migratory habits, and instead of travelling all the way to Spain or North Africa, now stay put for the winter.

Many of these birds head to the milder south and south-west of Britain, often gathering near water, where more insects remain active throughout the winter months. But whether they spend the winter here or around the Mediterranean, chiffchaffs have an obvious advantage over long-haul migrants such as the willow warbler, as they do not have to complete such a prolonged and hazardous journey to reach their breeding grounds. As a result, the eponymous song of the chiffchaff is more familiar now than ever before.

LAPWING
*

Tumbling through the air like an out-of-control kite, and uttering a sound like someone breathing helium, the lapwing certainly makes its mark on our rural landscape. Sadly, though, this colourful and charismatic wader is far less common than it used to be just a generation ago, and has now vanished from much of our countryside.

We can measure the lapwing's familiarity by the variety of names the species has garnered through the centuries. They are sometimes known as the 'green plover' because of a greenish tinge to their feathers. That distinctive call has also inspired the name 'peewit' – found throughout Britain – and the more local name of 'pyewipe', which in turn gave its name to a place near Grimsby in Lincolnshire, a reminder of a time not so long ago, when they were much more familiar on farmland.

Lapwings are one of the most stylish of all our farmland birds. About the size of a feral pigeon, they have long legs, white underparts, iridescent purplish-green upperparts and a long crest. When they take to the air they do so on wings that are broader at the ends than near the body, which give lapwings one of the most distinctive flight-patterns of any British bird.

They can look lazy in flight, as if barely making any effort, but that's deceptive: they are capable of

astonishing aerobatics, especially in the breeding season, when the males career madly over their territories, calling loudly.

For centuries, the lapwings' dark, freckled eggs would be collected each spring and taken to city markets by stagecoach and train, where they were served to discerning diners in expensive restaurants. These are the 'plovers' eggs' sent to Sebastian by his mother in Evelyn Waugh's novel *Brideshead Revisited*, set in the years between the First and Second World Wars.

Left to their own devices, the eggs hatch to produce tiny chicks that can leave the nest immediately to forage for food. The chicks are intricately marked to enable them to blend into the background, though their attentive parents still need to chase off marauding crows with plaintive cries accompanied by rapid dive-bombing.

But lapwings haven't been able to defend themselves against changes in the agricultural landscape, including the loss of mixed pasture and arable farms, and the drainage of much of our farmland. These have dramatically reduced our breeding lapwing population, so that there are now large areas of lowland Britain where you will no longer find them in spring.

Lapwings are more widespread in autumn and winter, when they gather in fields and marshes, often accompanied by their cousins, the smaller and longer-winged golden plovers, rising into the sky to utter a chorus of that mournful 'pee-wit, pee-wit' call.

NUTHATCH

*

A loud wolf-whistle echoing across your local park is a clear sign that spring is here – but not, perhaps, in the way you might think. These penetrating sounds are just part of the repertoire of a male nuthatch, whose varied calls and songs include squeaks, trills and twitters; more than enough to keep his mate happy.

But both male and female nuthatches have another trick up their sleeve. They are the only British bird that can climb down a tree as well as up: you'll sometimes see them descending the trunk or hanging beneath a branch as if the normal rules of gravity simply don't apply.

That's if you see them at all; for nuthatches are rather elusive, often out of sight in the leafy canopy of the tall trees where they feed and nest. March is a good month to get a decent view, as they are beginning their courtship and breeding activity, and can be easier to see when the leaves are not yet on the trees.

If you do get a good look at one, a nuthatch is easy to identify: blue-grey above, chestnut under the tail and with a black highwayman's mask across its face. They use their long, businesslike bills to prise away pieces of bark in search of insects, or to hammer open nuts and seeds; indeed the name 'nuthatch' derives from the phrase 'nut-hack'. Their bills are handy on the bird-table too, to fend off fellow diners such as tits and finches – a nuthatch may be about the same size as a great tit, but when one is about, there's no doubt who's in charge.

Nuthatches are also well known for gathering mud or dung in their bills and plastering it around their nest-hole to exclude larger predators such as woodpeckers. They don't excavate their own holes, but in mature woodlands and even town parks they have plenty to choose from, which they can customize to their own taste and design by adding mud.

But although there's plenty of wooded habitat available throughout the UK, nuthatches aren't found everywhere. They are rare in Scotland and completely absent from Ireland, as they are unwilling, or perhaps unable, to fly across large areas of open water. They seem to be doing well in much of England and Wales, and are well worth looking and listening for wherever there are mature trees.

TREECREEPER

*

A walk through a wood on a March afternoon can be a rather quiet affair. With the dawn chorus long since finished, most birds have already fed and are hiding away in the tops of the trees or dense undergrowth.

Then you spot a tiny creature, brown above and white below, creeping up and around the surface of a tree-trunk in short, jerky movements. At first sight, it looks more like a mammal than a bird – a mouse perhaps, or a vole. But it is a bird: one of the more modest of our woodland inhabitants, a treecreeper.

As their name suggests, treecreepers are perfectly adapted to life close to the trunk or branches of a tree. Indeed they rarely let go, preferring to inch their way upwards, belly hugging the bark and using their stiff tail-feathers to brace themselves. Only when they reach

the point at which they can go no further do they launch themselves off their anchorage and flit downwards to land at the base of another tree, to begin the whole process over again.

Treecreepers are common woodland birds but, because their high-pitched, almost whispering song is regularly drowned out by the dawn chorus, they're often overlooked. Once you're familiar with their song or tremulous calls, the secret is to look not among the foliage but along the tree-trunk. Here the treecreeper is easy to find even in silhouette, because of its distinctive long, narrow shape – a product of its tapering tail and curious bill.

In fact a glimpse of the treecreeper's downcurved, tweezer-like bill will clinch the identification. It's a delicate instrument, which the bird uses like a dentist's probe to locate tiny insects and spiders hidden deep in the crevices of the bark. Treecreepers love bark: they build their nests behind its peeling flaps, and even sleep in bark bivouacs.

They're adaptable birds too. Huge conifers known as 'Wellingtonias' were introduced from North America to parts of Britain in the mid-1850s, a dramatic centrepiece for a park or country estate. The bark of these evergreens is spongy and soft, and in the 1920s one observer was puzzled to find small holes scooped out of the surface. When he went back at dusk, he found a treecreeper sitting in each hole, its back level with the rest of the bark: warm, well insulated and beautifully camouflaged. This roosting habit soon caught on and now wherever there are Wellingtonias, treecreepers prefer these to all other trees.

PEREGRINE

*

A sheer cliff-face, rising well over a hundred metres into the sky. At the top, almost out of sight, a bird is surveying its territory. Far below, a flock of pigeons takes flight, and in a fraction of a second the watching bird has launched itself into the air in hot pursuit. As soon as one pigeon becomes separated from the flock, its fate is sealed: moments later, a loud, explosive crack goes off like a gunshot, and the pigeon is caught. Its nemesis? The peregrine.

That same scene may be played out on the coast, where waves crash against the rocks below; on a crag, halfway up a heather-clad mountainside; or more recently in the heart of a city, where the 'cliff' is a tall building made from metal and concrete. Nowadays the peregrine is equally at home in all three habitats.

We think of peregrines as specialist predators: partly because they were so rare, for so long; and partly,

perhaps, because they only kill birds. But with more than 200 prey species to choose from in Britain alone, they can hardly be called specialized. Indeed peregrines can survive almost anywhere, and are the world's most widespread raptor, found in all the world's continents except Antarctica. Wherever they are, they kill using the same, ruthlessly efficient technique, chasing down their prey in breathtaking dives, or 'stoops'.

Yet despite its skill and adaptability as a predator, this mighty falcon once almost disappeared from Britain. Raptors have been routinely killed wherever they pose a threat to game birds, or simply out of prejudice against any animal that kills as effectively as us. But during the Second World War hundreds more peregrines were shot, and many nests destroyed, to prevent them from intercepting the homing pigeons carrying messages from RAF pilots shot down across the Channel.

No sooner had the war come to an end, and one threat was over, than another soon arose. During the post-war era organochlorine pesticides such as DDT concentrated up the food chain, either killing the peregrines directly, or causing them to lay eggs with shells so thin they broke before they could hatch. Britain's peregrine population went into freefall, and by the early 1960s had been reduced to less than half its 1939 level.

Numbers stayed very low during the 1970s and 1980s, but gradually peregrines began to bounce back – and did so in style. By the millennium they had returned not just to their traditional nest sites on sea-cliffs and mountains, but also to an entirely new habitat: the urban jungle. Here it's still a surprise for older birders to glimpse that blue-grey form with its pale face and dark moustache soaring high over the city streets, or hear the grating cackle echoing off the walls of high-rise blocks.

Our city churches, cathedrals and other tall buildings turned out to be a perfect substitute for cliffs and quarries and, with a plentiful supply of pigeons, peregrines are thriving. But pigeons aren't the only item on the menu. Studies of their prey have revealed that urban

peregrines have been known to kill well over a hundred different species of birds, including ducks, gulls and parakeets. Less likely victims include migrating corncrakes and Leach's petrels, caught illuminated by the city lights as they fly overhead at night.

So whether you live in Worcester or Westminster, Bristol or Birmingham, Exeter or Edinburgh, look upwards next time you're in town; you might just be treated to a flypast from the fastest living creature on the planet.

ROOK

*

The chocolate-box image of an English country village, with church tower, cricket green and local inn serving foaming pints of beer, would hardly be complete without the sight and sound of one of our most quintessentially rural birds: the rook.

When forests covered much of our island nation, rooks must have been pretty scarce, confined, perhaps, to the grassy clifftops around our coasts or the treeless uplands. But since Neolithic times, when the first farmers began felling the forests and planting crops, rooks have thrived. Their requirements are fairly simple: open countryside where they can probe the pastures and ploughed fields for worms and grubs, plus a stand of tall trees where they nest together in colonies known as 'rookeries'.

Almost before the New Year has turned, they gather in noisy flocks, attending to last year's nests, and adding twigs to these loose, untidy structures in order to repair the ravages of winter and make them suitable for this year's breeding season. They bustle and squabble with one another, emitting a noisy babble of croaks, caws and yelps, as they establish who is nesting where, and how far apart they will tolerate each other's homes.

It can be mayhem up in the canopy, with birds arguing over who should have first pick of the best places to nest. As they pilfer twigs and protest loudly to each other, it's tempting to draw comparisons with humans, and indeed our ancestors believed that rooks held 'courts' or 'parliaments', where punishments were meted out to transgressors.

Nearby, ragged flocks of rooks congregate in arable and pastoral fields, often with carrion crows and jackdaws, and plunge their long, pointed beaks deep into the soil in search of food. To prevent their facial feathers from becoming matted with earth, they have bare skin around their bills, and this greyish patch is a good way to distinguish them from the all-black crows. In flight they look more ragged and looser-winged, and their central tail-feathers are longer, giving their tail a blunt diamond shape, differentiating them from crows which have a square-ended tail.

CETTI'S WARBLER

*

One classic rule of the bird world is that if you have a fairly drab plumage, you need an extraordinary song. Along with the nightingale and wren, a less well-known bird shares this trait: Cetti's warbler. Few birdsongs have the power to stop you in your tracks, but heard at close range, Cetti's warbler really can make you jump.

That explosive, almost heart-stopping burst of notes is a relatively new feature of our countryside. Until the 1960s, Cetti's warblers were unknown in the UK, though on the Continent they were common in marshy areas, especially dense scrub and the edges of reedbeds and ditches.

Named after an eighteenth-century Italian zoologist and Jesuit priest, Francesco Cetti, these birds first bred here in south-east England in the early 1970s. Unlike most of our warblers, Cetti's warblers don't migrate, which initially helped them to spread rapidly. However, relying on a diet of insects means they are badly affected by harsh winters, and two of these in a row in the mid-1980s checked their progress, for a while at least. But by the end of the century their loud and sudden song-bursts were making people jump out of their skins from Devon to Kent, through South Wales and as far north as Yorkshire.

If you're in the right place, hearing them is easy, especially as they sing almost all year round. But actually seeing a Cetti's warbler is a totally different matter. They tend to skulk about in thick vegetation near water, so often all you'll glimpse is a dark, mahogany-coloured bird rather like a giant wren, dashing between bushes, never to reappear.

There's no doubt that their song is by far the best clue to their presence. Once heard, it's hard to forget, but if you need a mnemonic to help you remember, there are several, including a memorable one from the *Collins Bird Guide*: 'Listen! What's my name? Cetti, Cetti, Cetti, that's it!' There is also: 'Me? Cetti? If you don't like it, naff off!' And perhaps the most apposite: 'Oi! Have you seen it . . .?! Have you seen it yet?!'

GREY PARTRIDGE
*

Of all our rural birds, no other species' fortunes are quite so closely tied to the way we farm the land as the grey partridge, which has aptly been described as the 'countryside barometer'. In the decades since the Second World War, since industrial farming methods have come to dominate our lowland landscape, the grey partridge population has been in freefall. The characteristic 'knife-sharpening' call is now a sound to savour, as this once common game bird has become a rarity across most of Britain.

From a distance, grey partridges look like brown clods of earth with orange faces. Look closely, though, and you'll see they have a dark, horseshoe-shaped patch on their bellies and are finely barred in shades of gunmetal grey and dark chestnut. They're true farmland birds, revelling in wide, open landscapes rich in weed seeds and insects – prime food for their growing chicks.

Partridges can be extremely sedentary: a pair will often hold territory across a few fields, seldom straying further during their whole lives. The hen partridges lay their enormous clutches – usually between twelve and sixteen eggs, more than any other British bird – in thick vegetation or under hedges. When the partridge family hatches, the chicks run around and are able to feed themselves almost immediately. In autumn and winter birds gather together in extended family groups known as 'coveys'.

With the ability to breed so prolifically, you'd think that grey partridges would be doing well. But they are one of our fastest declining birds and have vanished or are very scarce across large swathes of the countryside. The causes of this decline include increasing field sizes, which reduce nesting cover, and the widespread use of pesticides, which kill off the insects so essential for the growing chicks. There may also be competition from red-legged partridges and pheasants bred and released for sport.

Ironically, the partridge is only able to hang on in some parts of Britain because the birds are managed for shooting on large country estates. The provision of nesting and feeding areas and legal control of predators has helped the grey partridge to thrive in some places, but without intensive care its future across the rest of the farmed landscape is looking bleak.

GREAT CRESTED GREBE

*

On a gravel pit on the outer fringes of London, a pair of elegant waterbirds is gearing up for a very special court-ship display. First, one dives beneath the waters, and comes up to the surface with a tuft of waterweed in its beak. Its partner then does the same. What follows

is one of the most elaborate and ritualized courtship displays in the entire bird world. For great crested grebes, spring is definitely in the air.

Today, great crested grebes, ruffed like Tudor courtiers, are a regular sight on rivers, lakes and wetlands throughout southern Britain. But a century ago the bird was almost extinct here, driven to the brink of oblivion by the tastes of fashion-conscious, high-society women.

Grebes are the most aquatic of all the world's birds, living their whole lives on water, and virtually never coming to land. They even build a floating nest, where they lay their clutch of three or four narrow, elongated eggs. These start out white, but soon turn olive green because the adult grebes cover them up with waterweed to hide them when they are away from the nest. Once hatched, the stripy chicks often ride on their parents' backs, keeping up a constant clamour for small fish and even the occasional feather, which aids their digestion.

Ironically, feathers were almost the great crested grebe's downfall. To stay warm during their life on the water, grebes have very dense, soft feathers on their breast. It was this special plumage, known as 'grebe fur', and the birds' distinctive feathered ear-tufts, known as 'tippets', that were so prized by the fashion trade, which used them to decorate hats or to make into hand-muffs. At one stage in the late nineteenth century the breeding population of grebes was down to just forty pairs.

At the eleventh hour, fate intervened in the shape of a group of redoubtable women who strongly disapproved of the use of feathers in fashion, and campaigned to stop this cruel and destructive trade. This led, in 1889, to the founding of the Society for the Protection of Birds, which in 1904 gained a royal seal of approval and became the RSPB. Since then the great crested grebe has gone from strength to strength, and there are now more than 5,000 pairs breeding in the UK – mostly in England and Wales.

When they were still very scarce here, great crested grebes also played a crucial part in the birth of

a new science: ethology, or the study of animal behaviour. Until the First World War the kind of scientific observation of living creatures we take for granted today was simply unknown. Then, in the spring of 1912, a young man named Julian Huxley decided to spend a fortnight's holiday studying the courtship behaviour of great crested grebes on a reservoir at Tring, to the north-west of London. The resulting scientific paper changed the way we study nature for ever, helping turn it from the museum-based examination of dead creatures into the field observation of live ones.

Today, if we are lucky, on a fine early spring day we can observe a pair of great crested grebes indulge in the climax of their courtship display: standing chest to chest in the water with weed held in their beaks, each paddling furiously to stay upright in their elaborate 'penguin dance'. As we watch, we can share the wonder the young Julian Huxley must have felt a century ago, and also give thanks to the formidable women who campaigned against the cruel exploitation of this beautiful and fascinating bird.

SAND MARTIN

*

It's often said that 'one swallow doesn't make a summer'. But the sight of the flickering shapes of sand martins over the local lake or reservoir on a blustery March day is a welcome sign that spring is almost here, whatever the weather.

These small, pale brown relatives of the swallow arrive several weeks earlier than their cousins, having winged their way across the Sahara Desert and Mediterranean Sea to turn up some time in the first week or two of March. Partly this is because they don't have quite so far to travel: swallows come all the way from South Africa, whereas sand martins have spent our northern winter in the vast Sahel region, just south of the Sahara. Nevertheless, this is still a journey of almost

4,000 kilometres, which, given that a sand martin weighs about fourteen grams (roughly half an ounce), is a pretty impressive achievement.

Sand martins are the smallest of the three species of swallow breeding in Britain, and are brown above and white below, with a brown band across their chest, whereas swallows and house martins have dark blue upperparts. You can often hear their dry, buzzing calls overhead before you see them, but in cold weather they become very obvious as they hawk for low-flying insects over large stretches of water such as lakes and reservoirs.

As the month goes on, and the weather hopefully improves, sand martins begin to look for somewhere to nest. They're called sand martins not because of their brown colour, but because they breed in sandy soil, digging tunnels in quarries or steep riverbanks, using their tiny feet and bills. A tunnel seventy centimetres long will take them about a week to dig, depending on the density of the earth.

Sometimes hundreds of pairs will nest in a single quarry face, peppering its surface with their burrows. Sand martins are great opportunists and have been known to nest in temporary piles of building sand or even sawdust – a rather risky strategy. They will also use artificial burrows known as 'sand martin banks', which have been created on some nature reserves to allow visitors to get close-up views of this attractive little bird.

GOLDENEYE

*

A concrete-sided reservoir on the outskirts of a big city may not seem an obvious place to witness a courtship display more usually seen in the wilds of Scotland or Scandinavia. Yet on a sunny March morning, male goldeneyes are wooing their potential mates with a performance better suited to the West End stage. The suitor begins by approaching the female, getting her attention with a deep, grating call. Then he arches his neck and throws his head back against his mantle in an ecstasy of wooing – not that the females ever look terribly impressed.

For most goldeneyes, this is the start of a relation-ship that won't be consummated until they return to the Scandinavian lakes where most of our wintering birds breed. Since 1970 though, a small population has stayed on in spring to breed in Speyside, in the Highlands of Scotland. Female goldeneyes usually nest in holes in trees, but if these are scarce, they will readily use nestboxes. This habit was discovered in Sweden more than 200 years ago, when these boxes were initially used to harvest the eggs for food. Thanks to the efforts of Scottish ornithologists, who have put up dozens of nestboxes, today about 200 pairs of goldeneye breed there each year.

Because goldeneyes are diving ducks, feeding mainly on shellfish and crustaceans, they are sometimes the only winter duck found on bleak, open reservoirs. Unlike dabbling ducks such as mallard and teal they don't need muddy shorelines and lots of vegetation.

Both males and females have bright yellow eyes, but the drake is the snazzier dresser, with glossy black and white streaks down his back, a white collar, greenish-black head and a bold white spot under each eye. Females and youngsters have a chestnut-brown head and pale grey plumage, and share the male's distinctive, rather bulbous head shape.

SNOW GOOSE

*

Few geese stand out in a flock of other goose species quite so well as the aptly named snow goose, whose bright white plumage makes them as obvious as a golf ball in a coal scuttle. But even though this bird may be conspicuous and easy to identify, deciding whether it is a truly wild vagrant from across the Atlantic Ocean is guaranteed to cause a headache for any birder lucky enough to stumble across one.

Snow geese breed in their millions in the Canadian Arctic and fly south in autumn to feed on grain and other crops in the lowlands of the southern United States. Their migrations are eagerly awaited and the arrival of thousands of snow-white geese with jet-black wingtips is one of the world's greatest wildlife spectacles.

Here, on the opposite side of the Atlantic, one or two snow geese are seen every year, often with wintering flocks of birds such as white-fronted geese, in wild places such as the Outer Hebrides. It would seem reasonable to assume that these are genuine wanderers, which have made it across the ocean. But if only life were that easy. Snow geese are common in captivity in the UK, and escaped birds can and do breed in the wild. There is even a feral breeding population on the island of Coll, not that far from where supposedly wild birds are regularly seen.

So, when a distinctive white shape turns up among a flock of wild grey geese, its origins are always under scrutiny. The only way to confirm its credentials is to check if it's carrying a ring that was put on in North America. This has been done on occasion, so we can confirm that some snow geese do indeed reach here under their own steam.

Such niceties didn't bother the author Paul Gallico. His novella *The Snow Goose*, published in 1941, tells the tale of an injured goose found by a young girl named Fritha. She gives it to a disabled artist, Philip Rhayader (loosely based on the ornithologist and conservationist Peter Scott), who nurses it back to health.

Rhayader then takes his boat to help the evacuation at Dunkirk, but fails to return, and is presumed lost at sea. When, the following winter, the snow goose comes back to the wild Essex marshes, Fritha takes it as a sign of her lost lover. This parable of love, loss and the power of friendship became an unexpected bestseller, perhaps because its story so reflected the uncertainties of its time.

WOODLARK

*

Thomas Hardy's 'blasted heaths' are home to some of our most specialized birds, including the nightjar, stonechat and Dartford warbler. But another species also lives here, a small, brownish bird that more than makes up for its rather drab plumage with its delightful song: the woodlark.

Woodlarks are closely related to skylarks, but are far rarer in the UK, mainly breeding in southern England and East Anglia. They're much fussier than skylarks about where they live and are more or less confined to heathland or newly felled conifer plantations, where they hollow out a scrape in bare, sandy ground in which to lay their eggs. With her back level with the surrounding soil, the streaky brown female is superbly camouflaged as she broods her precious clutch.

As its name suggests, the woodlark will sing from the branches of trees in open areas or very young plantations, but like his relative the skylark his *pièce de résistance* is an elaborate song-flight, during which he flies slowly in a broad loop, high over his territory.

As the woodlark performs his aerial display, his broad wings and very short tail give him the appearance of a small, diurnal bat. While circling, he produces a string of bell-like notes, purer and less complex than the song of the skylark, with a series of liquid sounds descending down the scale. In France, its song has given it the name 'Alouette lulu', which is also echoed in its evocative Latin name – *Lullula*.

The French composer Olivier Messiaen, many of whose compositions were inspired by birdsong, considered the woodlark's song to be one of the most beautiful he had ever heard, while it also inspired poems by Gerard Manley Hopkins and Robert Burns. However, as woodlarks do not breed in Scotland it is more likely that Burns was writing about the tree pipit. Rather confusingly, this also used to be known as the 'wood-lark', but can't match the real thing for the quality of its pure, cascading notes.

EGYPTIAN GOOSE

*

A bird that appears in artwork on ancient Egyptian tombs and shares the limelight with crocodiles and hippos in wildlife films doesn't seem a likely candidate for *Tweet of the Day*; yet the Egyptian goose is officially a British bird – and indeed one that is doing rather well.

Egyptian geese are common and widespread throughout most of sub-Saharan Africa, including, of course, Egypt. They're striking and rather odd-looking birds: pinkish brown in colour, with a dark eye-patch and, in flight, large white patches on their wings. Unless you're familiar with them, your first reaction at seeing one in the English countryside is likely to be 'What on earth is that?'

It was the Egyptian goose's exotic appearance that brought them here in the first place, attracting the attention of wildfowl collectors as long ago as the late seventeenth century, when this species was introduced to Britain. Until the 1980s they were mostly found around the Holkham Estate in north Norfolk, where

several hundred birds fed and swam on the ornamental lake and surrounding grounds. Then, for no obvious reason, they began to spread across southern and eastern England – especially where lakes are close to ancient woodland, as they nest in tree-hollows.

As you might expect, a bird that's at home in a warm climate struggles to survive when we experience harsh winters. Egyptian geese can start to breed as early as February or March, and as a result often lose many goslings at this time.

Nevertheless, today more than 1,000 pairs of Egyptian geese breed here, and they can even be found in London's Hyde Park, with parakeets screeching overhead to add an exotic air to the nation's capital city. They are now spreading steadily northwards and westwards, so wherever you live there is an increasingly strong chance that these bizarre birds will turn up in your neighbourhood in the years to come.

ALPINE SWIFT

*

A large brown and white crescent scything through the spring clouds might just be an Alpine swift. If it is, then it's certainly your lucky day, for these giant cousins of our familiar common swift are a scarce visitor to Britain, with an average of about ten recorded sightings a year, mostly in spring.

Like a common swift on steroids, Alpine swifts are anchor-shaped, with a wingspan nudging sixty centimetres, about the same as a merlin. They are much paler than the sooty-brown swifts we usually see: coffee-coloured above and milky white below, with a brown band across the chest. Their name is slightly misleading, because they're common throughout southern Europe, from Spain in the west to Turkey in the east, where these superb aeronauts sweep across the skies above familiar tourist spots such as the Parthenon in Athens and the Colosseum in Rome. Their rolling screeches, lower-pitched than the screams of the common swift, are a feature of the soundscape of many Mediterranean towns and villages, as they trawl for airborne insects.

Each spring, a handful of Alpine swifts overshoot their intended destination on their way back from their African wintering grounds, and end up in southern Britain – especially when an early ridge of high pressure in March or April brings fine, sunny weather across western Europe.

They aren't the only ones: other exotic European migrants, including bee-eaters and hoopoes, also overshoot at this time of year, and occasionally even stay on to breed; though as yet the Alpine swift has not attempted to do so. But because they travel so fast, and cover huge distances with such ease, they can turn up almost anywhere from central London to Shetland, so it's worth looking up on a fine spring day; you might just see one as it arcs across the skies.

RUFF

*

There are no prizes for guessing why this bird is called a ruff – at least when you see a male in all his spring finery. Sporting neckwear that would put a Tudor nobleman to shame, they strut around with other males in an arena known as a 'lek', performing for the right to mate with the watching females. Just like a red deer rut, this is a 'winner takes all' display, in which the majority of males are going to end up disappointed.

As they assemble for these extraordinary displays, these extravagantly plumaged wading birds really do look impressive. For the rest of the year, however, they are just another medium-sized, brownish-coloured wader, about the size of a redshank, though more pot-bellied, and with a shorter bill and pale orange, rather than red, legs. Females – known as 'reeves' – are considerably smaller than the males; and side by side the two can look like completely different species, especially to the novice observer unfamiliar with the variation within the species.

Ruffs pass through Britain in autumn, on their way south from their breeding grounds in Scandinavia and the Low Countries. Quite a few spend the whole winter here, while others move on all the way to Africa, where they share their wetland homes with flamingos, egrets and crocodiles.

When they return the following spring, some males have begun to sprout colourful ruffs. These impressive neck feathers, which may be black, white, ginger, or a mixture of all these colours, are a crucial weapon in the business of courtship.

At the lekking sites, which are mostly on wet meadows where the birds will later breed, the majority of males hold small patches of ground known as 'residences', where they perform a series of elaborate displays designed to impress the watching females. But they do not always succeed, and around the edges of the lek other birds known as 'satellite males' watch and wait, hoping for their chance to entice one of the females to mate with them instead. To make things even more complicated, scientists have recently discovered that some birds, which lack a ruff and so look very like females, are in fact cryptic males, known as 'faeders' (from the Old English word for 'father').

A large lek is a lively scene as the exuberant males spar with each other, fluttering their wings and jumping in the air to strike out with their long legs. Sadly leks like this are rare in the UK, as breeding ruffs are very few and far between, with only a handful of records in recent years. But many ruffs do pass through our wetlands on the way north to breed, so there's always a chance of seeing them in their spring finery.

LITTLE RINGED PLOVER

*

A working gravel pit might be the last place you would look for one of our scarcest breeding birds. Yet it is here, amid the rumble of lorries and the constant to-ing and fro-ing of huge digging machines, that the little ringed plover chooses to nest.

The little ringed plover is, as its name suggests, the smaller and slimmer relative of the ringed plover, a familiar shorebird found around our coasts. It can be told apart by its smaller size, greenish (rather than orange) legs, lack of orange on the base of its bill and, if you get close enough, by the distinctive lemon-yellow ring around each eye. The call is distinctive too: a piercing 'pee-oo', which you can hear even above the din of the gravel lorries.

Unlike most ringed plovers, the little ringed plover shuns the seaside, preferring to breed inland. On the Continent, it usually nests on the shingle banks of fast-flowing rivers, which have been swept clean of any vegetation by winter floods. This enables its clutch of four eggs, speckled like the pebbles on which they lie, to be perfectly camouflaged, especially against aerial predators such as kestrels and crows.

Until the Second World War the little ringed plover was a very rare visitor, with only a handful of records. But in 1938 a pair bred on the exposed gravelly shoreline of a reservoir in Hertfordshire. Six years later, to great excitement among ornithologists, they returned there and to nearby Middlesex. The little ringed plover's colonization of Britain had begun.

These momentous events were immortalized in a novel by a young newspaper reporter, Kenneth Allsop, who would go on to become one of our best-known broadcasters and nature writers. *Adventure Lit Their Star* is told as a *Boy's Own* adventure yarn, in which an invalided RAF pilot and two teenagers fend off a dastardly egg-collector keen to acquire a piece of ornithological history, and by saving the nest enable the plovers to establish a permanent foothold in Britain.

What was so surprising about the colonization of the little ringed plover was that it happened not in some remote, wild place, but on the edge of suburbia; in Allsop's phrase, 'that messy limbo which is neither town nor country'. It did so because of the post-war construction boom, which proved ideal for a bird that nests on newly deposited gravel. Within a decade little ringed plovers were calling and displaying over gravel workings, rubbish tips and new reservoirs as far north as Cheshire.

Today there are about 1,200 breeding pairs, and these brown and white waders with black masks and collars are found on many gravel pits and nature reserves. In Wales they have even started to nest on their natural habitat of riverbanks. If you're lucky you may see and hear the males' 'butterfly display' flight on a fresh, breezy day in early spring.

BLACK REDSTART

*

A flash of fiery orange on a patch of urban wasteland is always a welcome sight, signifying the presence of one of our rarest breeding birds: the black redstart.

For one species of bird to colonize Britain during the Second World War, breeding in a completely new habitat as a direct result of human activity, is incredible enough. But for two to do so is truly extraordinary. That's the surprising story of the black redstart.

Like the little ringed plover, the black redstart was very rare in Britain until the early decades of the twentieth century. On the Continent, the species is a common sight, especially around the rocky slopes of hills and mountains, or on the edge of towns and villages. The first breeding record in Britain was in

the 1920s, but it only managed to establish itself permanently here as a result of one of the most terrible events in our nation's history: the Blitz.

During the early 1940s, bombing raids by the German Luftwaffe devastated many British cities, including London. The resulting bombsites were left abandoned during the rest of the war, and soon became overgrown with wild flowers such as rosebay willow-herb, which in turn attracted plenty of insects. By 1942 there were over twenty singing males in London alone, and a scattering of black redstarts began to colonize other towns and cities.

Although they've been tagged the 'bombsite bird' ever since, black redstarts also breed on a range of other brownfield and man-made sites, including power stations, old dockyards, railway sidings and cathedrals. Appropriately, even their song has a rather artificial, metallic tone, and is often likened to the sound of ball bearings being ground together, which helps it cut through the constant hum of urban traffic.

If you do catch sight of the bird itself, given good views you can't mistake it for anything else. About the size of a robin, though rather more slender, it is sooty grey, with a darker throat and a flash of white in the wings when it flies. But the most distinctive feature is, of course, its orange-red tail ('start' is the Anglo-Saxon word for tail), which it flicks up and down almost constantly.

Modern development has drastically reduced the availability of breeding sites in our towns and cities; so black redstarts have recently declined as a British breeding species. Today, only about thirty pairs nest here, mostly still in city centres in the south and east of the country, though the population is boosted in autumn when birds arrive here from continental Europe to take advantage of our milder climate. Some spend the winter on beaches along the south coast, searching for insects beneath the cliffs.

But there is one ray of hope on the horizon. Some urban buildings are now being covered with 'green roofs', alternative habitats rich in flowers and insects.

Black redstarts are already beginning to take advantage of these new homes, feeding and even breeding high above the bustle of the city.

RING OUZEL

*

Always check your spring blackbirds carefully. If you're fortunate, you may have found a ring ouzel. With a call like the clatter of scree tumbling down a mountainside, ring ouzels loudly announce their presence in the uplands of northern and western Britain. Known as the 'mountain blackbird', this is indeed closely related to our familiar garden resident. But unlike its much commoner cousin the ring ouzel is a summer visitor, arriving in early spring to establish breeding territories in some of the wildest and most beautiful scenery in Britain, often in gullies by mountain streams, where the males sing their clear, fluting whistles from rocky crags.

The male ring ouzel is very handsome indeed: sooty black with a broad white ring called a 'gorget' across his chest, which is very conspicuous even from a distance. Like female blackbirds, his mate is brown, but she also has a pale brown gorget. Young ring ouzels can look very like scaly blackbirds, but when they fly, adults and young both show subtle silvery patches in their wings, and their calls are harder and stonier than those of blackbirds.

Unfortunately ring ouzels are becoming harder to find even in their classic strongholds, which include the North York Moors, Dartmoor in the south-west and the mountains of Scotland and Wales. Just why they're declining isn't certain, but poor breeding success could be linked to drier summers, which make it harder for the birds to find worms and grubs for their chicks.

Ring ouzels spend the winter in the mountains of North Africa, where an increase in grazing or the felling of juniper scrub could be adding to the pressures on the birds, as juniper berries form an important part of their winter diet.

There's still a chance of seeing ring ouzels, though, wherever you live, as they pass through the lowlands in spring en route to their breeding grounds in Britain and Scandinavia. There are traditional stopover sites where the birds rest to refuel for the next leg of their journey, often on downland or hilltops where they feed avidly for earthworms. So in late March and April, do scan those blackbirds with an eagle eye; if you're lucky, you might see one with a broad white collar . . .

Woodcock
Black Grouse
Willow Warbler
Snipe
Curlew
Bittern
Grasshopper Warbler
Great Grey Shrike
Common Whitethroat
Green Woodpecker

 APRIL

Hoopoe
Little Owl
Little Grebe
Stock Dove
Capercaillie
Ruddy Duck
Goosander
Red-throated Diver
Fulmar
Stone-curlew

INTRODUCTION

A FLASH OF COBALT across a farmyard, accompanied by a burst of enthusiastic twittering, can only mean one thing: the swallows are back from South Africa.

No matter how grey and cold the spring weather may be, the first sight and sound of a swallow dispels winter blues at a stroke. April is the month in which to celebrate migration. While the flocks of winter ducks, geese and waders wing their way north, the African migrants pour in from the south.

We understand the purpose and rigours of migration now, but our less well-travelled ancestors had their own – sometimes rather bizarre – explanations for the sudden appearance of birds each spring. Some 2,400 years ago, the Greek philosopher and pioneering naturalist Aristotle claimed that swallows hibernated in holes in the ground or hollow trees. More than two millennia later, Gilbert White found it hard to let go of the hibernation theory, writing to his fellow naturalist Thomas Pennant that: 'I acquiesce entirely in your opinion – that, though most of the swallow kind may migrate, yet that some do stay behind and hide with us during the winter . . .' Only with the advent of modern ornithology in the twentieth century did we begin to understand how migrants find their way across the globe and marvel at their extraordinary achievements.

Back home, April is a time for relearning plumages, calls and songs as we re-acquaint ourselves with birds we haven't seen for six months or more. All our smaller migrants are insectivores and their arrival coincides with the great emergence of insects across northern Europe. Queen bumblebees, roused from hibernation, drone past searching for nest-holes. Caterpillars swarm over unfurling leaves. Furry bee-flies hang in mid-hover as they probe primroses for nectar.

The stage is set for the arrival of our most numerous summer migrant. In the month's first few days, you may hear a gentle cadence of notes from a sallow or birch sapling, at first gushing, then dying away. It's a willow warbler, and though its sweet, almost hesitant song is often drowned out by the louder thrushes and wrens, it is affirmation that the migratory pulse is still functioning. This bird whose recent neighbours may have been antelopes and zebras is now utterly at home in a British copse.

As April matures, the floodgates open. Whitethroats are suddenly everywhere, singing their explosive songs from tangled hedges. House martins appear high over the suburbs and the sound we all associate with spring echoes through woods and copses. Cuckoos have returned from their winter home in the rainforests of central Africa and though they're not as numerous as they once were, can still be heard across much of Britain, especially in the north. Their calls, which none of us needs to relearn, swell a dawn chorus that is growing louder each day.

The real excitement this month is seeing birds that may not breed in your neighbourhood passing through en route to their nesting areas. For the dedicated patch-watcher – and your patch may be your garden, local park or a chink of conveniently placed countryside – April can bring all kinds of dividends. Whether they are overflying yellow wagtails betraying themselves with a loud 'wheesp', redstarts along a woodland edge, or northern wheatears landing on the local playing fields, sometimes it's hard to know where to look next.

Marshes are vibrant with life in April. Reed warblers straddle the desiccated canes of last year's reeds while sedge warblers launch themselves skywards from the fringing bushes. Near large reedbeds, you may be lucky enough to hear the low boom of a bittern, whose tigerish form is hidden somewhere out there among the rustling stems. Other well-camouflaged birds throw caution to the winds in brief but necessary spells of spring fever. As night falls, woodland clearings become the stage for the weird roding display of woodcocks, which twitter and burble as they patrol their aerial flyways, while snipe bleat like goats above fens and bogs, switch-backing across the darkening skies.

At a few upland sites in northern England, Wales and Scotland, where moors meet the edge of woodland, if you're up early you may hear bubbling and sneezing sounds as dawn breaks over the bleak landscape. This is one of the most memorable wildlife spectacles in the British Isles: black grouse displaying at their lek. These lyre-tailed, red-combed, blue-black males strut and fret upon their grassy stage, their breath rising in wisps in the chill morning air as they bustle around like fairground bumper-cars, trying to impress the watching females. As a sound experience, it's second to none, a cross between a pigeon loft and a steam engine rally.

We each have our favourite spring sounds, and for many of us they're closer to home. It may be a garden wren, singing lustily as he gathers nesting material, or a blackbird warbling from the rooftop while his mate broods her clutch of speckled greenish-blue eggs nearby.

Or coming full circle, it may be a swallow, back on the same wire as last year and singing in the hope of attracting a mate. We now know that this may be the very same bird that was here last summer and although the lively twitters that we hear in April are technically about establishing a territory, it's hard not to think of them as a triumphal celebration of a successful homecoming, and marking the true arrival of spring.

WOODCOCK

*

As dusk falls over a wood in springtime, dark shapes flicker over the treetops like remotely controlled model spaceships, emitting weird, unearthly sounds: not a Martian invasion, but displaying woodcocks.

Woodcocks are technically waders, but they don't do much wading because they live mainly in woods and forests. They're substantial birds, like a large, stocky snipe and are well adapted to the sylvan scene: thickset, long-billed and superbly camouflaged. On the woodland floor where they hide by day, their plumage – a patchwork of rusts, fawns, browns and blacks – enables them to blend into the leaf-litter until they almost become part of the forests in which they live.

Often your first sign that a woodcock is about is a blur of russet, followed by a rapid whirr of wings as the bird rises from almost under your feet, twisting away between the tree-trunks as if fired by a catapult – the speed and suddenness causing you to miss a heartbeat.

On the woodland floor woodcocks are very vulnerable to predators, but they don't rely on camouflage alone to protect them. Their large dark eyes, set high and far back on their heads, provide 360-degree vision, perfect for detecting intruders.

In winter there may be more than a million woodcocks here in the British Isles, though these elusive birds are not often seen. Tagging has revealed that some travel from as far away as Siberia to take advantage of our relatively mild winter.

In spring and summer, woodcocks are more localized, especially in the south. If you know where and when to look, they are more conspicuous. From March until July, woodcocks swap a life of secretive skulking for blatant self-advertisement. At dusk and dawn males patrol their woodland territories in a courtship display known as 'roding'. Flying at treetop height, with halting wingbeats, they grunt and whistle their way around a large circuit, often pursuing other males or intercepting females as they go.

Young woodcocks hatch in May and also rely on their cryptic colours to keep them safe. If a female bird is flushed from her nest she will scatter droppings over her brood to deter predators with the unpleasant smell and taste. A female woodcock can also pick her chicks up between her legs, or even in her bill, and fly away with them to a safer spot, although this aspect of a highly secretive bird's life has rarely been witnessed by human eyes.

BLACK GROUSE

*

At first light on a frosty northern moor, the bubbling calls of black grouse echo over the heathery ground. Sounding rather like a chorus of homing pigeons interspersed with the hissing of steam engines, these bizarre sounds are made by a gathering of males at their courtship ground, known as a 'lek'.

Charged with testosterone, the males, known as 'blackcocks', compete on jousting lawns to win the attention of the sombre-coloured females, or 'greyhens', mottled like dead heather and lichen. Fanning their lyre-shaped tails and exposing a flurry of white petticoats – their undertail feathers – the males rush towards their rivals with harsh, scouring sneezes and bubbling cries, known as 'roo-kooing'.

As the display becomes more and more intense, the birds flutter wildly, jumping at each other or flying in small circles around the lekking arena. It would be easy to assume that the males are the ones in control here – after all, they are the ones taking the lead in this complex courtship ceremony.

But, as in so many cases in nature, it is the female birds – watching modestly from deep within the purple heather – that actually make the important decisions. The females ultimately decide which male they will mate with, and which male, therefore, will win the prize of passing his genes down to the next generation. Studies have shown that the females tend to prefer the bigger males, especially those that spend more time displaying, and whose territories are the largest and closest to the centre of the lek: a sign of their dominance.

To see a lek in its full glory, you need to be up before first light and in the right place. Black grouse need a mosaic of habitats, including moorland, boggy ground and forests, and usually lek on the edge of the trees in an area of more open ground. But as we have homogenized our landscape, many of these areas have been lost, and numbers of black grouse have diminished.

Back in the eighteenth century black grouse could be found in every English county, but after a long and steady decline they are now confined to the wilder uplands of Britain. In recent years dedicated conservation work and habitat restoration has boosted numbers in parts of northern England such as Teesdale, and also in North Wales, while black grouse are being reintroduced to the Peak District, so now more people can witness that fabulous dawn display once more.

WILLOW WARBLER

*

A fine April morning, on the edge of a woodland or heath. A sound pierces the dawn air: a sweet, rather plaintive cadence sliding gently down the scale. It is both familiar, yet strangely unfamiliar, for it hasn't been heard here for half a year or more: the song of our commonest summer visitor, the willow warbler.

With well over 2 million breeding pairs, comfortably outnumbering more showy migrants such as the swift, swallow and house martin, the willow warbler really does deserve to be better known. But this unassuming little bird keeps itself to itself; and its song, though rather beautiful, is not as memorable as that of its cousin the chiffchaff.

The first willow warblers return here from Africa in late March, but the bulk of the arrival is in the first couple of weeks of April, when a wave of these tiny birds spreads gradually northwards across the country, often stopping to sing for a day or two and then moving on.

In their winter homes they may have been catching flies in forests full of monkeys or among antelopes browsing thorn-scrub, before flying across the Sahara, to arrive in northern Europe with the first flush of spring. They prefer open, fairly young woodland and plantations, and a better name for them might be 'birch warbler' because birch saplings are their favourite trees.

Willow warblers belong to the genus *Phylloscopus*, which means 'leaf-inspector', and that's exactly what they do as they search the fresh foliage for emerging insects. At first sight the bird itself is nothing special: a typical 'leaf-warbler', olive green above and pale below, with a distinctive pale stripe just above the eye. But as you watch, its subtle grace begins to reveal itself. Those long wings, needed to take it all the way to west Africa and back, give it a poised, elegant appearance as it flits around the hawthorn blossom in search of tiny insects.

The wistful song is also something that grows on you. It helped the pioneering eighteenth-century naturalist Gilbert White tell the willow warbler apart from two of its closest relatives, the chiffchaff and wood warbler, in the woods around his village home at Selborne in Hampshire. Modern birders may scoff at the idea that these birds are similar to one another, but we must remember that White and his contemporaries were watching them with the naked eye, not with the high-powered optics we are able to use today.

Willow warblers remain the most frequent summer visitor to Britain, but in the last couple of decades numbers in the south and east of England have dropped by as much as two-thirds in some places. Fortunately in Scotland, Ireland, Wales and much of western England they seem to be holding up. The jury is still out on why they have declined so rapidly, but many believe it is a result of changes in climate and habitat, both here on their breeding range and in Africa where they spend the winter.

SNIPE

*

On a fine spring evening, on the wild and windswept Outer Hebrides, a male snipe is perched on a wooden fence-post, uttering a loud 'chipping' call. In the fading light he rises into the air, flying high over his territory on winnowing wings, then plummets down towards the ground in a kamikaze dive, before sweeping upwards again. Throughout this madcap display, he produces a distinctive bleating noise known as 'drumming', which

sounds rather like someone blowing across the top of a beer-bottle while waggling a finger across their lips.

It is easy to assume that this unusual sound is emerging from the bird's bill, whereas in fact it is coming from the other end. Snipe have a special hinge in their outer tail-feathers, which when they fly rapidly through the air, causes them to flutter like a flag. This produces one of the strangest sounds made by any bird; one that has earned it a Gaelic name meaning 'little goat of the woods', as well as the English folk-name 'heather bleat'.

It's a sound you'd once have heard widely in bogs, fens and marshes throughout the British Isles, but in the past few decades snipe have declined as breeding birds in many places, especially in the south and east of England where they are now very local. Even where new wetlands have been created, snipe have not returned to breed, which may mean that their range is shifting northwards for other reasons, possibly linked to climate change.

In autumn and winter they are much more widespread, which gives us a chance to savour the intricate patterns of their plumage. Snipe are brilliantly camouflaged with streaks of dark brown and straw yellow, ideal for concealment among the tufts of marshland grasses. They are not much bigger than blackbirds, but have enormously long bills, with which they probe for worms and other creatures in soft, sticky mud. In autumn and winter you'll often see them feeding at the edge of shallow pools, their bills buried in the ooze right up to their eyes as they feed, while keeping a wary eye out for predators.

When they're disturbed, snipe dash off in a frantic zigzag flight, making a rasping call like a wellington boot being sucked out of sticky mud. A flock of snipe is known as a 'wisp' and will fly around the sky in high, wide circles, before pitching once more into the safety of the tussocks to resume feeding.

CURLEW

*

Few bird sounds summon up the spirit of wild places quite so poignantly as the haunting call of the curlew. Our largest waders lead a double life: in autumn and winter they gather on estuaries and saltmarshes, while in spring and summer they head to the hills.

Curlews can reach prey that other waders can't, digging deep into the mud for lugworms and cockles, locating them with the flexible tip of their very long, curved bill, which is richly supplied with nerve-endings to enable them to feed by touch. If disturbed they take to the air, their brown plumage giving them the look of immature gulls – until, that is, you spot that huge bill.

But by April, most curlews have left their winter homes and have returned to their breeding territories on moorland or upland pastures, where they probe for worms and grubs in the slowly thawing ground. A few will nest on boggy lowland heaths or even on farmland, but wherever they breed, you'll hear the male birds singing and displaying.

When he performs, the male curlew climbs high above his territory, uttering a distinctive bubbling call. At the peak of his ascent he hangs like a paraglider, using thermal air-currents to stay aloft; then, as his courtship display reaches its climax, he parachutes slowly down to the ground. Sometimes he will perform aerial switchbacks, dropping and rising several times as he sings.

Although they don't switchback like their partners, female curlews will also sing during gliding flights and even from the ground. Once they have laid their quartet of speckled eggs, however, they are less vocal, and slip silently away from the nest while their mate stands guard.

According to legend, a seventh-century holy man named St Beuno accidentally dropped his book of sermons into the water off the coast of Wales. A curlew rescued the book and brought it safely to the shore, so in gratitude, St Beuno prayed for the protection of the bird. That is why, tradition has it, finding a curlew's nest is so difficult.

Certainly curlews are now increasingly scarce as breeding birds in many parts of Britain, but the UK is still an important wintering ground for flocks from as far away as Russia, probing our coastal mudflats and thrilling us with their mournful cries.

BITTERN

*

On a misty April morning, as a light breeze rustles the tops of last year's reeds, you might hear one of the most peculiar sounds in nature: a deep, lowing call more like a distant foghorn than a bird. This is the famous boom of one of our rarest and most elusive breeding birds: the bittern.

The bittern's boom is lower-pitched than any other UK bird, and also carries further: as much as five kilometres when the air is still. Before the seventeenth century, when the draining of the East Anglian fens began in earnest, this booming must have been a familiar sound, although people weren't exactly sure how the birds made it.

Some thought that the bittern amplified its voice by exhaling down a hollow reed stem. Others, including Chaucer, believed that it blew directly into the water. In *The Canterbury Tales*, the Wife of Bath says of a character: 'And as a bitore bombleth [booms] in the myre, She leyde hir mouth unto the water doun.'

We know now that bitterns do indeed produce the booming sound by exhaling loudly, expelling air from the oesophagus, which is surrounded by powerful muscles. The poet John Clare wrote in the early 1800s that 'the first part of its noise is an indistinct muttering sort of sound very like the word butter uttered in a hurried manner and bump comes very quick after . . .' hence the folk-name 'butter bump'. Other local names include 'bog drum', 'bumble' and 'bull o' the mire'.

You are far more likely to hear a bittern than see it, for this relative of the familiar grey heron prefers to spend its time deep in the heart of reedbeds. Its cryptic plumage, streaked dark and light brown like the reeds themselves, makes it very hard to see, especially if it adopts its characteristic defensive pose of standing stock-still with its beak pointing vertically upwards.

From time to time, bitterns do take to the air for a minute or two, their slowly flapping wings and brown plumage making them look more like an owl than a species of heron. Normally, though, they disappear almost as soon as you spot them, flopping back down into the safety of their reedbed. Over the past two centuries or so, bittern numbers have declined severely with the drainage of their wetland homes. They became extinct as breeding birds in Britain by the year 1900, though they soon returned to nest in small numbers, mostly in East Anglia.

Nevertheless, towards the end of the twentieth century numbers were very low, with just eleven booming males counted in 1997. For a while, it looked as if we might lose the bittern as a British breeder once again, especially as many of their reedbed homes were on or near the coast, and were threatened with flooding from breaches in sea walls.

But conservationists were determined to save this unique bird, creating new wetland reserves, complete with vast reedbeds, in order to do so. Their foresight and efforts paid off remarkably quickly: there are now well over a hundred booming male bitterns in Britain, with more than thirty at just one site, the Avalon Marshes in Somerset. Here, a vast new wetland has also attracted rare herons such as the bittern's diminutive relative, the little bittern, to breed. So now, on a fine spring morning, you have a greater chance of hearing – and perhaps even seeing – a booming 'butter bump' than at any time in living memory.

GRASSHOPPER WARBLER

*

Not all birdsongs sound like birds, and one elusive species sounds far more like an insect: the aptly named grasshopper warbler, from the equally appropriate genus *Locustella*.

Like the paying out of an angler's line from a reel, the grasshopper warbler's song spills out from the bush or bramble clump where he hides away in the deep, dense foliage. Hearing one sing can be an almost unconscious experience; only when you finally 'tune in' do you realize it has been playing out around you for some time.

You'll mostly hear the grasshopper warbler's extraordinary song at dawn or dusk in overgrown scrubby or marshy areas, although the bird itself can often be very hard to locate. That's because he turns his head this way and that, so the stream of song appears to change direction, making it almost impossible to pinpoint. This intrigued the eighteenth-century naturalist-parson Gilbert White: 'Nothing can be more amusing than the whisper of this little bird, which seems to be close by though at a hundred yards distance. And, when close at your ear, is scarce any louder than when a great way off . . .'

Grasshopper warblers are indeed superb

ventriloquists, and sound more like some species of bush-crickets than a bird. But you can be sure that if you hear one in April or May it can't be a grasshopper or cricket, because they're not yet mature and don't sing in spring. An added frustration for many older bird-listeners is that this is one of the first songs we cannot detect as our hearing deteriorates, and we lose the ability to distinguish high-frequency sounds.

When it's not singing, spotting a grasshopper warbler can be a real challenge, and calls for patience or careful stalking. They are rather local birds, scattered throughout the British Isles and often in very young conifer plantations or damp scrubby areas near streams or reedbeds. If you do finally track one down you'll see that it's a small, slender bird, not much bigger than a blue tit; khaki-brown with dark flecking on its back, a pale throat and a broad tail. And when it sings, you can't help noticing that its whole body vibrates with the effort of delivering that incredible reeling song.

GREAT GREY SHRIKE

*

As you walk across a heath or moor in spring, you might expect to see a stonechat bobbing up and down on a gorse bush, or meadow pipits rising from the tussocks. But one bird, which the chats and pipits have good reason to fear, will never fail to make the day special: the great grey shrike.

Unlike the red-backed shrike, a rare migrant which also breeds fitfully here, the great grey shrike is exclusively an autumn and winter visitor, although in most years fewer than a hundred visit Britain from their breeding grounds in Scandinavia.

Scarce they may be, but they're imposing and often very obvious, as they have a convenient habit of perching on top of prominent small trees or shrubs in a forestry clearing or tract of heath. They are the largest European shrike, about the size of a blackbird but with a characteristic upright stance, accentuated by a long, white-fringed tail.

Great grey shrikes are smart birds with frosty grey upperparts, luminous white underparts and a black mask, which gives them a rather stern appearance. Their black bill is hooked at the tip – a sign that even though they are songbirds, they are also highly effective predators.

In winter, they are solitary, feeding on small birds, which they can catch in flight – a neat trick if you're lucky enough to witness it. They also eat mice, voles and shrews and, as spring approaches, they'll include bees and larger beetles in their diet. Shrikes are known as 'butcher birds' because of their habit of impaling their prey on thorn bushes, just as a butcher hangs his meat on hooks.

By late March and early April great grey shrikes are preparing to leave us, and as the breeding season approaches they may start to sing before heading off across the North Sea to find a mate, delivering a rather hesitant, chirping sound from the topmost point of a tree or bush.

Very occasionally a solitary bird will stay on into May or even later, but so far, despite rumours, they have not yet been proved to nest in Britain. Why they do not do so is something of a mystery, given that they are found across a wide range of the temperate northern hemisphere including North America, Europe and Asia. Perhaps one year a pair will decide to stay on here and ornithological history will be made.

COMMON WHITETHROAT

*

From the middle of April onwards, hedgerows, commons and untidy corners of fields are alive with the scratchy, frenetic song of whitethroats. One moment they are absent, the next almost everywhere, celebrating a safe return from their wintering grounds just south of the Sahara.

Whitethroats are members of the warbler family, but like the blackcap and chiffchaff they have the distinction of being so well known that they acquired their vernacular name long before their official one. They are one of the commonest and most widespread summer visitors to Europe and more than 1 million pairs breed in Britain each year.

This abundance doesn't mean that they are easy to see, however, as they spend much of their time skulking in hedgerows and tangled vegetation, a habit that earned them the old name of 'nettle creeper'. If they do emerge after scolding you loudly, you'll see that their throats are indeed pure white, their heads and cheeks soft grey (browner in the female) and their wings chestnut.

Fortunately the males don't just creep among nettles. When they arrive in April, they establish their territory by singing from hedgerow perches or, more spectacularly, launching themselves into the air while uttering that rapid, scratchy song to try to secure a mate. According to one Victorian naturalist, the

Revd C.A. Johns, this dancing song-flight gave rise to another country name – 'singing skyrocket'.

Whitethroats are so common in our countryside that their return each spring has always been taken for granted. Yet in April 1969, to the surprise of many birdwatchers, about three-quarters of all Britain's whitethroats failed to reappear. Investigations revealed that the cause was a severe and widespread drought across the Sahel Zone, the narrow strip of land extending from west to east across Africa just south of the Sahara. In some ways the whitethroat acted as an early warning system for us all, alerting us to the violent effect of changes in weather and climate on our precious migrant birds.

Fortunately the whitethroat did recover, and today the hedgerows of our lowland countryside still echo to its sound. On a fine, sunny spring day, it's a pleasure to watch the males launching themselves skywards, as they loudly declare temporary ownership of the small patch of greenery below.

GREEN WOODPECKER

*

As you walk through a wood, the strengthening breeze and greying skies suggest that fickle April is sending showers your way. Before the raindrops start to fall, you will sometimes hear a loud, laughing call: a green woodpecker.

This maniacal sound gave the green woodpecker its old country name of 'yaffle', but it may not be pure coincidence that you hear one before a shower. Another folk-name for our largest woodpecker is 'rain bird', as its call is supposed to herald the onset of showers.

It's a sound you can hear in woods, parks, heaths and large gardens throughout most of Britain, though not in Ireland, as the Irish Sea proved too much of a barrier for these birds as they headed north and west after the end of the last Ice Age.

You might expect to find woodpeckers in trees, but although green woodpeckers do nest there, they spend far more time on the ground, probing lawns and meadows for their main food: ants and their pupae. Bracing themselves on their stiff tail-feathers, they flick their long sticky tongues into the heart of anthills, and then retract them coated in tiny insects. Disturb one at this activity and it bounds off into the distance, yelping loudly, flashing a lemon-yellow rump as it goes. Seen in flight like this they can sometimes be mistaken for golden orioles or even escaped parrots.

Unlike great spotted and lesser spotted woodpeckers, green woodpeckers hardly ever drum. They use that loud, laughing call instead as a warning to rivals and a proclamation of territorial rights. Before mating, male and female green woodpeckers raise their red crown feathers and fan their wings and tails while playing a game of hide and seek around a tree-trunk, a comical and fascinating sight. When the young woodpeckers emerge from the darkness of their nests in late summer and crouch near their favourite anthills, they are mottled and greyish, looking rather like washed-out versions of their parents.

HOOPOE

*

The far-carrying, triple-noted 'poo-poo-poo' hoot of the hoopoe instantly transports us to a dusty Mediterranean vineyard, or an eastern European

woodland. This gaudy, outlandish-looking bird looks completely out of place on an English lawn. Yet the hoopoe is more than a sporadic visitor to Britain: occasionally they even pair up and breed here.

The hoopoe is about the size of a mistle thrush, and is quite simply unmistakable. It is salmon-coloured, with a long curved bill that it uses to probe short, grassy areas for grubs, and a flamboyant black-tipped crest, which it can spread like a fan when excited. In flight it transforms into a giant black and white butterfly, with broad, banded wings. Because of this hoopoes rarely go unnoticed even by non-birders, especially when they turn up on a manicured garden lawn, as they occasionally do.

Hoopoes are not actually all that rare in Britain: more than a hundred turn up here every year, mostly in southern counties during April or May. These have overshot their intended destination as they return to Europe from Africa, and are usually single birds, but sometimes a pair gets together and breeds. So far though, the hoopoe hasn't managed to colonize Britain permanently as a breeding bird.

On the Continent the species is fairly common and widespread in orchards and the open countryside, where they breed in holes in trees. Their unsavoury sanitary habits are legendary: young hoopoes defecate all over their nest, and the parents seem unable or unwilling to clean up after them. It is often said that you can find a hoopoe nest just by smell.

Elsewhere in the world, hoopoes have long-standing cultural associations. In ancient Egypt they were respected as sacred birds and appear on many tomb paintings. The hoopoe is the king of birds in Aristophanes' play *The Birds* and in 2008 was voted the National Bird of Israel.

LITTLE OWL

*

A loud yelping sound, coming from the branches of an ancient oak tree jutting out from a hedgerow, betrays the bobbing silhouette of a little owl – by far the smallest of our five breeding owl species.

Greyish-brown with white spots, little owls really are little, only about as long as a starling, but much stockier, with a large head, short tail and rounded wings. If you disturb one it will bound off low over the ground before swinging up on to a telegraph pole or gate-post where it bobs up and down, glaring fiercely at you with large, yellow and black eyes.

Little owls prefer mature trees in farmland and parks, although they will also nest in quarries and old farm buildings, where they raise their youngsters on a diet of small mammals, worms and insects. At dusk, if you're lucky, you may see one running across the furrows of a field to grab surfacing earth-worms or crawling dung-beetles, in a most un-owl-like way. In common with other owls, they are active at night, but you'll also often see them by day, perched on top of telegraph poles, on dead trees and around old farm buildings.

Although they're now widespread in lowland Britain and seem very much at home here, little owls are not native to our islands, but were introduced here from continental Europe.

The first record of this species here was one caught alive in a chimney in the Tower of London in the mid-eighteenth century, but this may have been an escaped cagebird. A century later, in 1843, an eccentric Yorkshire squire, naturalist and explorer named Charles Waterton imported little owls from Rome and released them on his estate near Wakefield in Yorkshire. Apparently he thought that they would be useful in his kitchen garden, where he hoped they would eat insect pests.

These first released birds didn't survive for long, but further attempts by landowners were more successful, and ornithologist Lord Lilford is credited with the successful introduction of birds from the Netherlands, which led to the first pair breeding in Northamptonshire in 1889.

By 1900 they had already spread to several southern counties, and by 1930 they had become wide-spread south of the River Humber, though they didn't breed in Scotland until 1958, and are still scarce there. Today, you can hear the yelps of little owls and their loud, almost melodious spring song across the fields and parks of much of lowland England and Wales.

LITTLE GREBE

*

A wetland in spring is not necessarily the place where you would expect to hear a sound like the whinnying of a small pony. But this is not the prelude to some aquatic equestrian experience, but the territorial call of the little grebe.

Our smallest waterbird, much smaller even than the diminutive teal, little grebes are rather dumpy creatures. In winter they are plain brown and buff, but during the breeding season they look rather smart, with a deep chestnut patch on their cheeks and the sides of their neck, and a bright yellowish-green spot just behind their bill, as if someone has daubed them with a touch of luminous paint.

Throughout the year, they fluff up their tail-feathers, making them look like bathtub rubber ducks as they float on the water. But such sightings are often fleeting because little grebes can be very secretive, especially during the breeding season when they lurk in reeds and rushes, or dive to avoid being seen. This diving ability was noticed by Shakespeare:

Like a dive-dapper peering through a wave,
Who, being looked on, ducks as quickly in . . .

As well as 'dive-dapper', another old name was 'dabchick', which refers to the little grebes' disappearing act, as well as to their superficial resemblance to the offspring of other waterbirds.

Being so small, little grebes can breed on small ponds and canals as well as larger lakes, slow-flowing rivers and gravel pits. Like other grebes they build a nesting platform from pondweeds and waterside plants on which they lay their clutch of white eggs. These are soon stained olive green by the waterweed the adults cover them with to conceal them from predators. The humbug-headed youngsters hatch in late spring and beg noisily for small fish or freshwater invertebrates, either following in their parents' train or hopping on to their backs for a free ride.

STOCK DOVE

*

Few other British birds are quite so overlooked, yet at the same time so common and widespread, as the stock dove. These slate-blue birds look rather like wood-pigeons, and can also resemble feral pigeons, so are often misidentified. But as soon as you learn their soft, low-pitched cooing sound, you'll realize just how common they are.

The terms 'pigeon' and 'dove' are largely interchangeable, though pigeon usually refers to larger members of the family, in which case 'stock pigeon' might be a better name for this species, as they are only slightly smaller than the familiar woodpigeon. They can be told apart from woodpigeons by the lack of white markings on their necks and wings, and their darker, more blue-grey shade. Seen close to, they are rather attractive, with iridescent green patches on the sides of their neck, beady black eyes and a short, yellow bill.

In flight, their triangular grey wings are edged with black, and they look rather solid – 'stocky', you might say. But their name has nothing to do with their appearance, deriving instead from their nesting places in the hollow trunks of old trees, also known as 'stocks'. A folk-name for the species is 'hole dove', and stock doves also breed in disused farm buildings, old haystacks and large nestboxes, including those put up to attract barn owls.

Unlike woodpigeons, stock doves haven't taken to a life in town. They are mainly birds of wooded farmland where they glean weed seeds among cereal crops. In spring and autumn, they gather in flocks, numbering tens or exceptionally hundreds of birds, to feed on newly sown cereals.

But you're most likely to notice them on fine days in spring, because that's when the birds perform their graceful display flights. The male doves fly at treetop height, then lift their wings in a shallow V-shape and glide in broad arcs like paper aeroplanes. Sometimes the female joins in, urged on by her mate in a precisely choreographed aerial ballet, a virtuoso performance from a bird many people hardly ever notice.

CAPERCAILLIE

*

The old pine forests of Speyside, which once covered much of Scotland, can be an eerie place; especially at first light, when the early rays of sunshine filter through the dense canopy to the forest floor beneath. As dawn breaks, all you see beneath the sheltering pines are knee-high hummocks of heather and bilberry, furred with grey lichens. Your breath clouds in the still April air.

Then you hear one of the weirdest sounds made by any British bird: a series of sneezes, grindings and what sounds uncannily like the popping of champagne corks. This is the spring display of the male capercaillie.

The name 'capercaillie' comes from the Gaelic for 'horse of the woods' – a reference to the cantering sound that is the overture to their extraordinary mating display. 'Capers', as they're sometimes known, are the largest grouse in the world – even bigger than a turkey – and the only places you can see them in Britain are these ancient Caledonian pine forests lining the Scottish straths and glens.

But if you do want to witness their extraordinary display, you're going to have to get up very early. The huge black males perform at dawn at 'leks' where they strut like turkey cocks, fanning their tails and stretching their necks skywards. Around them, on the ground or perched in pine trees, are the much smaller and less obvious hens, whose brown and russet camouflage makes them less noticeable to predators.

With a captive audience, the male capercaillie swaggers up and down, wheezing, sneezing and popping to his heart's content, in order to impress as many females as he can. Very occasionally, fuelled by an excess of testosterone, a 'rogue male' will attack people and sometimes even vehicles.

But this bold ritual is a declining one, becoming harder and harder to see every year. The capercaillie has a chequered history as a British bird, its numbers waxing and waning over time. Once widespread throughout the Scottish Highlands, numbers were massively reduced by shooting, and by the late eighteenth century the species had become extinct here.

From the 1830s onwards capercaillies were reintroduced from Scandinavia, and at first were very successful, recolonizing much of their former range. But towards the end of the twentieth century capercaillie numbers began to go into freefall, due to a combination of cold springs and wet summers, which reduce the chicks' ability to feed and waterlog their downy plumage. As well as this, many adult birds are dying from collisions with the fences erected to keep the growing deer population out of the forests.

Add an increase in predators – including the gradual return of the pine marten after centuries of persecution – and the future of the capercaillie in Scotland is looking less than rosy. With as few as 1,000 pairs remaining, we will need to act fast if we are not to lose this magnificent bird – and its extraordinary sounds and displays – for a second time.

RUDDY DUCK

*

The debt we owe the great conservationist, ornithologist and wildlife artist Sir Peter Scott is a huge one. Yet, unintentionally, he also created one of the greatest headaches in modern conservation, involving a small but charismatic species of wildfowl, the ruddy duck.

Ruddy ducks are jaunty little birds, part of a group known as 'stifftails', from their habit of cocking their tails at right angles to their body when they swim. The drake is a deep russet-red in colour, with white cheeks, a black cap and a sky-blue bill, while the female and youngsters are a drabber shade of brown. Male ruddies perform an unforgettable courtship display, drumming their bill rapidly down on to their chest, which releases the air trapped in their breast feathers to produce a sea of bubbles and a hollow, drumming sound.

Like grey squirrels, mink and Canada geese, ruddy ducks are not native to Britain and Europe, but were brought here from North America, originally by Peter Scott to his wildfowl collection at Slimbridge in Gloucestershire. Unfortunately during the 1950s a handful of birds managed to escape, and gradually established themselves across a swathe of the English Midlands, breeding on lakes and gravel pits and wintering on larger reservoirs.

By the late twentieth century the ruddy duck had become firmly established as a British breeding bird, with a seemingly permanent presence here; it had even been adopted as the logo of the West Midlands Bird Club. But then the problems started. Ruddy ducks are adaptable birds, and over time, as the population grew, they began to disperse in search of new homes. Some headed south through France, eventually reaching Spain where they encountered a very rare native cousin, the white-headed duck. With fewer than 10,000 individuals in the whole world, the white-headed duck is considered to be globally endangered.

To the horror of conservationists, ruddy ducks soon began to hybridize with their white-headed relatives, and there was a strong risk that unless drastic action were taken, the Spanish white-headed duck population would effectively die out, undermining years of conservation work to save the species from extinction.

After taking advice from scientists at home and abroad, the British government took the highly controversial decision to eradicate the ruddy duck, and within a decade numbers have fallen from several thousand birds to just a few dozen. Today those last survivors are clinging on, but it is surely only a matter of time until they too are gone, and the short but colourful history of this charismatic species in the British Isles will be over.

GOOSANDER

*

Ahead of you on a river swollen by spring rains, a low-slung, brilliant-white shape is riding the currents. As you approach, you see that it is a duck, and not really white at all, but a soft, almost pale peach colour. Then it dives beneath the surface, and vanishes from view.

Few British ducks are quite so handsome and striking as a male goosander in full breeding plumage. From a distance, he is black and white, but his true beauty is revealed close up, from his bottle-green head and dark back to pink-washed flanks and breast. Females and youngsters are striking too, with soft grey bodies, foxy-brown heads and obvious shaggy crests – earning them the nickname 'redheads'.

Goosanders, along with their cousins the red-breasted merganser and smew, belong to a group of ducks known as 'sawbills', whose long slender bills are lined with backward-pointing 'teeth', all the better for gripping wriggling, slippery fish. Underwater they're as agile as otters, pursuing their prey through raging currents or nosing for fish under riverbanks. This habit has made goosanders unpopular with some anglers and water-bailiffs, though few people would dispute the beauty of these elegant birds.

They nest in hollow trees, and if disturbed the duck will twist her neck and hiss menacingly to ward off intruders. When the ducklings hatch they leap fearlessly down from their nest and head straight to the water. A string of young goosanders riding the white-water rapids behind their mother is an impressive sight, on large streams and rivers throughout the north and west of Britain.

There's more chance of seeing goosanders now, because they have increased both their breeding range and numbers in the last few decades, spreading eastwards from Wales and southwards into central England. They also occur more widely outside their breeding range in autumn and winter, when you may see them on reservoirs, lakes and gravel pits as well as on rivers. In some places these regal-looking birds can become quite tame and will occasionally deign to consort with mallards. At one site, Windermere in the English Lake District, they've even been photographed taking bread at the feet of visitors.

RED-THROATED DIVER

*

On a blustery spring day in our northernmost archipelago, Shetland, rain is threatening to fall. As the sky darkens to graphite and the heavy clouds prepare to shed their load, the air fills with the eerie wails of one of our most beautiful waterbirds, the red-throated diver.

On these windswept, treeless islands, sandwiched between Scotland and the Arctic Circle, the red-throated diver is known as the 'rain goose', because when it calls, rain is supposedly imminent. But a more plausible explanation is that, as cynics have pointed out, in this part of the world rain is never far away.

Like all divers, 'red-throats' are handsome birds with slender, streamlined bodies and long, sharp bills, perfect for catching fish. In summer they have a rusty throat patch which can look almost black at a distance or in poor light, and zebra stripes on the back of their neck, but in winter they're mainly pearly grey and white. You can tell them from black-throated divers at any time of year by their tip-tilted bill and their habit of carrying their head at a slightly raised angle to their body.

Like all members of their family, red-throated divers have their feet set so far back on their bodies that they can't travel far on land, so they usually choose to nest at the very edge of lochans, the small pools scattered throughout their moorland homes in the remote highlands and islands of Scotland.

They don't need fish in their breeding pools, though, because the parents regularly travel several kilometres to larger lochs or even the open sea to catch food for their chicks. Most divers need a long stretch of water to get airborne, but the red-throated diver is the only species able to take off directly from land. As the birds fly to and from their nests, they utter a very different sound, cackling rather like geese.

In summer, the best places to see red-throated divers – and hear their haunting calls – are in the north and west of Scotland, especially the Outer Hebrides, Orkney and Shetland. But outside the breeding season they're much more widespread, and you can see them riding the winter waves around much of our coastline.

FULMAR

*

Watching from the top of a cliff, the movement of a bird catches your eye. At first sight it looks like just another gull, but as it turns towards you in mid air, something about its stiff-winged flight action makes you realize this is something different. A closer look reveals a snow-white bird with grey wings, a dark smudge around the eyes and a short, stubby bill: not a gull at all, but a fulmar.

You can't help but admire fulmars as they soar and wheel around these vertiginous sea-cliffs. They're accomplished aeronauts and can hang effortlessly in the air-currents around the cliff-ledges where they nest, almost grazing the rock with their wingtips before circling out into the void once more. Eventually one settles to greet its mate with a chorus of cackles like a particularly manic witch.

Despite their superficial resemblance to gulls, fulmars are members of the petrel family. They belong to the order of 'tubenoses', true seabirds that have long, tubular protuberances on top of their bills, through which they expel excess salt from the seawater they drink.

Each pair of fulmars rears a single chick, which they feed by regurgitating fish offal gathered from their feeding trips out at sea. The chicks may look downy and defenceless but are far from helpless. Any intruder reckless enough to approach a young fulmar chick risks a face full of stinking, greasy oil which the bird vomits over them; a habit that gave the species its name: 'fulmar' comes the Old Norse meaning 'foul gull'.

Fulmar oil is notoriously difficult to remove from our clothing, but for avian predators, it's far more than an inconvenience – it can even spell death. If a peregrine or sea eagle gets the sticky oil on its feathers, it may be impossible to remove, so a brush with a fulmar can be fatal for even these mighty predators.

Back in the Victorian era, fulmars were very rare in Britain, confined to the remote northern archipelagos of St Kilda and Shetland. But over the following century the fulmar expanded its range more than any other native breeding bird, colonizing virtually the whole of the British and Irish coastline. This may have been due to the expansion of the offshore fishing industry, or perhaps a result of some new genetic mutation. But whatever the reason, the species' success means that we can now all enjoy the sight and sounds of a colony of fulmars gliding and wheeling over a clifftop in spring.

STONE-CURLEW

*

Night-time on a sandy heath in East Anglia can be unnerving when a sound like a wailing banshee pierces the clear, still air. This is the courtship cry of one of our most peculiar wading birds, the stone-curlew.

Despite its name, the stone-curlew shouldn't be confused with the more familiar curlew, as the only similarity between the two birds is their call. Their old country name of 'goggle-eyed plover' suits them better, as they have huge, staring, yellow eyes to enable them to see better at night, when they're at their most active.

By day, they lie up on sparse grassland or heath

camouflaged superbly by their streaky brown and white plumage. If you think of waders as active, running around on the mud to snatch up morsels of food, then by comparison the stone-curlew seems positively slothful. Watch them by day and they hardly move for hours on end as they squat on Breckland heaths surrounded by grazing rabbits.

The stone-curlew is the only European representative of a family known as 'thick-knees', mysterious, nocturnal birds found in the arid regions of Africa, Asia, Australasia and South America. They spend the winter around the Mediterranean region south to the Sahel Zone on the lower edge of the Sahara, and return to Britain early in the spring, usually by March.

Their breeding range is mostly in the south and east of England, on the dry, sandy heathlands of the East Anglian Brecks, and on Salisbury Plain, where they are inadvertently protected from disturbance by the army, whose presence here means that vast tracts of land are out of bounds to visitors.

They still breed on some agricultural land, but only where the farmer is sympathetic to these mysterious birds, as they cannot survive on intensively cultivated fields. Although numbers have declined, stone-curlews are now recovering and the population has stabilized at about 350 pairs. This is in no small part thanks to partnerships between conservationists and landowners, who have encouraged stone-curlews back on to their land by leaving protected patches on which the birds can feed and nest without being disturbed.

A VOYAGE to the outermost reaches of the British Isles has never been for the faint-hearted. Heading out to St Kilda, battered by the wind and waves of the North Atlantic, sailors once kept a particularly keen lookout for our most impressive seabird: the great auk.

As its name suggests, the great auk was the largest member of its family, not just in Britain but in the whole world. In appearance, it resembled a giant razorbill. Standing almost a metre tall and weighing five kilograms, it was jet-black above and white below, with a prominent white patch across each eye, its thick, powerful bill marked with narrow, white streaks. Great auks made a range of calls, including a low, croaking sound and a hoarse scream. On land, they stood up straight, with a regal pose, accentuated by that huge bill; in water they swam rather like penguins.

This resemblance is no coincidence: like penguins, great auks were flightless, having no need to take to the air as they pursued their fishy prey beneath the waves. The great auk's scientific name was originally *Pinguinis impennis*, and it was this mighty seabird that lent its name to the southern hemisphere penguins, not the other way around.

Great auks – also known as 'garefowl' – were once found throughout the North Atlantic, with millions of birds nesting in huge, noisy colonies on low-lying islands from Newfoundland in the west to Norway in the east. In Britain, they were confined to the extreme north and west, with their stronghold on St Kilda, though birds were seen as far south as Lundy in Devon, where an astonished observer described seeing 'the King and Queen of the razorbills . . . standing up bold-like . . .'

Sadly, this splendid seabird became extinct – not just in Britain but in the whole world – in the middle of the nineteenth century. The last British sighting was in 1840, when a great auk was captured off St Kilda. When, soon after it was taken, a terrible storm arose, the fearful islanders, thinking it was a witch, beat the bird to death. But by then the great auk had long been doomed: its flightless-ness made it incredibly easy to exploit, and millions of these birds were caught and plucked for their feathers, then either eaten or boiled to produce oil.

As the only British bird to go extinct since records began, the great auk has achieved iconic status matched only by the legendary dodo. It has appeared in literary works ranging from Charles Kingsley's *The Water-Babies* through James Joyce's *Ulysses*, to Enid Blyton's *The Island of Adventure*. We can describe its appearance and sounds from the accounts made by fascinated nineteenth-century naturalists. Once its scarcity had been recognized, ironically enough many of the last remaining birds were caught to add to the collections of Britain's museums and rich bird enthusiasts.

A century and a half after the last great auk vanished from our planet, we can only speculate about how differently things might have turned out. What if just a handful of these birds had managed to survive in some remote part of the North Atlantic for just a few decades longer? What if, at the eleventh hour, the embryonic conservation movement of the late nineteenth century had managed to protect the great auk? And what if, with hunting banned and its breeding islands protected, numbers had gradually begun to rise once more, allowing the species to repopulate the northern seas?

As it is, we can only grieve for the magnificent, tragic and ultimately irre-placeable great auk. But its demise offers the valuable lesson that it's all too easy to take our birds for granted. Many of the birds written about in this book are under threat (the RSPB estimates that one British bird in five is in peril) and we should – and must – do everything we can to ensure that no other bird in this book ever suffers the same fate.

THE BOOK

*

When it came to turning the short radio scripts into the book you are holding, we would like to thank everyone at John Murray Press and Saltyard for all their skill and hard work. In particular, the discerning eye of Caroline Westmore, the creativity of Sara Marafini and Ami Smithson, and the meticulousness of copy-editor Morag Lyall and indexer Douglas Matthews. In publicity and marketing, we'd also like to thank Rosie Gailer and Vickie Boff for their enthusiasm and hard work. MD Nick Davies and the brilliant sales team led by Ben Gutcher and Lucy Hale have also been highly supportive – thanks especially to Lucy, a keen birder, for taking this book under her wing.

Overseeing a book like this from conception to delivery takes real talent, which we fortunately have found in our editor, Georgina Laycock. She has had the vision and drive to make this project a success, and her editorial skills have improved our text no end.

Carry Akroyd's illustrations have transformed the book into something truly beautiful. Carry is one of Britain's finest illustrators and her skill in distilling the essence of each bird in colour and in black and white has more than answered our (high) expectations. Carry would especially like to thank Steve Brayshaw, for his very helpful advice on the featured birds.

FINALLY

*

Brett would like to thank friends and family for their patience and endurance over a short but intense period during which he has talked of little but tweets. Stephen would like to thank, as always, his wife Suzanne and children Charlie, George and Daisy for their inspiring enthusiasm for birds.

THE SERIES

*

The radio series of *Tweet of the Day* could not have been made without the hard work and dedication from many inside and outside the BBC. Brett Westwood would like to thank his colleagues at Natural History Radio and Radio 4 for their unstinting support.

Special mention should be made of Julian Hector, Sarah Blunt, Sarah Pitt, Andrew Dawes, Jamie Merritt, Jim Farthing and Philip Mattison. Rob Collis provided invaluable support by fact-checking and rounding up the latest information.

Without the sound recordists the book and the series would not have been possible and we are very grateful in particular to Chris Watson, Geoff Sample, Gary Moore and Simon Elliott.

Thanks also to the presenters who brought the scripts to life. In order of appearance: Sir David Attenborough, Miranda Krestovnikoff, Steve Backshall, Michaela Strachan, Brett Westwood, Chris Watson, Martin Hughes-Games, Chris Packham, Kate Humble, John Aitchison and Bill Oddie.

Tweet of the Day would not have happened without the support of Radio 4 and we are grateful to the Controller Gwyneth Williams and commissioning editor Mohit Bakaya for championing the project.

Special thanks also go to Paul Stancliffe of the British Trust for Ornithology for answering a multitude of queries at short notice with such good humour and efficiency.

FURTHER READING AND LISTENING

With so many bird books, covering so many subjects, on the market, this is inevitably a personal selection. It concentrates on books that give an insight into our human relationship with birds, from a historical, cultural and social as well as a scientific point of view.

BOOKS

*

Beguiled by Birds, Ian Wallace (Helm, 2004)

A Bird in the Bush, Stephen Moss (Aurum, 2004)

Birds and People, Mark Cocker and David Tipling (Jonathan Cape, 2013)

Birds Britannia: How the British Fell in Love with Birds, Stephen Moss (HarperCollins, 2011)

Birds Britannica, Mark Cocker (Chatto & Windus, 2005)

Birdscapes: Birds in Our Imagination and Experience, Jeremy Mynott (Princeton, 2009)

A Birdwatcher's Year, Leo Batten, Jim Flegg, Jeremy Sorensen, Mike J. Wareing, Donald Watson and Malcolm Wright (Poyser, 1973)

The Charm of Birds, Sir Edward Grey (1927, new edn Weidenfeld and Nicolson, 2001)

Collins Bird Guide, Lars Svensson, Killian Mullarney and Dan Zetterström (Collins, 2nd edn, 2009)

The Crossley ID Guide: Britain and Ireland, Richard Crossley and Dominic Couzens (Princeton University Press, 2014)

The Natural History of Selborne, Gilbert White (1789, new edn Thames & Hudson, 1981)

The Poetry of Birds, ed. Simon Armitage and Tim Dee (Viking, 2009)

The RSPB Handbook of British Birds, Peter Holden and Tim Cleeves (Helm, 3rd edn, 2010)

The Shell Bird Book, James Fisher (Ebury Press and Michael Joseph, 1966)

Silent Spring, Rachel Carson (1962, new edn Penguin Modern Classics, 2000)

Ten Thousand Birds: Ornithology since Darwin, Tim Birkhead, Jo Wimpenny and Bob Montgomerie (Princeton University Press, 2014)

This Birding Life, Stephen Moss (Aurum, 2006)

Was Beethoven a Birdwatcher?, David Turner (Summersdale, 2011)

Why Birds Sing, David Rothenberg (Allen Lane, 2005)

Wild Hares and Hummingbirds: the Natural History of an English Village, Stephen Moss (Square Peg, 2011)

The Wisdom of Birds, Tim Birkhead (Bloomsbury, 2008)

AUDIO

*

Collins Bird Songs and Calls, Geoff Sample: book and three CDs (Collins, 2010)

A Guide to: Garden, Woodland, Water, Coastal, Farmland, Mountain and Moorland Birds, Brett Westwood and Stephen Moss: six CDs (BBC Audio, 2007–13)

Page numbers in **bold** indicate the main entry for
  specific birds

Adams, Richard: *Watership Down*, 142
Adolph, Peter, 102
Aesop, 125
African Queen, The (film), 186
Aitchison, John, x
Akroyd, Carry, xii
albatross, black-browed, **63–4**
Allen, Woody, 123
Allsop, Kenneth, xxx
  Adventure Lit Their Star, 245
Aristophanes: *The Birds*, 262
Aristotle, xviii, xxiii, 259
Attenborough, Sir David, x
auk
  great, **270–1**
  little, 137, **153**
auks (group), 28
Avalon Marshes, Somerset, xxxiii, 257
avocet, **222–3**

Backshall, Steve, x
Barnes, Simon, 85
Bass Rock, 63
Bates, H.E., 4
Beaver, Sir Hugh, 143
Bede, Venerable, 73
Bedgebury Pinetum, Kent, 149
bee-eater, 244
Beethoven, Ludwig van, xx
Beuno, St, 255
Bewick, Thomas, 188
  History of British Birds, xxiii–xxiv
Big Garden Birdwatch, xxvii
binoculars, xxv
Birding for All (*formerly* Disabled Birders'
  Association), xxvii

BirdLife International, 106, 128
birds
  collecting, xxiv
  recognizing, xx–xxi
  singing and other sounds, xiv–xxx
  threats to survival, xxviii, 271
birdwatching (birding)
  history of, xxii–xxix
  starting and practice, xxx–xxxvi
bittern, xxxiii, 251, **256–7**
  little, 257
blackbird, xiii, xvi, xxi, xxxv, 24, 47, 70, 136, 156, 178,
  180, 204, 227, **228–9**, 247
blackcap, xvii, **11–12**, 24, 71, 93, 156, 259
blackcock *see* grouse, black
bluethroat, **105**
Blunt, Sarah, x–xi
Blyton, Enid: *The Island of Adventure*, 271
bobolink, xiii, **132–3**
Book of St Albans, 66
Boys, William, 50
brambling, **120–1**, 204
British Birds (magazine), xxv, 102
British Birds Rarities Committee, 133
British Broadcasting Corporation (BBC): Natural
  History Unit, Bristol, ix, 193
British Ornithologists' Union, xii
British Trust for Ornithology, 179
  Atlas of Breeding Birds, 187
broken-wing display, 74
Brown, Leslie: *British Birds of Prey*, 152
Browning, Robert: 'Home Thoughts, From Abroad',
  175
bullfinch, **78–9**
bunting
  cirl, 46, **59**
  corn, xxxv, 46, **48**
  Lapland, 131
  little, xxxiv
  ortolan, **117**
  reed, xxi, **15**, 204

bunting (*continued*)
   snow, xxxii, 131, 157, **167**
buntings (group), 46
Burns, Robert, 243
bustard, great, **220–1**
Buxton, John, 78
buzzard
   common, **50–2**, 66, 75, 84
   rough-legged, xxxii

'caching', 55
Cainism (or Cain and Abel Syndrome), 87
Canute, King, 173
capercaillie, **264–5**
Catesby, Mark, 77
Catullus, xviii
Cetti, Francesco, 237
chaffinch, xxi, 93, 112, 204, **209**, 227
Chance, Edgar, 6
Chapman, Alfred, 192
Charles II, King, 214
Chaucer, Geoffrey: *The Canterbury Tales*, 257
chiffchaff, xv, xvii, xxi, 47, 71, 179, 226, **229–30**, 253–4, 259
China: tree sparrows persecuted, 151
chough, xxi, **215–17**
Clare, John, xix, xxiv, 53–4, 145, 257
   'Birds in Alarm', xix
   'The Skylark', xx
Collins Bird Guide, 237
coot, 19, 137, **193–4**
cormorant, xxxv, 15, **37–8**, 71
corncrake, **53–4**, 162, 236
crake, spotted, **19**
crane, common, **143–4**
crossbill, 178, **183–4**, 217
   parrot, **217–18**
   Scottish, 218
crow
   carrion, xxi, **124–5**, 236

   hooded, 125, 160
crows (group), 138
cuckoo, xiii, xxi, xxxv, 5, **6–7**, 24–5, 42, 99, 251
curlew, xxxiv, 96, 122, 137, 147, 191, 227, **255**
Cuthbert, St, 116

Daniels, Jeff, 214
Davies, W.H., 170
dawn chorus, x, xvii–xviii, 5, 25, 251
dipper, 157, **169–70**
diver
   black-throated, **221–2**, 267
   great northern, 179, **200–1**
   red-throated, **266–7**
divers (group), xvi
DNA technology, xxviii
dotterel, **62**
dove
   collared, 178, **187**
   mourning, xiii, 113, **133**
   rock, **123**
   stock, **263–4**
   turtle, xviii, **49–50**
duck
   long-tailed, **161**
   mandarin, **192**, 220
   ruddy, **265–6**
   tufted, xii, 70, 137
   white-headed, 266
   see also eider; garganey; goldeneye; mallard; pintail; teal, wigeon
du Maurier, Daphne, 124
dunlin, 137, **146–7**
dunnock, 46, 70, 178, **211–12**, 227

eagle
   golden, **87**, 89
   white-tailed (sea eagle), **87–8**, 189, 269
eclipse plumage, 70

egret
  cattle, **129–30**, 191
  great white, xxxiii, 39, **188–9**, 191
  little, **39**, 43, 130, 189, 191
eider, common, **116–17**, 161
England, Derrick, 186
ethology, 190, 240
European Union Birds Directive, 117
Evelyn, John, 214

Feynman, Richard, xxx
fieldfare, xxx, 112, 136, 156, **159–60**, 204
firecrest, xxxii, 112, **131–2**, 179
Fisher, James, xviii
  Watching Birds, xxii
Fly Away Home (film), 214
flycatcher
  pied, **8–10**
  spotted, xvii, **59–60**, 71
Foulness, Essex, 163
Frickley Colliery, Yorkshire, 73
Frisch, Karl von, 190
fulmar, **267–9**

gadwall, **161–2**, 196
Gallico, Paul: *The Snow Goose*, 242
gannet, **33–5**
garganey, **17**
Gay Birders Club, xxvii
Gerald of Wales, 140
godwit, 86, 112, 137, 147
  bar-tailed, **140–1**
  black-tailed, 140, **149–51**
goldcrest, 47, 112, **125–6**, 131–2, 179, 219, 226
goldeneye, 137, 179, **241**
goldfinch, **29**, 149, 156, 204
Gooders, John: *Where to Watch Birds*, xxviii
goosander, 179, 205, **266**

goose
  barnacle, 112, 137, **138–40**
  brent, 112, **163–4**
  Canada, 112, 193, 206, **214**, 220
  Egyptian, **243**
  greylag, **189–90**, 206
  lesser white-fronted, **192–3**, 206
  pink-footed, xxxiv, 93, **117–18**, 179, 206
  snow, **241–2**
  white-fronted, 179, 192, **206**
goshawk, xxxiv, **152–3**, 205
Great Bustard Group, 221
Great Crane Project, 143–4
grebe
  black-necked, **190–1**
  great crested, xxxi, 190, **238–40**
  little, 190, **263**
  Slavonian, 190, **218**
greenfinch, **16**, 204
greenshank, 47, **96**
greyhen *see* grouse, black
grouse
  black, 251, **252–3**
  red, **97**
guillemot, **20**, 25, 47, 153, 227
Guinness Book of Records, 143
gull
  black-headed, 70, **142**
  common, **85–6**
  great black-backed, **75**, 76
  herring, xvi, **56–7**, 60
  lesser black-backed, **60**
  Ross's, xxxii

Hardy, Thomas, xxxv, 14, 242
  'The Darkling Thrush', 175
harrier
  hen, 97, 179, **199–200**
  marsh, xii, xxxiv, 179
  Montagu's, xii
Harrison, Beatrice, 5

Hartert, Ernst, 148
hawfinch, 137, **149**
Heathrow airport, London, 73
Hector, Julian, ix, xi
Hendrix, Jimi, 186
heron, grey, **12–13**, 205
Hines, Barry, 66
Hitchcock, Alfred, 124
hobby, xxxv, 46, 93, **101–2**
honey-buzzard, xxxiv, **84–5**, 93
hoopoe, xxiii, 226, 244, **260–2**
Hopkins, Gerard Manley, 64, 243
Hosking, Eric, 108
Hudson, W.H., 78, 142
Hughes, Ted, xxxvi
Hughes-Games, Martin, x–xi
Humble, Kate, x, 196
Huxley, Sir Julian, xxv, 240

ibis, glossy, **191**
Imberdis, Father Jean, 198
imprinting, 190
International Dawn Chorus Day, x, xviii, 5
irruptions, 184

jackdaw, xi, xxi, **138**, 215, 236
Jackson, Michael, xx
Jagger, Sir Mick, 14
jay, **103–5**, 215
Johns, Revd C.A., 260
Johnson, Samuel, 124
Jonson, Ben: *The Alchemist*, 140
Joyce, James: *Ulysses*, 271

Keats, John, 11, 92
    'Ode to a Nightingale', xix
Kempton Park nature reserve, xxxiii
kestrel, 52, **64–6**

kingfisher, **57**, 205
Kingsley, Charles: *The Water-Babies*, 271
kite, red, xxxi, xxxv, 157, **171–2**
kittiwake, xxi, **26–7**
Kleinschmidt, Otto, 148
kleptoparasitism, 80, 162
knot, 113, 137, **173**
Koch, Ludwig, x
Krestovnikoff, Miranda, x

Lack, David: *The Life of the Robin*, 170
lapwing, xxxiii, xxxv, 25, 142, 156, 205, 227,
    230–2
lark
    shore, **130–1**
    see also skylark
Latham, Dr John, 50
leks, 244–5, 251–3, 265
Lilford, Thomas Lyttleton Powys, 4th Baron,
    263
linnet ('lintie'), **144–5**, 152
Livingstone, Ken, 123
Lockley, Ronald, 32
Lonsdale Road Reservoir, London, xxxiii
Look (TV programme), 293
Lorenz, Konrad: *King Solomon's Ring*, 190
Lynford Arboretum, Norfolk, 149

Mabey, Richard, 86
MacCaig, Norman, 71
McCartney, Sir Paul: 'Blackbird', xx
MacPhail, Maire, 133
magpie, 61, **183**
Magpie (TV series), 183
mallard, 16, 70, 137, 160, 161, 193, **206–7**, 241
Mao Tse-tung, 151
martin
    house, 47, **54–5**, 113, 240, 251, 253
    sand, xxxiii, 205, 226, **240–1**

martins (group), 93
Mary, Queen of Scots, 196
Meredith, George: 'The Lark Ascending', xx, 215
merganser, red-breasted, xii, 266
merlin, 173, **195–6**
Messiaen, Olivier, xx, 242–3
migration, xxv–xxvi, 250
mimicry, 25, 41
Minsmere, Suffolk, 222
Mitterrand, François, 117
Moore, Gary, x
moorhen, xiii, 19, 162, **194–5**
Moss, Stephen, xxx–xxxiv
   A Bird in the Bush, xxii
   Wild Hares and Hummingbirds, xxxiii
moulting, 70
Mousa (Shetland island), 21
Murray, Donald, 35

Nene Washes, Lincolnshire, 54, 149
Ness (Isle of Lewis), 35
Nethersole-Thompson, Desmond, 62, 167
Nicholson, Max, 13
nightingale, xv, xviii, 4, **10**, 24
   thrush, **103**
nightjar, 25, **26**, 46, 242
nuthatch, 47, 219, **232–3**

Oddie, Bill, x, xxxi, 21, 48, 187
Oneword (radio station), xx
oriole, golden, 25, **36**, 260
Orwell, George, xxv
osprey, **52–3**, 93
ouzel, ring, 226, **247**
owl
   barn, xxxv, **29–31**, 157
   little, **262–3**
   long-eared, 46, **212–13**

   short-eared, **123–4**, 136, 179
   tawny, xix, 5, 145, 178, **180**, 212
owls (group), xvi
oystercatcher, **75–7**, 96, 122, 227

Packham, Chris, x
Paquin, Anna, 214
parakeet, rose-ringed, 179, **186–7**, 243
Paris, Matthew (monk), 183
partridge
   grey, xxxv, *237–8*
   red-legged, xxxi, **114–16**, 238
Pennant, Thomas, 85, 250
peregrine, 173, 174, **234–6**, 269
Peterson, Roger Tory, xxix
petrel
   Leach's, **129**, 236
   storm, **20–1**
phalarope, red-necked, 5, **62–3**
pheasant
   common, **119–21**
   golden, x, **220**
   Lady Amherst's, 229
pigeon, 234
Pike, Oliver, 6
pintail, xii, xxxiv, 112, 137, 179
pipit
   meadow, 93, **97–9**, 179, 195, 199
   rock, **79**
   tawny, **108**
   tree, xxxv, 46, **55–6**, 243
Pitt, Sarah, xi
Pliny the Elder, xviii, xxiii
plover
   golden, 136, **142–3**, 156, 205, 232
   grey, 113, **120–2**
   Kentish, 50
   little ringed, xxxiii, **245–6**
   ringed, **74**, 76, 245
Porro, Ignacio, xxv

Protection of Birds Act (1954), 79
ptarmigan, willow (formerly willow grouse), 97, 157, **166**
puffin, 25, **27–8**, 70, 153, 227
Pullen, Norman, 208
Pullman, Philip: *His Dark Materials*, 183

quail, 25, **32–3**

rail, water, x, **162**
Ransome, Arthur: *Great Northern*, 201
raven, xxi, 178, **181–2**, 205
razorbill, **28–9**, 70, 153, 227
redpoll
    common, 169, 204
    lesser, 109, **168–9**
redshank, **17–19**, 96, 137, 227, 244
    spotted, xxxiv, 5, 71, **86**
redstart, 71, **78**, 251
    black, **246–7**
redwing, xxx, 112, **114–15**, 136, 160, 185, 204, 227
René, Leon: 'Rockin' Robin', xx
reverse migration, 128
robin, xv, xvii, xxi, xxx, 47, 70, 93, 112, 157, **170–1**, 178, 182, 209
roding, 251–2
roo-kooing, 253
rook, xi, **236**
Rossini, Gioacchino Antonio: *The Thieving Magpie* (opera), 183
Royal Society for the Protection of Birds (RSPB), xxiv, 29, 53, 106, 222, 238
rubythroat, Siberian, 113
ruff, **244–5**
Rutland Water, 53

St Kilda, 228, 270–1
Sample, Geoff, x
sanderling, **166–7**

sandpiper
    common, **39–40**, 71, 99
    green, 25, 71, **99–100**
    purple, **168**
    wood, 5, 25, 71, **100**
Scilly, Isles of, xxvi
scoter, 161
Scott, Dafila, 188
Scott, Sir Peter, 188, 193, 242, 265
'Seafarer, The' (Anglo-Saxon poem), xviii
Selous, Edward, xxiv
serin, **108–9**
shag, **13–15**, 25, 71
Shakespeare, William, xix, 263
    King Lear, 212
    Love's Labour's Lost, 180
    Macbeth, 30, 54–5
    A Midsummer Night's Dream, 229
    The Winter's Tale, 171
Shapwick Heath National Nature Reserve, Somerset, 189
'sharming', 162
shearwater
    great, **100–1**
    Manx, **30–2**, 71, 75
    sooty, **128–9**
shearwaters (group), xvi
shelduck, **164–5**
Shelley, Percy Bysshe, 204
    'To a Skylark', xix
shoveler, 137, 161, 179, **196–8**, 207
shrike
    great grey, xxxii, **258–9**
    red-backed, **67**, 259
Simms, Eric, 123
siskin, 109, **141**, 169, 204
Six Birds of Fate (folk-tale), 16
skua
    Arctic, **80**
    great, **35–6**
skuas (group), 71

skylark, xvii, xx, 93, 156, 195, 204, **214–15**, 242
Slimbridge *see* Wildfowl and Wetlands Trust
snipe
 common, xxxiv, 123, 251, **254–5**
 jack, **122–3**, 205
Snow, David, 175
Society for the Protection of Birds *see* Royal Society for
 the Protection of Birds
Somerset Levels, xxxiii
Song of Solomon, xviii
sonograms, 218
sparrow
 hedge *see* dunnock
 house, xxi, **72–3**, 151, 174
 tree, xxxv, 73, **151**
sparrowhawk, xxxv, 52, **61**, 66, 152, 174, 196, 205
'speculum', 160
Spice Girls: 'Wannabe', xxi
starling, xv, 47, 61, 136, 157, **174–5**, 188, 209
stonechat, 64, 71, **72**, 136, 242
stone-curlew, **269**
stork, white, **82–4**
storm petrels (group), 71
Strachan, Michaela, x
swallow, **94**
swallows (group), xxxiii, 24, 71, 93, 113, 240, 250–1,
 253
swan
 Bewick's, 112, 137, 159, 179, **188**
 mute, 159, **163**, 193
 whooper, 112, 137, **158–9**, 188
swift, xxxvi, 4, **7**, 47, 71, 243, 253
 Alpine, 226, **243–4**

Tchaikovsky, P.I.: *Swan Lake*, 159
teal, 112, 157, **160**, 207, 241
Tennyson, Alfred, Lord, 73
tern
 Arctic, **33**, 71, 130
 common, **85**

little, **66–7**
 roseate, **94–6**
 Sandwich, **50**, 147
Theroux, Paul, 163
Thomas, Edward: 'Adlestrop', 229
thrasher, brown, xv
thrush
 mistle, xvii, 156, 175, 179, **184–5**, 204, 227
 song, xvii, xxi, 24, 70, 112, 157, **175**, 178, 180, 185,
 204, 227
thrushes (group), 112, 156
Tinbergen, Niko, 190
tippets, 238
tit
 bearded, x, **118–19**
 blue, xxx, 24, 46–7, 147, 182, **197–8**, 227
 coal, 46, **55**, 156
 crested, **127**
 great, xxi, 24, 46–7, 147, 157, 178, **185–6**, 227
 long-tailed, 5, 46, **77**, 156, 227
 marsh, 137, **147–8**
 willow, 137, **148**
tits (group), xvi
treecreeper, 47, **233–4**
Turner, David, xx
turnstone, **102**, 168
Tweet of the Day (BBC radio series), ix–xii
twitching, xxvi
twite, **152**

waders (group), xvi
wagtail
 grey, 179, **199**
 pied, xxi, **145**, 179, 199
 yellow, **80–1**, 199, 251
warbler
 aquatic, **105–6**
 barred, **88**
 Cape May, 113
 Cetti's, xvii, xx, **236–7**

warblers (*continued*)
    Dartford, **13**, 50, 147, 242
    garden, **11**, 93, 147
    golden-winged, xxvi
    grasshopper, 26, 40, **258**
    great reed, **107–8**
    icterine, **81**, 107
    marsh, xv, xvii, 25, **40–1**
    melodious, **106–7**
    reed, xxxiv, **41–2**, 251
    Savi's, **40**
    sedge, **21**, 42, 251
    willow, xxxiii, 47, 71, 230, 250, **253–4**
    wood, xxxv, **7–8**, 24, 254
    yellow-browed, 113, **127–8**
    see also blackcap; chiffchaff, lesser whitethroat,
       whitethroat,
warblers (group), xix, 4, 46–7
Warton, Joseph, 10
Waterton, Charles, 263
Watson, Chris, x, 5
Watson, Donald, 74
Waugh, Evelyn: *Brideshead Revisited*, 232
waxwing, 185, 204, **213**
West Midlands Bird Club, xxxiv
Westwood, Brett, x, xxx–xxxi, xxxiv
wheatear, northern, xxxv, **82**, 93, 205, 226, 251
'whiffling', 137
whimbrel, **16**
whinchat, xxxv, 47, **64**
White, Gilbert, xiv, xviii, xxiii, 8, 28, 56, 209, 250, 254
    The Natural History of Selborne, xxiii, xxxiii
whitethroat
    common, **259–60**
    lesser, xxi, 24, **37**, 71, 251
wigeon, xxxiv, 112, 137, 157, 179, 205, **207–8**
Wildfowl and Wetlands Trust, Slimbridge,
    Gloucestershire, 144, 188, 193, 265
Williams, Ralph Vaughan, 215
    'The Lark Ascending', xx
Woburn Abbey, Bedfordshire, 192

woodcock, 136, 251, **252**
woodlark, **242–3**
woodpecker
    great spotted, 205, **208–9**, 260
    green, **260**
    lesser spotted, 205, **219**, 260
woodpeckers (group), xvi
woodpigeon, **73–4**, 136, 264
Wordsworth, William, 6
    'To the Cuckoo', xix
wren, xxi, 46, 70, 178, 209, **211**, 227, 251
    St Kilda, **228**
Wren, P.C.: *Beau Geste*, 185
wryneck, **38**

yellowhammer, xxi, 4, 46, **48–9**, 51, 58, 204

Zeiss, Carl, xxv